AF575094

The Horse and The Tiger

Also by Muriel Anne Lennox

E.P. Taylor: Horseman and his horses
Northern Dancer: The legend and his legacy
Dark Horse: Unravelling the mystery of Nearctic

The Horse and The Tiger

Muriel Anne Lennox

Beach House Books
Toronto

Beach House Books
25 Leuty Avenue, Toronto, Canada M4E 2R2

Library and Archives Canada Cataloguing in Publication
Lennox, Muriel, 1942-
The horse and the tiger / Muriel Anne Lennox. -- 1st ed.
Includes bibliographical references.
ISBN 978-0-9699025-5-3

1. Nijinsky (Race horse). 2. Race horses--Ontario--Oshawa--Biography. 3. Race horses--Ireland--Biography. 4. O'Brien, Vincent. 5. Horse trainers--Ireland--Biography. 6. Ireland--History. I. Title.

SF355.N5L45 2010 798.40092'9 C2010-905540-3

Editorial Advisor: Judith Mappin
Design: Francine O'Halloran - Zarka Design
Tiger photo: Christine Gehrig

Fonts: Garamond
Aon Cari Celtic - Designed by Cari Buziak

First edition

I owe a great debt of gratitude to the friends and family who galloped alongside me offering critical advice and encouragement throughout this very long journey. Thanks especially to the most enduring outriders — Judy Mappin, Bridget Bimm and my dad. This one's for you.

"When Allah willed to create the horse, he said to the South Wind, I will that a creature should proceed from thee. Condense thyself.' And the wind condensed itself. Then came the angel Gabriel saying, I have called thee horse. I have attached good fortune to the hair that falls between thine eyes. Thou shall be the lord of all other animals, and men shall follow thee where ever thou goest. Good for pursuit as for flight, thou shall fly without wing and upon thy back shall riches repose and through thy means shall wealth come.'"

— *A Bedouin Legend*

Prologue

At the close of the 20th Century and beyond all expectations Ireland mysteriously bounded from one of the most impoverished European Union members to one of the wealthiest. Almost over-night. Or so it would appear. The phenomenon was named the Celtic Tiger and a battalion of analysts set out to discover the secret behind Ireland's success story. While the experts attempted to decipher the mitigating factors, other EU members dispatched missions to Dublin in an attempt to understand, and with luck, emulate Ireland's rampant prosperity.

Economists, scholars, financial journalists, politicians, authorities of every shape and stripe published papers, articles and books offering a vast range of theories. Some pointed to low corporate taxes and foreign investment; others to the Irish educational system and the decision in 1967 to offer free secondary schooling to all. Some argued the boom was precipitated by a shift in demographics resulting from the legalization of contraceptives in 1979. Another theory was that the visit of Pope John Paul II in 1976 lifted the nation's spirit and self-esteem. Still in the end it appears that determining the underlying cause, the spark that actually triggered Ireland's renaissance, proved as illusive as snaring a leprechaun and his pot of gold.

"To be brutally frank, nobody is quite sure why all of this happened," offered Michael McKenna, assistant secretary, Department of Enterprise, Trade and Development. "The best that can be said is that a number of factors came together at the same time to produce what has turned out to be a happy situation."

Curiously, until now, no one has suggested that this Celtic Tiger might well have galloped into town on the back of a horse — or at the very least been a contributing factor in this *happy situation.* Horses are, after all, thoroughly entwined in Ireland's past, present and future. A steadfast part of the Irish landscape, the age-old magic of the horse — its majesty and unbridled spirit — help to define the people of this land. And this, the story of the horse and the tiger, is one that runs deep through the soul of Ireland.

The Celtic Tiger surely took *The Economist* by surprise. In 1988 the magazine predicted the Irish were scorching head-long into the great dark abyss of economic catastrophe. Nine years later the publication revisited this presumed sleepy backwater land of blarney and leprechauns only to emerge awestruck by the country's dramatic turn-around. *The Economist* now heralded Ireland as Europe's shining light and this Celtic Tiger was lauded as a beacon of economic brilliance.

Yet in 1988, amid those reports of doom and gloom, the Celtic Tiger had already begun to roar. Members of this once impoverished society were well on their way to becoming millionaires and billionaires and their astounding financial successes were inspiring countless other Irish men and women. The source of the bonanza? Horses, of course.

According to those experts tracking the fortunes of Ireland there have been several incarnations of Celtic Tiger. The first was spotted in the 1990s — only to pad back to its lair in 2001 during the global economic downturn. Then in 2004 the grand cat was back with a fury only to vanish once again when the world economies began to tumble in 2008.

There is, however, every likelihood there was an earlier Celtic Tiger — the one that would result in Ireland's global domination of the high stakes world of Thoroughbred horses and in its wake create gargantuan wealth.

Is it possible *The Economist* and all the rest missed this, the original Celtic Tiger? Perhaps they were looking in all the wrong places. Instead of searching Dublin's boardrooms, the answers could be found at The Curragh of Kildare, Ireland's ancient and storied racecourse. For this the heart of Ireland. The rhythmic sound of horses hooves pounding the soft turf, the pulse of this dynamic, yet timeless land.

As early as 1 AD, The Curragh, a level stretch of grasslands in County Kildare, was the site of horse races. Later the area was home to the Aenach Colmain (Curragh fair), an annual ceremony for the people of Leinster. It is said that all of Ireland journeyed to this grassy plain to participate in the popular festival. The event spanned three days. New laws were drawn and announced, goods were bartered, gossip shared, friends reunited, funeral rites performed, marriages solemnized, and, of course, horse races conducted.

Legend suggests in the year 480 Saint Bridget, daughter of an Irish chieftain, asked the King of Leinster for a piece of land to build a monastery. The King, unaware of her powers, scoffed at her request and told her she could have as much land as her cloak could cover. When Saint Bridget placed her cloak on the ground, it spread across the entire immemorial grasslands — almost 5000 acres. The saint then decreed the land a *common*, to be for all the people of Ireland. And for all time.

There are those who believe that just before sunrise, the soft breeze that drifts across The Curragh carries the secrets of countless generations of Irish. So whether sitting quietly at dawn, or shouting encouragement to your choice in the 5th race of the afternoon, The Curragh is where the inquisitive are most likely to discover the secret behind Ireland's extraordinary renaissance. They will learn that the raging Celtic Tiger was inspired by a horse — a grand horse to be sure, but a horse nonetheless.

The Economist and other business papers reported Ireland's economic boom a *rags-to-riches* tale. Technically it is *riches-to-rags-to-riches.* Beyond or about the fringes of civilization, the wealth of this island nation was staggering. Her land, abundant and fertile; her forests vibrant; her rivers teeming with salmon; her river beds awash with precious minerals.

Herds of Irish horses grazing lazily against the distant horizon complete the portrait of this utopian splendor. The rich soil laced with limestone, coupled with a gentle, temperate climate, was perfect for raising horses. And so it was that Ireland became renowned, the world over, as *the land of the horse.*

Then for several millennia Ireland was assaulted and plundered by countless invasions; wars; terrorism; famine; genocide; exploitation and poverty. It began in 500 BC with droves of mounted Celtic warriors. Next, longboats laden with Vikings began landing on Ireland's rocky shores. Then the Danes. Followed by waves of Norman foot-soldiers and cavalry. Finally, and most devastatingly, the English.

Many of the Celtic, Viking and Norman invaders remained in Ireland. They soon assimilated and often became more Irish than the Irish. It would appear, however, that when the English hoisted their flag on Irish soil assimilation was not considered an option. For some peculiar reason, the English thought themselves vastly superior to the Irish. So superior, in fact, that they deemed it immoral and, ultimately, illegal to be Irish. To that end they began composing laws to, if not eradicate, surely diminish the native Irish. Among these, the Statutes of Kilkenny prohibited colonists from marrying the native Irish or learning their language.

Prior to the English aggressions traditional Irish law was passed orally from one generation to the next. During the time of St. Patrick (438-441 AD) the laws were compiled into a single document and became known as Brehon Laws or laws of free farmers. Written in Irish, for the Irish, by the Irish, the Brehon Laws stood unaltered for 800 years.

The English laws governing the Irish, incidentally, were not written in Irish as the English had decreed that the Irish were no longer allowed to speak Irish. Before long the Irish were branded as the enemy, in their own country.

What manifested as eight centuries of Irish misery began 17

October 1171, the day England's King Henry II landed on the shores of Ireland accompanied by a formidable army of 500 knights and 4000 archers. The Irish had no hope of resistance and by the time the king departed he had anointed himself 'Lord of Ireland'.

In 1185 Ireland was subjected to its second royal visit — Henry's youngest son, Prince John. Arrogant and cunning, he made it his mission to impose British order on the now occupied island. Native Irish were thrown out of their homes to make way for the dark prince's loyal henchmen. Over the next century or so they were followed by droves of Anglo-Norman barons who, by 1300, controlled much of Ireland. The Irish, however, received a reprieve during the bitter conflict between England and Scotland. The trend to colonization was reversed and before long the native Irish began to regain lost territories. At least temporarily.

In the mid-1500s, around the time Elizabeth I ascended the British throne, the English launched a new scheme to appropriate the homes, farms and properties of the native Irish. The rationale behind this blatant land-grab, according to the history books, which, for the most part, were written by the English, was that the vast majority of native Irish were Catholic. Thus with a Protestant God on their side, and a set of Commandments that presumably excluded the *"thou shalt not steal"* clause, the English began systematically removing the Irish from their homes. Homes that had been in their families for centuries. The fortunate among the dispossessed had enough money for passage to North America. Others were sold as slaves to the West Indies. The rest were forced to subsist in hovels. Yet the native Irish managed to survive.

In the late 1600s the English, who by now were the absentee landlords of most of Ireland, began writing, and enforcing, the infamous Penal Code. This time around, they took away all possible rights they could think of from the native Irish. Law upon law was drawn. Native Irish were denied the right to vote; to bear arms; to educate their children. They were not allowed to buy land, nor were they allowed to own a horse worth more than £5. By 1700, the native Irish owned less than 15% of the land of their country. Still, the Irish survived.

The first severe famine hit Ireland in 1728-29; the second, ten years later. The third struck with a vengeance in 1741. The Irish called this *bliadhain an áir*, the year of the slaughter. Roughly 300,000 native Irish starved to death.

In 1801 amid a storm of bribes, threats and corruption The Act of Union was passed uniting Ireland to England. The theory was things would improve, instead it simply strengthened an already villainous system of absentee landlords that toppled all that remained of Irish commerce.

Beyond the grand country estates and castles of the English overlords, Ireland, the once great and abundant utopia, devolved into a bleak landscape of windowless mud huts. The people subsisting on little more than potato and milk diets.

Then in the late 1840s came the *Great Hunger*. Clearly the Act of Union proved a one-way street. Not only did this travesty occur on the doorstep of what was, at the time, the world's wealthiest nation, there was widespread belief among the British upper classes that the famine was an act of God — no doubt a protestant God. The leading voice in the theory was Sir Charles Trevelyan, the British civil servant responsible for doling out relief to the Irish during the famine. In his book *The Irish Crisis* (1848) he champions the famine as 'a direct stroke of an all-wise and all-merciful providence.' Thus he advised that what little aid provided to the starving men, women and children be terminated. At least a million native Irish died of hunger and disease.

"There never was a country," testified Irish-born Duke of Wellington, "in which poverty existed to the extent it exists in Ireland."

Then at about the dawn of the 21st century a strange new

sound was heard coming from the streets of Dublin. Above the fiddles and pipes and drums and lilting Irish voices it was the reverberating roar of the Celtic Tiger. But stop, listen ever more closely, for there was a more subtle sound — the rhythmic and unmistakable clip-clop of horses hooves trotting along the cobblestone street. For this is music to the Irish soul. Certainly if anyone, or anything could inspire the Irish to turn the tide it would be a horse.

Where the Industrial Revolution transformed the very fabric of Ireland's European neighbours, the upheaval seemed to have blown right past Ireland. Thus the country and its commerce remained as it had for several thousand years — essentially agricultural. In fact, until the middle of the 20th century, for many Irish, owning a horse was imperative. These versatile animals plodded and tilled the fields; swapped the plow for a cart to fetch produce to town on market days; and on Sundays ferried family to church.

Irish horses also provided entertainment. The Irish concocted steeplechasing and show jumping. And probably horse racing. During the Middle Ages Ireland boasted more horse racing than any other. But, most significantly, to a legion of Irish, the horse was (and continues to be) business — their sole source of income. Generation after generation of horse-traders have assembled at Irish horse fairs like Ballinasloe, an annual event that dates back to the High Kings of Tara.

If the EU delegates seeking the secret to the Irish success stumbled upon the answer, would they have believed it? Would they trust that the original Celtic Tiger trotted boldly into town on the back of a horse? Furthermore, would economists deduce that observing Irish horse-traders would provide insights into Ireland's renaissance? Unlikely. Yet these masters of the ancient art of horse-trading are the most shrewd, cunning entrepreneurs on the planet. And as such played a major role in Ireland's economic growth spurt.

There is, of course, every chance that no logical, linear text-book explanation behind Ireland's giant leap from dire poverty to rampant wealth exists. Instead, the situation may well have fallen into another branch of mathematics — the *chaos theory*, which states that a small change in the primary conditions can drastically alter the long-term behaviour of a system.

"The flapping of a single butterfly's wing today," explains Ian Stewart in *Does God Play Dice? The Mathematics of Chaos*, "produces a tiny change in the state of the atmosphere. Over a period of time, what the atmosphere actually does diverges from what it would have done. So, in a month's time, a tornado that would have devastated the Indonesian coast doesn't happen. Or maybe one that wasn't going to happen, does."

In this case the butterfly was a horse and when this very special horse galloped effortlessly across the soft turf of The Curragh of Kildare, he ultimately, yet inadvertently, altered Ireland and her people.

The horse that inspired the renaissance was special. He was noble. He was magical. He granted wishes, made dreams come true. That this extraordinary horse even ended up in Ireland was due to any number of curious circumstances — if not a minor miracle.

The horse was named Nijinsky and he was quite possibly the most magnificent and exciting Thoroughbred racehorse of all time. Whenever he graced an Irish racecourse the number of his admirers grew exponentially. He was treated like a rock star. Huge crowds gathered everywhere he went. To simply be in the company of Nijinsky was to touch the stars.

When it was proclaimed that Nijinsky was to be retired from racing to stand at stud, the Irish turned themselves inside out trying to raise the money to keep him in Ireland. But to no avail. They were categorically and easily outbid by the Americans.

Nijinsky inspired all who saw him, but no more than a band of Irish horse-traders who believed there might just be another that shone with the brilliance of Nijinsky. If that was the case they would find him and bring him home to Ireland. They would find the money. They would find a way. No one would stop them this time. To that end they set sail for America in search of the next Nijinsky.

Unhampered by orthodoxy. Blessed with imagination. Armed with determination and the genius of generations of Irish horse-traders, they turned the world of the Thoroughbred on its ear, gleaned pots of gold, and unleashed the original Celtic Tiger from its lair.

The Horse

This extraordinary horse was named for the celebrated Russian dancer Vaslav Nijinsky. Born on a cold and snowy February 1889 in Russia, Vaslav Nijinsky made his dance debut at age four. By the time he was seventeen he was considered the greatest male dancer the world had ever had seen. Audiences were mesmerized by his breath-taking leaps propelling himself skyward — rising and rising to astounding heights. At the zenith he seemed to remain suspended, hovering in the air high above the stage. Then, like an autumn leaf floating from a tree, he'd drift ever-so slowly back to the earth.

As Vaslav Nijinsky defied gravity as a dancer, he defied convention as a choreographer and again was adulated as a genius. Yet the story of Vaslav Nijinsky is one of dualities: one of brilliant light, and extreme darkness. A story that echoes ancient myth — like the tale of Icarus who flew too close to the sun. Vaslav Nijinsky was but twenty-nine when he suffered a nervous breakdown and retired from the stage. The second half of his life was spent, for the most part, in a sanitarium and shrouded in a veil of gloom and melancholy. Prior to his death in 1950 Vaslav Nijinsky announced that he would return — reincarnated as a horse.

The incarnation may well have happened on a cold and snowy February 1967 in Canada when the mare Flaming Page gave birth to a long-legged bay colt with a distinctive heart-shaped marking in the centre of his forehead just beneath his curly black forelock. When he came of age this colt would be named Nijinsky.

Perhaps the inspiration for the name simply was a spin on that of the colt's sire, Northern Dancer. Still, and quite curiously, there are many parallels between the dancer and the horse that bore his name.

Nijinsky, the horse, was but two when he made his debut — as is often the case in Thoroughbred racing. Yet from the very first time he stepped on to an Irish racecourse, he too left his audiences spellbound as he appeared to transcend the capabilities of ordinary Thoroughbreds. Where all horses have four gaits — walk, trot, canter and gallop — Nijinsky possessed a magical fifth gait. His long stride was so fluid that he appeared to cruise across the turf and in full-flight, he too, gave the impression of hovering above the ground. Then, at the end of his spectacular but brief racing career, the horse's highly-strung disposition began to unravel and he experienced the equine version of a nervous breakdown.

Heralded as *god of the dance*, Vaslav Nijinsky, forever changed the world of dance. This horse named Nijinsky forever changed the world of the horse. Celebrated as *lord of the Dancers* it was his spectacular superiority and the ensuing mania to find the next Nijinsky that caused his sire's offspring to become more valuable than gold. Today more than half the world's Thoroughbreds descend from this one horse, Northern Dancer. But perhaps more important was that Nijinsky touched something deep in the Irish soul. An ancient art was rekindled. Ireland's age-old reputation as *land of the horse* was restored. And in the process the original Celtic Tiger began to roar.

Still, the story of how this remarkable horse actually came to exist is marked with more twists and turns than the slalom course at Whistler in the 2010 Olympics. If indeed the destiny of Nijinsky was guided by forces unseen, the fates would have worked overtime simply staying on course. Time and again the lengthy and winding road that led to Nijinsky was fraught with a myriad of challenges from human error to near calamity. Still, all along the way, the route was also strewn with an uncanny collection of serendipitous events.

The ballad of Nijinsky, this horse that carried the tiger, is a song that spins full circle — beginning and ending in Ireland. The first verse tells of two young Irishmen who set sail for Canada in the mid-1880's. Charles Magee departed the family home in Fermanagh, one of the six Counties of Northern Ireland and not far from Binlauglin Mountain, the peak of the Laughing Horse. The other, Thomas Dixon Taylor, hailed from County Wicklow in the South. Both young Irishmen eventually settled in Ottawa, the Canadian capital. Taylor, a civil engineer, to work on building Canada's railways. Magee, a shrewd entrepreneur, to find his fortune by engineering deals.

Years later the two Irishmen met at a wedding. Magee's daughter, Frances, married Taylor's son, Plunket. The couple had two sons. The younger, Fred, became an accomplished artist. Their first-born, Edward, seems to have embodied the traits of both grandfathers: an engineer by training; an entrepreneur by intuition.

Edward Taylor's passion, however, was for horses. This singular reality evolved as the driving force in an uncommon life. All that he did, all that he was, reflected back to his love of horses — of riding them, and racing them, and working unwaveringly toward the day when his Windfields Farm emerged as the home to the world's greatest Thoroughbreds. In fact no one person in the long history of the Thoroughbred has bred more champions than this grandson of two Irish immigrants. Nijinsky, the greatest of them all, was as a result of his colossal commitment.

Born and raised in Ottawa, a conservative government town, Taylor's entire world was shaken and stirred when he traveled to Montreal to attend university. The antithesis of staid Ottawa, Montreal was vibrant, cosmopolitan and daring. The four years Taylor enjoyed in Montreal impacted his life profoundly.

Until then horses were but the sturdy creatures that plodded submissively hauling delivery wagons along Ottawa's quiet streets. Montreal, an eclectic mixture of French and English cultures offered a different kind of horse — high-strung Thoroughbred racehorses. Taylor was instantly besotted. The course of his lifetime was established. From thereon he marched to his own drummer, all the while striding a path that would lead to Nijinsky.

According to US philosopher Joseph Campbell:

> *"If you follow your bliss, you put yourself on a kind of track that has been there all the while waiting for you and the life that you ought to be living is the one you are living. Wherever you are — if you are following your bliss, you are enjoying that refreshment, that life within you, all the time."*

Eddie Taylor clearly followed his bliss and it would appear that he was given all the gifts required to fulfill whatever destiny had in store for him. Tall, fair-haired, blue-eyed, clever and extremely handsome, he could charm the birds out of the trees. One of his most telling character traits was that once committed to a project, he simply refused to quit. Yet, while on one side he was steadfastly determined, he was also unusually patient. It was as if he always knew he would eventually reach his destination.

It seemed, however, that this absolute devotion to his quest allowed Taylor to see and experience the world differently from most. When you were with him often-times he was not there. Instead it was if he frequented another dimension or parallel universe. Like the absent-minded professor, he was a genius, yet flummoxed by the mundane or ordinary aspects of day-to-day living. At mealtime as a young man his fraternity brothers made it a game to pass him salt when he asked for sugar, then watch as he not only spooned the salt into his tea, but drink the tea — totally oblivious to the joke.

This life-long absentmindedness was due in part to the fact that his mind operated on any number of tracks at a time. One afternoon he and I were out on our horses taking a relaxing stroll around Windfields estate. He was explaining his plan to rejuvenate horse-racing in Quebec. The dollar figures were staggering. The concept, complex. Suddenly his horse stumbled and in that one horrible moment I realized he was so involved in his vision he had neglected to remember that he was on the back of a horse. I saw the confusion in his eyes. The next moment he was tumbling to the ground. He was seventy-six at the time.

After what seemed like an hour, but was probably only a minute or so, Taylor stirred and attempted to get to his feet. I held out my hand and offered to assist him. He refused. I thought of the riding accident he had years earlier and his fractured pelvic bone and his doctor's warnings that another fall would leave him crippled and I felt sick. Once on his feet he brushed himself off and assured me that he was fine.

That afternoon I watched in awe, relief, and eventually amusement as he approached any number of Jockey Club directors and employees. He'd ask them what they had done that morning, then chuckled as he told them that he had fallen off one of his horses.

"I haven't had a fall like that for years," he confided.

"I try not to, but it happens now and then," he chuckled, his blue eyes sparkling with delight, " but I don't intend on falling off my horse tomorrow morning."

He'd leave them flummoxed. Not knowing what to say. Many of these men were at least half his age yet visibly blanched at the notion of actually riding a horse, much less falling off one. Taylor continued to ride right up until this side of his eightieth birthday. The concept of quitting simply because the doctors warned him not to or because he had fallen off were not in his nature.

The road to Nijinsky was an uphill journey, but it is unlikely the man noticed. Instead, Taylor took the whole thing in his stride and was clearly invigorated by the challenges. It would appear that with every step along the way he became more and more captivated by his horses and not just his courageous Thoroughbreds. It was not uncommon for Taylor to arrive for a business meeting at his office in the coach house on one corner of Windfields estate on horseback.

At plateaus all along this uphill journey stood a remarkable Thoroughbred horse enticing him deeper into their world and that of horse racing. His prize, the holy grail of this one man's pilgrimage, was the horse named Nijinsky.

Taylor's enchantment began with a pair of outstanding Thoroughbreds named Sir Barton and Billy Kelly. Both were owned by Commander JKL Ross, a prominent Montreal sportsman and heir to Canadian Pacific Railroad fortunes. In 1918, the year young Edward Taylor arrived in Montreal to study engineering at McGill University, Billy Kelly was the talk of the town. Time and again he carried Ross' black and orange racing silks to glory in the big US horse races. A two year old gelding, Billy Kelly prevailed in all manner of conditions, including against older horses and was made to carry huge weight. Billy Kelly's only loss came in a match race with Eternal, the leading US money winner. The ultimate victor, however, was the Red Cross as both Ross and Eternal's owners put up $10,000 with all the proceeds to go to the charity.

Each and every one of Billy Kelly's races was reported in the Montreal press and his numerous victories made front page news. During the winter months high anticipation began building over the next encounter of Billy Kelly and Eternal — the 1919 Kentucky Derby. To make things even more sensational, his owner had been duped into wagering a massive amount on the outcome of the race.

Several months before the Derby Ross and his son were having lunch in a New York restaurant when they were approached by what Ross' son described as "an insignificant, yeasty-faced little man." The little man proposed a wager. He was betting that Eternal would beat Billy Kelly in the Derby. Ross put his fork down and asked "How much?" The fellow said, "How about fifty?" Thinking he meant $50 Ross agreed. Before leaving the fellow added the stipulation that in order for either to win the wager his horse must finish among the first three across the wire. Ross concurred and returned to his lunch.

Ross did not know that the "little man" was Arnold Rothstein, a notorious gambler who later that year would be connected to baseball's Black Sox scandal. When Rothstein said fifty, in gambler-speak he meant $50,000. Before long the story of the wager was leaked to the press. By the time Ross and his horses arrived at Churchill Downs in Louisville they were met with a barrage of reporters and photographers.

Churchill Downs was originally built to host the Kentucky Derby which in turn was aimed at showcasing Kentucky horses. The inaugural Derby was run in1875 but by the turn of the century the track was losing money and about to close down taking the fledgling Derby with it. Then along came Colonel Matt Winn, the portly, cigar-chomping Louisville promoter.

Winn's first challenge was to lure North America's best Thoroughbreds to the Derby. A man who thought on a grand scale, Winn optimistically billed the race as contest between the best of the East and the West. That the parochial little race was actually a romp between horses hailing from east and west of Louisville did not hamper his sales pitch. Still, none of the big stables on either coast took the bait so Winn took a new tack — he began a campaign to win over the sports columnists. It was after all, life before television, hence the age of newspapers and the beginning of Golden Age of Sports Writers. In the US columnists like Damon Runyan and Grantland Rice were enormously popular and powerful. Their every colourful word was devoured by their fans.

And so it was that every winter Winn made the trek to New York where he lavishly wined and dined the columnists and reporters; they reciprocated by writing lavishly about the Derby. 1n 1914, when Old Rosebud won the Derby, Grantland Rice coined the phrase "the run for the roses" which Winn turned into the theme of his race — one that remains in place to this day.

The following year a filly from New York won the race. Her name was Regret. After Regret's great triumph her exuberant owner, Harry Payne Whitney, declared, "I don't care if she ever wins another race, or if she even starts in another race. She has won the greatest race in North America." A win for the prominent New York-based Whitney stable — and with a filly — made headlines across the country. Whitney's words "the greatest race in North America" were quoted over and over by Winn's journalist friends.

Now, four years later, with Billy Kelly and Sir Barton soon to enter the starting gate, the hoopla surrounding the Kentucky Derby had grown exponentially and all Montreal was rooting for Commander Ross' horses to win 'the greatest race.' Almost everyone had their money on Billy Kelly and paid little, if any, heed to Sir Barton. And with good cause. Where the previous year Billy Kelly won almost every time he walked on to a track, Sir Barton was yet to win a race. To add to the prevailing excitement the Kentuckians had chosen Eternal and his running mate as favourites. The Ross entry was selected to finish second.

On the day of the race Eddie Taylor and his friends created a betting pool and like so many Montrealers, were hunkered down by a wireless radio to listen to the broadcast of the big event. Much to everyone's surprise, the moment the starting barrier was dropped Sir Barton bounded right out into the lead. The rangy chestnut colt didn't look left or right. He just kept running and running like a great, gangly teenager. When it was all over the bewildered colt had won the famed US event by five lengths. Billy Kelly was second. Eternal finished a dismal and distant tenth.

Sir Barton's his first taste of victory was not his last. No flash in the pan, the colt suddenly began to quite enjoy horse racing. That year Sir Barton was never out of the money in thirteen starts, eight of which he won, and he banked more money for his owner than any other horse in North America. Sir Barton was also the first horse in history to have won the US Triple Crown: the Derby, the Preakness and the Belmont.

If Eddie Taylor was indeed destined to devote his life to the creation of extraordinary horses, fate could not have placed him in a more exciting time in the history of horse racing in North America. For starters there was a rugged campaigner called Exterminator that won the hearts of all who saw him run. Huge and angular, Exterminator was not a pretty horse. Walter S. Vosburgh described him as "an unattractive gelding ... as lean and hungry looking as Caesar described Cassius. High in bone and low in flesh." His craggy conformation inspired his fans to affectionately dub him "Old Bones." Nothing seemed to bother Exterminator except the absence of his constant companion, a diminutive pony named Peanuts. Starting in 1917 the indomitable Exterminator raced for eight years and was sent to the post 100 times. He won 50 races, including — to the surprise of most — the Kentucky Derby. Starting as the longest price on the board, the ungainly animal splashed his way around the muddy track to triumph over a collection of far more fashionable runners. Exterminator was seldom out of the money and would go down in history as one of the most beloved of all American runners.

In 1919 while Sir Barton was dominating the winner's circles of the top US races, a youngster by the name of Man o' War had begun his march toward immortality. His legion of fans nicknamed him "Big Red" and he would eventually reign in the minds of many as the most exciting Thoroughbred in the history of US horse racing.

A holy terror to handle when he was young, Man o' War was an awesome creature. A muscular glowing chestnut he stood over 16 hands and he possessed an enormously long stride. Although never officially measured it was said to have been somewhere between 25 and 28 feet. Big Red was also known for his voracious appetite. When in training his first meal of the day — 2-1/2 quarts of oats with a side entree of hay — was served at 3:30 a.m. Because he tended to hoover every morsel in a single gulp they opted to feed him with a bit in his mouth to slow the process. His final meal of the day arrived promptly at 5:15 p.m. and varied between 5 quarts of oats for a daily total of 12 quarts, or a mixture of crushed oats and bran. He also had a fondness for oranges.

All the while the big red horse exuded supercharged energy: "Even when he was standing motionless in his stall, with his ears pricked forward and his eyes focused on something slightly above the horizon which mere people could never see, energy still poured from him," observed Joe Palmer. "He could get in no position which suggested actual repose, and his very stillness was that of the coiled spring, of the crouched tiger."

Man o' War was entered in 21 races and except for his single defeat (by Upset in the Sanford Stakes), the colt won all of his races by open daylight. Almost every time he touched a hoof on a racetrack Man o' War shattered an existing record. Not because he was being pressed by another. No, he simply ran for the sheer joy of speed. Man o' War won one of his races by 100 lengths.

It was a time of heros. The horse had been named by Eleanor Belmont for her husband August Belmont II who was abroad fighting during the first world war. The war was now over and in the aftermath Man o' War joined a succession of outstanding US sports figures — Babe Ruth, Jack Dempsey, Bill Tilden that would burst on the scene.

Film newsreels capturing each and every one of Man o' War's

thrilling performances were played in movie theatres across North America. His final race was publicized with all the excitement and ceremony of a coronation and Canada's Sir Barton was chosen the most appropriate adversary in this, Man o' War's swan song. Kenilworth Park, in Windsor, Ontario put up $80,000 for this highly-anticipated match race.

En route to the Windsor event Sir Barton had fought and won four consecutive, and very demanding, races. Carrying as much as 134 pounds, Sir Barton prevailed over fields of tough competitors that included the mighty Exterminator. In fact Sir Barton not only vanquished Exterminator, he set a track record in the process.

Nonetheless, on the eve of the match race Commander Ross announced he was replacing Sir Baron's regular jockey. "I have determined to substitute jockey Frank G. Keogh for Earl Sande in today's race, for the reason my boy (Earl Sande) is not in good form." quoted *New York Times*, "Keogh is at the top of his form at present and I want to take advantage of it so there will be no excuse after the race is won or lost."

At the crack of the starters pistol Sir Barton bounded into the lead and was a good length ahead of Man o' War, but not for long. Man o' War won the match race with ease, but then Man o' War generally won his races with ease. After the event his owner, Sam Riddle, was handed the $75,000 cheque for Man o' War's final triumph and a $5,000 gold trophy filled with champagne. Riddle poured the champagne on the ground, filled the trophy with water and presented it to his horse.

Eddie Taylor had become an instant and avid fan of horse racing and followed the careers of Man o' War and Sir Barton and Billy Kelly and the rest with uncommon devotion According to his fraternity yearbook of 1921, Taylor was more than prepared to back his hunches:

> *" ... If you wish to place some money on the Derby or King's Plate,*
> *And the papers give the odds upon your horse as one to eight,*
> *Don't believe the sporting circles for they'll do you every time,*
> *Go to Edward, he'll compute the odds at "ten to eighty-nine."*

One morning at breakfast in his first winter at McGill Taylor was struck with a notion that ultimately would fund his frequent forays to Montreal's racetracks. At the time toasters browned only one side of a piece of bread at a time. The process was time-consuming and he was, after-all, a young man in a hurry. Why couldn't someone invent one that toasted both sides at the same time? he reasoned. So, he did. On Valentine's Day 1919, a fortnight past his eighteenth birthday, he applied for a patent to his electric toaster. He then approached a Montreal firm and negotiated the rights to manufacture his invention along with a royalty for every *Household* toaster sold. The money went towards his university tuition and his new fixation, horse racing.

There were seven racetracks in the Montreal area. The most prestigious was Bluebonnets at the foot of Mount Royal. Owned by Commander Ross this was where the elite of Montreal's society could be found strolling the manicured lawns of the members' enclosure on Saturday afternoon. Every weekend throughout the summer and into the fall Eddie Taylor was among the throngs that caught the streetcar that rattled up to Bluebonnets, or the ferry across the river to another of his favourites, King Edward Park on Ile Gros Bois.

As it would turn out the four years young Taylor lived in Montreal coincided with the golden age of Thoroughbred sport in Quebec. When he graduated from McGill University in the spring of 1922 with a B.Sc. in mechanical engineering he returned to Ottawa. He never practiced as an engineer, not even one day

— but his new-found passion for horses endured all the days of his life.

Horse racing in Ottawa surely paled compared to the panache of Montreal. So when he returned to Ottawa after graduation Taylor decided to pursue his new-found passion for horses from another angle — in the saddle. He joined the Princess Louise Dragoon Guards, a mounted ceremonial regiment, and learned to ride. On a number of occasions, resplendent in full military regalia, he served as one of the two officers escorting the governor-general's landau to the opening of parliament. Eventually he and a few friends purchased horses of their own and he rode at every opportunity.

One Saturday afternoon Taylor brought his bride-to-be to the races at Ottawa's Connaught Park. It was Winifred Duguid's first visit to a Thoroughbred meet and the excitement and colour appealed to her great sense of humour and adventure. At the end of the day Taylor had wagered and lost his money and she was dismayed that they might not ever return to the races. She need not have worried.

Taylor and his bride moved to Toronto in 1928. His father had convinced Taylor to work for him as a bond salesman for the brokerage firm McLeod, Young, Weir. A natural born promoter, Taylor was soon their top salesperson and before he was thirty was able to convince the board that he should be given a junior partnership in the firm. The following year the stock market crashed.

Taylor was a restless man. To fulfill the mission that would lead to Nijinsky he was going to need a whole lot of money. Unlike Commander Ross, he would not inherit the necessary fortune. He would have to create it himself, hence was not prepared to sit around and wait for the market to right itself. Instead, he scanned the bleak horizon for an opportunity.

During the first world war his father was stationed in London, England and Taylor and his brother were dispatched to local schools. Thirteen year-old Eddie, however, was forever running off, bent on joining the army. Finally his frustrated parents sent him back to Canada to live with his entrepreneurial grandfather, Charles Magee. Among Magee's many acquisitions was an interest in Bradings, a small Ottawa brewery. After university Magee gave his grandson a seat on the board of the company. Several years later, following the repeal of the Temperance Act, Taylor proposed a grand scheme for expanding the brewery. The other directors said *No*.

This time around he didn't ask permission. Instead off he went, with his bride in tow, to amalgamate Ontario's forty-or-so breweries. It was a version of the plan he had suggested to Bradings directors wherein he argued that one large operation would function more efficiently than a motley collection of independent brewers. The country was in the devastating grip of the great depression. Taylor had no money but along the way he met an US promoter, Clarke Jennison who had a similar idea — except that Jennison had money — about half a million dollars he had raised from British investors. Before long the Brewing Corporation of Ontario was incorporated with Taylor as president and Jennison as chairman.

There were seven racetracks within an eighty mile radius of the city. The most prominent was Woodbine Park in the east end and Eddie and Winnie Taylor were often among the crowds, cheering on their favourites. Still Taylor longed to have racehorses of his own but had neither the time nor the money.

In short order he had amalgamated about a dozen small breweries, but it was against the law to advertise beer, which, of course, hampered sales. Then in the spring of 1936 another of his big ideas came to him. He would merge his passion for horses with his business interests and start up a small racing stable and name it Cosgrave after one of his newly acquired breweries. Again, he had no money, but characteristically, was disinclined to allow small details get in the way of his grand scheme.

Next Taylor needed a trainer. Somehow he not only managed to convince the wily Bert Alexandra into coming out of retirement, he managed to finagle Alexandra into backing him financially. Before long Alexandra had rounded up a small herd of race horses. The road that led to Nijinsky had begun.

For the most part Alexandra ran the entire racing operation. Taylor came to the track when one of their horses was running and the rest of the time he was at the office attempting to build the company, and his bank account.

One afternoon an Irishman named Callahan phoned Taylor offering to sell him a filly — a grand filly to be sure — for six hundred dollars. Without consulting his trainer, he bought her, sight unseen. Named Mona Bell she was swift, determined and courageous and probably the most important purchase he made, for Mona Bell led him to the next stage of his journey. The bravery of this exquisite filly convinced Taylor to take the giant leap from horse owner to horse breeder.

Mona Bell and the colt Bunty Lawless emerged the stars of the Ontario horse racing circuit. Still they got off to an inauspicious start. The first time they met was in Mrs. Orpen's Cup and Saucer Handicap, named for the track owner's wife. The year was 1937 and there were eighteen horses in the race. Mona Bell finished sixteenth and less than a length behind her Bunty Lawless ambled across the finish. The pair eventually got the knack of racing

While Taylor simply handed over a fist-full of cash for Mona

Bell, the story of how Toronto tavern owner, Willie Morrissey, came to own Bunty Lawless, is considerably more colourful. It all started when Morrissey heard that Jack Whyte was selling a horse called Gift Roman for eight hundred dollars. It sounded like a good deal, so he gave a friend the required cash and dispatched him to buy the horse. When Whyte discovered the transaction was being made on behalf of Morrissey, he raised the price to twelve hundred dollars. Morrissey was furious and became obsessed with getting revenge.

"Morrissey was a fiery little Irishman who had been born in Toronto's gaslight district, known as Cabbage Town," wrote Jim Coleman, "and he had single-handedly fought his way to a comfortable financial plateau. He was a non-drinking, non-smoking bachelor, he was a gambler and a hotel owner, he was scrupulously honest, but his strong character was flawed by an Irish passion for nurturing life-long grudges ... Willie was a dedicated hater ..."

When Morrissey saw his new enemy was running a filly called Mintwina in a two-thousand-dollar claiming race the die was cast. The theory behind claiming races is that the owner of the horse determines the value of their horse, hence its level of competition. Entering a horse worth $20,000 in a race slated for horses valued at $2,000 simply to win a race would be a bad idea since horses in claiming races may be purchased by another owner or trainer at the meet for the amount it is running under.

Strictly for spite Morrissey claimed Mintwina but his period of revenge was short-lived. The first time the filly raced in his colours she broke the sesamoid in her right forefoot. Morrissey's temper erupted once again. He was going to have the filly put to her death. Fortunately his friend, Doc Hodgson, managed to convince the irate Irishman that Mintwina's life should be spared.

The filly eventually recovered but her racing days were over so Hodgson suggested she would be a good broodmare. Morrissey had no interest in breeding Thoroughbreds. Hodgson persevered, and somehow persuaded the Irishman to have her bred to the stallion, Ladder. The result of the mating was a colt Morrissey named for his childhood hero James "Bunty" Lawless.

Time and again Mona Bell and Bunty Lawless were pitted against each other on Ontario racecourses. Bunty Lawless was the stronger racehorse still Mona Bell outran Bunty Lawless on a number of occasions, with a portion much of the credit going to her cunning trainer, Bert Alexandra.

It wasn't long before grand colour photographs of Mona Bell were displayed on the walls of Ontario taverns. Beneath her photo, in very large letters was the word: COSGRAVE. Taylor had not only discovered a way of circumnavigating the province's law against advertising beer and spirits but had launched a racing stable that would grow to become home to the world's greatest Thoroughbreds.

The rivalry between Mona Bell and Bunty Lawless was such that when, in the summer of 1939, their owners announced that upon retirement from the track the two horses would be bred, the news was headlined in the local Toronto newspaper.

Sadly, in August of the same year, Mona Bell slipped on the muddy Stamford Park track and broke her leg. For almost an hour after the accident Taylor and Alexandra talked with the veterinarian about the possibility of saving her, so that she might live out her days as a broodmare. But there was no hope that she would walk again. Mona Bell was euthanized and buried in the infield of Stamford Park, not far from where the accident had occurred.

Bunty Lawless was retired to stud in 1940. While saddened by the death of Mona Bell, Taylor agreed that Nandi, one of the original string of Cosgrave horses, be sent to Bunty Lawless. In the spring of 1942, Nandi gave birth to a filly, the first offspring sired by Bunty Lawless. Nandi was bred back to Bunty Lawless, this time she produced a brown colt.

Winnie Taylor named the colt Windfields after their farm, which was, in retrospect, quite appropriate. In years to come the designation *Windfields-bred* would become synonymous with the very finest Thoroughbreds in the world. So while Mona Bell encouraged Taylor to take the plunge into the world of horse breeding, this colt named Windfields heralded a whole new plateau in the journey that led to Nijinsky.

Now if this were a work of fiction or a screenplay where events simply happen in order to carry the story along, a certain suspension of verisimilitude would be acceptable, if not anticipated. But this story actually happened. It is, nonetheless, peppered with highly improbable events. Windfields, the horse, is but one of these many occurrences.

To have been rewarded with an exceptional horse like Windfields in only their second attempt at the inexact science of horse breeding was quite remarkable. Many have spent an entire lifetime and a fortune-or-two in pursuit of such Thoroughbred excellence. No doubt a portent of things to come, Windfields also catapulted Taylor on to centre stage and into the eye of the storm of controversy.

Windfields was a striking-looking horse. His conformation was flawless. His coat, a rich brown and his eye was bold and intelligent. As a two year old, Windfields showed tremendous potential as a race horse. He was quick, agile, and appeared to love to run. He easily won his first three starts, establishing, and re-establishing records along the way. Then one morning when he was attempting to out-race the wind, he wrenched a muscle-or-two and was side-lined for the rest of the season.

Bert Alexandra's antipathy for the directors of the Ontario Jockey Club was legend. At the least provocation he opted to race his horses anywhere but under their jurisdiction. So following Windfields's injury he packed up the tack trunks and moved the Cosgrave horses to Belmont Park in New York State for the winter. However, according to rules of the Jockey Club, racing anywhere beyond the Ontario border meant Windfields was ineligible for their most prestigious horse race, the King's Plate. This suited Alexandra dandily, but would cause some considerable consternation to Eddie Taylor.

The King's Plate was run under Royal ascent and featured a prize of guineas straight from the coffers of the reigning British monarch, who at the time was King George VI. A monarchist through and through, it had not occurred to Taylor that Windfields, only the second horse they had bred, was capable not only of running in the big race, but of winning. Nor was Taylor cognizant of the rules of racing. Nor was he familiar with the designers of the rules of racing who were considered at best a stodgy elitist club.

In the meantime, Colonel Sam McLaughlin's Kingarvie had won the King's Plate six lengths ahead of his nearest rival by splashing his way through the sloppy Woodbine track in a torrential downpour. It wasn't long before Canadian turf writers and racing fans alike began speculating whether Kingarvie or Windfields was the better horse. Supporters of Kingarvie were convinced the only reason Taylor was not racing Windfields in Canada was that he was afraid of having his colt beaten by the reigning King's Plate winner.

One evening at a dinner party Taylor was confronted by two ardent Kingarvie fans. The ensuing banter over which was the better horse resulted in some serious wagering. Kingarvie's backers stipulated that their wager be a *play or pay*, meaning that Taylor would have to pay up if he did not run Windfields against Kingarvie.

The next morning Taylor called Alexandra at Belmont Park and explained that everywhere he turned people had an opinion about his horse. Most were reflecting the sports writer's theory that he was afraid to run Windfields against Kingarvie. Even his daughters, Judith and Louise, had joined in the speculation and written a letter beseeching him to run Windfields against Kingarvie. As a rule Taylor did not interfere with the management of the racing stable, but now he felt he had no choice so he told Alexandra they were going to have to bring Windfields to Canada to run in the Breeders' Stakes.

Alexandra was reluctant and argued that Windfields had endured an arduous winter campaign. Furthermore, he debated, the race was being held that coming weekend, two days hence. But Taylor was adamant and eventually Alexandra conceded. Because there was little time they decided they had to fly Windfields to Toronto.

Alexandra arrived at the New York airport with Windfields and immediately deduced the plane was not large enough. The ceiling was too low and he reasoned that if Windfields were to become nervous on the flight and possibly rear up, the horse would crack his head. Alexandra didn't want to run Windfields in the Breeder's Stakes in the first place. The size of the plane was a perfect excuse. There was not enough time to trailer the horse to Canada, so he abandoned the project and whistled Windfields back to Belmont Park.

When Taylor phoned to make sure that his horse had arrived safely in Toronto he was flabbergasted to discover that Windfields was still in New York. Scant few horses were shipped by air at the time. During WWII Taylor was stationed in Washington, D.C., where as director-general of the British Supply mission, he was responsible for maintaining a constant supply of war supplies from the US to Britain. During his tenure Taylor made countless contacts, among them was the president of American Airlines. So he phoned the fellow to discover that the airline did indeed have a four-engine plane that could be equipped for the job. The plane, however, was in New York, but the stalls for shipping horses were in California. With no other options Taylor instructed them fly to California, pick up the stalls, then return to New York and collect Windfields and convey him to Canada. The junket would cost Taylor over five thousand dollars. The first four horses in Breeder's Stakes would divide a purse that was about three thousand dollars.

Hordes packed into Woodbine Park's wooden stands to witness the highly-publicized contest and were backing Windfields at odds of 2-5 to triumph over Kingarvie. The motivation being, no doubt, that if Taylor was going to all that expense to bring Windfields back to Canada for the race, he must be confident that his horse was going to win.

In the paddock before the race Bert Alexandra warned jockey Herbie Lindberg that Windfields was not a "whip horse." Under *no circumstances* was he to use his whip on the colt. To say that Windfields got off to a bad start is an understatement. First he balked at going into the starting gate, and eventually had to be backed in. Once in the gate Windfields was accustomed to being held by a member of the starting crew, as happened when he ran in the US. The Ontario Jockey Club, however, did not allow the practice.

When the bell sounded Windfields ambled out of the gate. He then cantered along blissfully unaware of the sense of urgency building among his supporters, and particularly his owners. A loud, collective moan rose from the stands when Kingarvie, who had slipped and fallen coming out of the starting gate, breezed past Windfields at the half-mile pole. Seemingly unaffected Windfields now trailed the field and toddled along as if out on a leisurely stroll in the park. Taylor was crestfallen.

All the while Windfields' jockey sat perfectly still in the saddle obeying Alexandra's order not to touch the colt with his whip. Then suddenly, as if awakened and lifted by the wind, Windfields became airborne and soared across the wire five lengths ahead of second-place Kingarvie.

Eddie Taylor heaved a great sigh of relief.

At some level horse racing mirrors ancient myths and humanity's enduring need for heros, or at the very least, heroic acts that we mere mortals are unable to create in our day-to-day existence. When the starting bell clangs a transference takes place and during the brief time it takes to run a horse race, at some level, we become our horse — the horse carrying our wager, our hopes, our dreams. On that sunny July afternoon at Woodbine Park, Eddie Taylor surely experienced the exhilaration of life on the edge vicariously through this quite remarkable horse.

Windfields continued his winning ways for years to come. He won several races at California's Santa Anita when he was six and then was retired to stud to become one of the most important stallions in the early days of the farm after which he was named.

The next horse ready to raise Taylor's sights was named Epic:"I spent a lot of time trying to find a name for this fellow," Taylor explained, "Finally I decided to thumb through the dictionary. I saw this name. It appealed to me, as it was short and easily remembered, an epic being a poem or event of importance."

And that he was, for this colt reigns as the first of the horses bred on the Taylor's farm to win the King's Plate — hence entry into the glamourous and regal side of this, the sport of kings and queens. Yet up to three months prior to the 1949 King's Plate, it was doubtful Epic would make it to the starting gate, much less run and win the race.

He was a big rangy colt with dodgy ankles and Alexandra didn't hold out much hope that he would ever be able to race, but his assistant, Johnny Collins, refused to give up on the colt. Collins spent hours and hours working with Epic and the colt eventually responded to his devotion.

In fact his recovery was so remarkable that the once pessimistic Alexandra was now boasting to anyone who would listen that he had the best horse in the country. Pretty soon both he and Taylor had a great deal of money riding on the race.

Epic made his debut in the first division of the King's Plate Trials. Although he ambled slowly from the gate, Epic soon figured things out. By the time the horses had reached the homestretch Epic had taken the lead and won with relative ease. The second division of the King's Plate Trials was won by Speedy Irish, Canada's champion two year old. Headlines billed the forthcoming King's Plate as a match race between Epic and Speedy Irish. Since Epic had only run one race in his life he was clearly the underdog up against the champ.

On the morning of the big race all hell broke loose when Alexandra learned Epic had drawn a post position outside the regular starting gate. The Jockey Club owned a 12-stall gate but there were seventeen entries so they elected to accommodate twelve horses in the gate. The remainder, including Epic, were to start from an open barrier outside the gate.

Alexandra argued that all the horses should start from the old open barrier, thus giving them all an even chance. The Jockey Club refused to budge, so Alexandra announced that Epic would be scratched from the race and stormed off to find Taylor. As it happened this marked the very year Taylor was invited to become a director of the Ontario Jockey Club. Since Alexandra had such disdain for the directors the two men now inhabited two very divergent camps. Taylor would be obliged to side with the directors. Fortunately several of the owners pulled their horses out of the race thereby moving Epic up to the last stall of the starting gate. The thirteenth entry would start from outside the gate.

A record crowd crammed into Woodbine Park and gave Speedy Irish an edge in the wagering. In the early running jockey Chris Rogers kept Epic about three lengths behind the pacesetter while Speedy Irish was content to coast along at the back of the pack.

Epic was anxious to run so Rogers let the colt take the lead. At the same moment Speedy Irish, a horse famous for his last-minute drive, started to make his move and as the horses hit the homestretch he was fast gaining on Epic. It was the moment the fans were waiting for.

Speedy Irish had rocketed his way to second place and was chasing Epic for all he was worth. Eddie and Winnie Taylor and the rest of the massive crowd were on their feet shouting and cheering. But Epic refused to be intimidated and staved off the challenge. Before long Epic was in the winners' circle and Windfields Farm had won its first 'Plate. The first of many.

Waiting patiently at the next bend on this uphill road to Nijinsky stood quite possibly the most courageous horse in the history of US horse racing. His name was Citation and seldom has more been asked of a great champion. He also plays a starring role in this saga for Citation's influence on Eddie Taylor, hence that of Nijinsky, was enormous.

During WWII horse racing in North America had been conducted under wartime conditions. Meets were subject to approval of local commissions which established ceilings on the numbers of employees to ensure none were vital to jobs in the war effort. There were restrictions on crucial commodities like petrol and rubber tires. Any number of tracks closed. When the war-time blackout was lifted close to 65,000 fans flocked to Jamaica Park on Memorial Day 1945.

By the time Citation began his gallop into the history books several years later the sport was experiencing a growth spurt. The world was recovering from a devastating war and it was not uncommon for people to look to sport for escape. There is nothing like the majesty and courage of a great horse to lift ones spirits. Citation, the hero many were searching for, filled the bill perceptibly.

Foaled 11 April 1945, the little bay colt won almost every time he entered a starting gate. Time and again he was compared to Man o' War. Yet from all fronts the two were worlds apart. Man o' War was a big red powerhouse that exuded massive energy on his every stride. Conversely Citation was a small compact dark bay with none of the flash and dash of Man o' War. Instead Citation was like a compact sports car with sleek lines and the acceleration of a Maserati.

Where Man o' War's muscles fairly rippled and bulged, Citation weighed little more than 1000 pounds. His nostrils were noticably large and his eyes were set wide apart and brimming with intelligence, which according to trainer Jimmy Jones was a major factor in how Citation went about things. A horse with manners and an excellent disposition, Citation was very easy on himself and those around him. After each and every race Citation was nonchalant. He took his celebrity in his stride and simply looked forward to a good meal after which he laid down and had a nap. And, according to his handlers, he snored.

His owners, Calumet Farms, dispatched Citation to the races in February of his two year old season and brought him back to the farm for a brief rest in mid-December. Citation had run in twenty races and won all but one and that was when he finished second to a filly named Bewitch. Since she was also owned by Calumet Farms, as was the third-placed horse, there was speculation that Citation might not have been asked to run very fast that day.

After Christmas Citation was shipped to Florida. He easily won the first three races including the Flamingo Stakes. Considered a prep race for the Kentucky Derby Citation romped to a six-length victory. To celebrate his jockey, Al Snider, and two friends set out on a fishing trip off the Florida Keys the following day. Lost in a storm, they never returned. The boat was eventually discovered, but no trace of the men was ever found. Snider was replaced by champion jockey, Eddie Arcaro

Citation's next race was over a hopelessly muddy track. A horse called Saggy splashed to the lead and when Arcaro positioned Citation to challenge one of the other horses scooted into his way. Citation finished second, a length behind Saggy. It was Citation's only defeat of the year. After the race Arcaro admitted that with the major races coming up, he didn't want to demand the utmost from his horse on the muddy track. Five days later Citation won the Chesapeake Stakes handily. Saggy finished last.

Only five horses, including stable-mate, Coaltown, had the temerity to face Citation in the 1948 Kentucky Derby. The track was sloppy, but Citation paid little heed and before long the little colt was standing in the winners circle. A huge blanket of red roses was draped across his withers and trailed along the ground. Eddie and Winnie Taylor were in the stands that afternoon and among the fans applauding horse racing's new hero.

A fortnight later Citation was in Baltimore for the Preakness. As was just about everyone of importance or notoriety in the nation. According to the Baltimore Sun: "(under) billowing white clouds hung suspended in an azure sky, an all-star crowd of 32,244 crammed into Old Hilltop to witness the 72nd running of the Preakness Stakes." Once again, Eddie and Winnie Taylor were among the throng that included countless celebrities being entertained by a bright and breezy red-coated 75-piece band. The excitement generated by Citation's appearance also was cause for the race to be televised for the first time in a program put on jointly by CBS and the local Baltimore station.

Only four horses were entered in the race. According to Joseph B Kelly, former *Washington Star* racing editor: "Citation was such a versatile horse that could overcome muddy tracks or fast tracks, short races or long races. He could adapt to any and all circumstances. None of the Derby horses came up to Pimlico.

They had to dig up horses to run against Citation because he scared them all off."

With Eddie Arcaro in the saddle, Citation led from wire-to-wire and won in a romp by six lengths. As the traditional blanket of Black-eyed Susans were draped over Citations withers Arcaro said: "It was a privilege to ride such a horse." Years later when Arcaro was about to retire from racing he continued to describe Citation as the best horse he ever rode: "he had more gears than a sports car."

Instead of resting Citation over the three weeks between the Preakness and the Belmont, final race in the US Triple Crown, Citation's owners shipped the colt to Garden State Park to run in the Jersey Stakes. Carrying 12 pounds more than the others Citation won by eleven lengths and set a track record.

Thinking Citation should be a bit fatigued seven owners sent their best and freshest horses out to the Belmont to challenge this great champion. Before the race Arcaro told the news media that the only way Citation could lose the race was if he fell off. And, he almost did. When the horses came flying out of the starting gate Citation stumbled and went down on his nose. Arcaro rode *acey-deucy* with the right stirrup two inches higher than the left. The theory was that it offered better balance on the turns. But when Citation went down, Arcaro was thrown off balance and left clinging for his life.

Still he managed to climb back into the saddle and Citation galloped on to win the Belmont Stakes by an astounding eight lengths. Once again Eddie and Winnie Taylor were among the crowd at the New York track.

The following week Citation was shipped to Chicago to run against older horses in the Stars and Stripes handicap. One of his toughest races, he pulled a hip muscle, but still won by two lengths and in track record time. Eddie and Winnie Taylor missed that race. Instead they had traveled to Kentucky and were among of buyers at the annual Keeneland horse auction.

The excitement generated by the sheer brilliance of the little bay colt resulted in an exceptionally large crowd roaming the stabling area. All were in search of the next Citation, but none more committed than Eddie Taylor.

Citation was, by far, the greatest horse Taylor had seen. In his opinion the horse was perfect. From the ease with which Citation galloped — with his ears perked forward it was as if the little bay colt was carried around the course on the wings of angels — to his agreeable disposition. If Taylor was going to breed truly outstanding horses, Citation was model he sought.

Taylor eventually settled upon five yearlings, two colts and three fillies and the shopping spree cost him $92,000 which was a colossal amount at the time. His most prized purchase was a dark brown yearling son of Bull Lea, sire of Citation. Taylor paid $38,000 for the colt. It seemed a king's ransom. In 1948 the average price for a yearling at public auction in the US was $3,600. But then, Taylor was a man on a mission.

He chose to purchase fillies whose families were rife with hardy US bloodlines. One was a daughter of Flaming Top and sported Man o' War and two Kentucky Derby winners in her pedigree. Winnie Taylor named the colt Bull Page and the filly, Flaring Top. In years to come these two yearlings would become distinguished as the maternal grandparents of Nijinsky. It would, however, be years before their custodians got it right.

Still, the odds of the grandparents of possibly the greatest Thoroughbred in history being a) at the same sale b) selected and purchased by the same individual and c) loaded on a horse van bound for Canada are as remote as finding two needles in one haystack.

When the five yearlings arrived in Canada Alexandra was particularly interested in Bull Page and was quick to point out the animal's conformation defects and shortcomings. In his opinion Bull Page was unlikely to endure the rigours of constant pounding on the hard racing surfaces. Yet when Alexandra started working with Bull Page he soon had a change of heart. Alexandra was impressed with the colt's natural speed and ability. "This colt will make the world forget Citation — if he remains sound," trumpeted Alexandra for all to hear.

Bull Page did not remain sound. He was not raced as a two year old and was out of action for most of his three year old season because of a broken bone in his foot. At four Bull Page began to blossom and mature. Alexandra had, once again, locked horns with the stodgy Jockey Club directorate — which now included Taylor. This time Alexandra retired for good and handed the reins to Gordon 'Pete' McCann.

A former jockey, McCann possessed a genius for understanding the mental and physical fragilities of so many Thoroughbreds. McCann was especially good at handling those with overly high nervous energy — the ones that, despite physical ailments, will run until they collapse. Most trainers have to rely on the opinions and instincts of jockeys and exercise riders. Not McCann. Instead he climbed into the saddle of all the horses under his care and continued to ride the ones that needed special care through their early morning exercises. Bull Page was one of the special cases. Over the 1951 season Bull Page went to the post 16 times. He won six including the Canadian International Championship. He was second five times; third, three times. He carried top weight, equaled track records and inspired the Canadian edition of the *Daily Racing Form* to conduct a poll to select Canada's first Horse of the Year. Bull Page was the unanimous winner. But most significantly Bull Page was grandsire to the horse named Nijinsky.

Nijinsky's grand-dam, Flaring Top, also began her racing days under the tutelage of Alexandra. She ran her first race in Detroit 2 June, 1949 and showed little inclination to work up a sweat and finished ninth. Several weeks later she was back in the starting gate. This time she picked up the pace and was fifth. She was a little faster out of the gate in her third race, but eventually faded back to sixth. In her final race of the year she was ridden by Ted

Atkinson. Known as 'the slasher' for his brutality with the whip, Atkinson drove the filly to the front of the field and steadily drew away from the rest. Flaring Top won the race by nine lengths.

It was surely a hollow victory. Whatever damage was inflicted records show that Flaring Top did not race again for almost an entire year. When she returned to the track Bert Alexandra had retired and she too was in the capable hands of Taylor's new trainer, Pete McCann.

Back at the races Flaring Top won several contests but her real place in history was as grand-dam to Nijinsky. Yet it took many, many years before the Windfields decision-makers got it right and stumbled upon the winning formula.

While Eddie Taylor was busily building a team of exceptional horses, he also decided to build a stadium worthy of Windfields runners. When Taylor made the transition from racing fan to horse owner he soon understood why columnist Jim Coleman called Ontario horse racing the "leaky roof circuit." The tracks and stabling were in very poor condition. The buildings were falling down and easily could be labeled fire-traps, so Taylor set out to change things. Over the next couple of decades he totally overhauled horse racing in Canada which included constructing Woodbine racetrack. When it opened for business June 1956 it was the most modern racing facility in the world, yet Taylor's detractors called it "Taylor's White Elephant." Built on what was, at the time, the outskirts of Toronto, his critics suggested they would need a horse just to get there. Today it is surrounded by urban sprawl.

It is impossible to simply sit down and map out a plan that would result in the creation of the perfect racehorse. The prevailing theory is "breed the best to the best and hope for the best."

Which was precisely what Taylor was doing. And at a fairly good clip. In the scant thirteen years since Mona Bell inspired Taylor to enter the world of horse breeding his Windfields Farm herd had mushroomed to about 100 horses and included thirty-eight broodmares, countless foals and yearlings and several stallions.

To house this ever-burgeoning horse empire Taylor purchased land adjoining their 40-acre estate and proceeded to build the most impressive and elaborate horse farm in the country. The horses were housed in three large red-brick stables. The luxury extended to their stalls which were made of highly polished oak. There were several smaller barns and staff houses and all were surrounded by green pastures and a maze of white board fences outlining countless paddocks.

The previous fall Colonel Sam McLaughlin phoned Taylor to announce that he planned to sell Parkwood, his stately horse farm located north of Oshawa, Ontario. Nearing his eightieth birthday McLaughlin felt it was time to retire. He had received lucrative offers from real estate developers, but he was anxious to have Parkwood continue as a horse farm. To that end he was prepared to make substantial price concessions.

Parkwood came with over two hundred acres of paddocks, five horse barns, a half-mile training track, a huge indoor arena, an office, fully equipped dispensary, five houses for staff, and a number of cattle barns. Also included were stallions, broodmares, foals, yearlings, horses-in-training and a herd of robust beef cattle.

Taylor began phoning friends and colleagues and exploring various options. While he surely did not need another horse farm, it wasn't long before he was as anxious as McLaughlin that the property not go to developers. Furthermore, McLaughlin was almost giving the place away — as long as horses continued to roam its paddocks. In the end Taylor bought the place himself. It was an offer he couldn't refuse.

It was also a significant sign-post on the road to Nijinsky. Now

Taylor had two farms and hundreds of horses. He could handle the financial responsibility of one farm, but not two. Because of the added pressure Taylor was compelled to go in search of the final piece of the genetic portrait that would result in Nijinsky.

Essentially Parkwood raised the bar of Taylor's aspirations — and well beyond even his lofty expectations. The place was going to have to pay for itself and Taylor was going to have to come up with a solution.

Initially he thought he'd turn Parkwood into a Canadian version of England's National Stud. Hoping to encourage others to also improve the quality of Canadian Thoroughbreds, he changed the name to National Stud and offered facilities for breeding, foaling, raising and training at reasonable rates. He also reduced the fees of the five stallions which included his top horses Windfields and Bull Page.

In 1950, however, the whole idea of raising champion Thoroughbreds in Canada was considered a fools mission. Especially by Kentuckians, who, for the most part, had never been to Canada but were convinced the country was but one great ice hockey rink. It surely was no place for delicate Thoroughbreds. It was not a view shared by Taylor.

Still the whole thing had turned into an extremely expensive proposition. This onerous responsibility of hundreds of horse mouths to feed had inadvertently propelled Taylor beyond the realm of ordinary entrepreneur. Ever on the lookout for new challenges, hence sources of revenue, by the mid-1950's Taylor had evolved into a most remarkable businessman. Scant few Canadians were not affected by his vast and diverse collection of enterprises. Through his holding company, Argus Corporation, Taylor held interests in a collection of major Canadian companies that ranged from mining, pulp and paper, broadcasting, restaurants, food products, soya mills, to farm machinery, supermarket chains and breweries.

At the time people did not breed and raise horses to make

their fortunes. Quite the opposite. When Taylor bought Parkwood, the average Canadian-bred yearling was selling for about fifteen hundred dollars.

Taylor had been studying both the economics and the science of horse breeding and concluded that the mare dominates the genetic mix by as much as seventy-five percent: "With the greatest stallion in the world and a poor mare you will get a poor horse. With an ordinary stallion and a great mare, your chances are considerably better. With a great stallion and a great mare, your chances are excellent."

For the National Stud to pay for itself, he reasonsed, they were going to have to breed very good horses. To achieve this he was going to have to invest in the very finest broodmares. To that end he contacted the British Bloodstock Agency where the young agent, George Blackwell, was assigned to him. Taylor asked Blackwell to purchase the best broodmare in the 1952 December Newmarket sale. "It was really no problem," Blackwell recalled many years later, "Lady Angela was by far the best mare in the sale."

Eight years old, Lady Angela descended from a long line of England's finest matriarchs, due, for the most part, to the fact she was a daughter of Hyperion. Winner of the 1933 English Derby, his dam, Selene, was not only an outstanding racehorse, she reigns as the pre-eminent broodmare in the history of the breed. Like Selene, Hyperion was small and fine-boned. When he made his racing debut Hyperion stood a mere 14 hand 2 inches (4'-2"), the size of a child's pony. Yet the little golden colt with the four white socks could run a hole in the wind. As a stallion he sired a succession of outstanding mares, the most notable was Hydroplane, dam of the gallant Citation.

Blackwell informed Taylor that Lady Angela was likely to be very expensive as she was in foal to Nearco. Born in Italy in the spring of 1935, among horses Nearco was supreme. He was powerful, resolute, mentally impervious and had brilliant speed.

He won every time he stepped on to a racecourse with disregard, if not disdain, for the others. Eventually his owner and breeder, Federico Tesio, decided to test his colt against the best in the world. Tesio chose the almost two-mile Grand Prix de Paris at Longchamp. Nearco won with speed to spare. The year was 1938 and the clouds of war were hovering over Europe. Instead of returning the horse to Italy Tesio opted to sell Nearco to British interests. The horse was immediately spirited out of France to Newmarket, England where his owners built him his own bomb shelter.

Nearco and Hyperion were considered the most outstanding stallions in England, if not the world. Taylor assured Blackwell he would pay any amount for Lady Angela, on one condition — Lady Angela remain in England to give birth to her foal and then be bred back to Nearco before coming to Canada. Not only did the request seem quite curious to Blackwell, it caused him tremendous grief.

Mixing the blood of Hyperion and Nearco seemed the perfect genetic formula and almost every British Thoroughbred breeder who owned a daughter of Hyperion sent her to be bred to Nearco. Yet there was nothing to suggest the theory had merit at all. So far the combination had not resulted in even one topnotch racehorse.

Lady Angela had been mated with Nearco on two previous occasions. Both offspring were difficult to handle and showed no great success on the racecourse. The filly, Mary Martin, was disinclined to race. The other, Gabriel, won but one very minor contest.

Taylor's insistence that the mare be bred back to Nearco made absolutely no sense, at least not rationally. Along with the adage: "breed the best to the best and hope for the best" at the core of Thoroughbred breeding is a quest for fire. The combustion translates into both the will and the physical ability to win. Yet this combination was not working.

That Taylor would not be swayed by the failures or successes of others was key to his personality. Still why he insisted on Lady Angela being bred yet a fourth time to Nearco remains a mystery. Whatever the answer, this single act became *the* turning point in the history of the modern Thoroughbred.

Lady Angela's owner, British bookmaker Martin Benson, was also major shareholder in Nearco and he flatly refused Taylor's request. Initially. Taylor was adamant. If he was unable to secure a return breeding the deal was off. Over the next fortnight Blackwell bartered and pleaded and reasoned and bargained with Benson. Finally, with a little bribery on the side, a deal was struck and Lady Angela was bred back to Nearco. The foal from this mating would be grandsire to Nijinsky, but not without a crisis or two along the way.

In what would be the first close-call, the fates were assisted by Harry Green, Windfields stallion manager. Taylor had dispatched his top horse-handler to Montreal to collect several horses that were to arrive from England by ocean liner. The first off the ship was a gift from Lord Derby to Taylor. Green loaded the horse into his lorry and then sat down on a crate and kept a lookout for the rest of his passengers, Lady Angela and her foal.

In time Green was asked to come on board as the crew were experiencing difficulty getting Lady Angela off the ship. The first mate was standing at the rim of a large aperture and suggested Green take a look below. Three stories down he could see the mare slipping and sliding on the steel deck. Lady Angela was in a profuse lather and refusing to enter the crate that would carry her to the top deck. Green suggested they put the mare back into her stall until he got there.

The trouble was, he reasoned, that Lady Angela would not go anywhere without her foal. When he reached the ship's hold Green took the foal out first and led him into the crate which would be hoisted up and out by a crane. Concerned that the netting the crew was putting over the top of the crate might frighten the little fellow, Green asked if he could ride with the horses. He took the foal up first and then returned for Lady Angela. This time she walked right into the crate and Green stayed with her as they were lifted from the ship's hold and swung on to the dock. What could have been a disaster was averted. Apart from the danger of slipping on the steel deck and doing irreparable damage, Lady Angela could easily have aborted. But she didn't.

Lady Angela gave birth to her fourth foal to be sired by Nearco at 10:30 a.m. 11 February 1954. Windfields Farm broodmare manager, Bill Reeves, was on hand in case of complications. Because most mares prefer to give birth between 11:00 p.m. and 2:30 a.m. Reeves worked the night shift patrolling the barns until daybreak, ever on alert for early indications of a mare in labour.

Generally Reeves left the barn around 7:00 a.m. but Lady Angela was showing signs of being close to foaling. Still the process can take some considerable time before the mare actually lies down and begins to deliver the baby so Reeves, a former jockey, thought he'd stroll over to the stallion barn and take Bull Page out for a gallop while he waited.

"I was just about to go out with Bull Page when someone hollered that Lady Angela was getting ready to foal. She was out in a paddock close to her barn and walking around and around. They brought her in to her stall and not long after I arrived she lay down.

"I don't remember any complications. I think it must have been an easy foaling. Lady Angela was a really nice mare. She was easygoing. A pleasure to work around. She had no problems. No bad habits. You'd remember her just for her personality. And she was a good mother."

Lady Angela's foal was a sturdy colt with good bone and solid hindquarters. His coat was dark, almost black. He had a small vee-shaped white marking in the centre of his round forehead and a snip of white at the top of his muzzle. Short white socks capped his hind legs from the top of his tiny hooves to over the fetlocks.

"He was a big black colt." recalled Reeves. "And he had *the look*. He would stare at you — as if to say 'I am the king.'"

And indeed he was. Winnie Taylor named this aristocratic colt Nearctic. By the dawn of the 21st Century more than three-quarters of the world's Thoroughbred population traced their lineage back to this one horse. He was the sire of Northern Dancer; grandsire of Nijinsky. But perhaps more significantly, he was also the horse Nijinsky resembled more than any other.

As a youngster Nearctic left an indelible mark, and a few bruises, on the staff at Windfields. After many decades, and thousands of Windfields Farm foals later people still remembered the colt that acted like he was the ruling monarch. According to former yearling manager, Andre Blaettler, this one colt was particularly difficult: "a real tough son of a gun: I remember this time when we had to give him some shots. He was four months old. There was this big guy who was supposed to hold him. But the guy couldn't hold him. The colt was just that tough!"

Nearctic was also unusually independent. Early on foals seldom stray far from their mothers' sides. It is as if there is an invisible boundary around the mare within which the foal feels safe. Initially the zone extends but a few feet away from the mare. Foals may wander beyond this circumference but will suddenly come running back to safety.

Nearctic, however, trotted to his own drummer. This unusual

independence, no doubt, was a character trait he inherited from his own sire, Nearco, who was an extremely self-willed horse. Indeed of all Nearco's sons Nearctic bears the closest physical resemblance: the same head, the same expression and carried himself in a similar manner.

Nearctic also reigns as the sole successful mating between Nearco and daughters of Hyperion. Quite possibly the genetic combination proved far too combustible. Thoroughbreds are, after all, hybrids — the result of crossing two very distinct bloodlines. On one side there is the hot-blooded Arabian, a fine-boned horse able to endure extreme heat, and designed to carry its Bedouin rider across endless desert sands. On the other side of the equation is the cold-blooded Scottish Galloway, a rugged animal able to endure damp and cold weather of Scotland, race through bogs and over hill and dale.

The most obvious characteristic of Thoroughbreds is an abundance of nervous energy. This is what makes them run. If there was a barometer to measure nervous energy in Thoroughbreds, Nearctic would have been off the scale. Throughout his life he was always teetering on the edge, hence not an easy horse — not on himself, nor on his caretakers. Yet the very characteristics that made Nearctic so difficult were the very ones that made him the supreme stallion. He was strong, courageous and feared no one. Neither pain nor exhaustion stopped him from running his heart out.

The reason Nearctic prevailed was, in three words, Gordon 'Pete' McCann. The vast majority of horse trainers would not even consider climbing on to the back of a racehorse. But McCann, a former jockey, rode the more challenging horses. Riding any horse brings a valuable dimension, one that enriches understanding of that individual, especially if the animal is a racehorse. With an animal as complex and combustible as Nearctic, this depth of understanding was critical. Pete rode the horse daily.

"Pete talked to the horses with his hands," explained Bill

Reeves. "Pete was smart, intelligent, but his greatest gift was his hands. Pete also had the greatest knack in the world of picking a yearling. When you came into the barn and saw Pete's tack outside a stall, you had to know that this horse was going to be a good one. How did he know? I can't say, but I saw it over and over. Pete just *knew*."

Nearctic was a fighter. Pete didn't believe in fighting his horses. When he rode Nearctic out in the mornings he fitted the horse with a double bridle. Generally used on powerful Grand Prix dressage horses, the bridle consists of two sets of reins, two bits and a curb-chain that runs beneath the horse's chin. The bridle gave Pete much-needed leverage which meant he could contain Nearctic's abundant and generally volatile nervous energy on their early morning gallops. When Nearctic was entered in a race they went back to using a simple racing snaffle.

Nearctic grew into a tall and elegant colt. His shining dark coat and unusually high head carriage gave him a regal appearance and he could outrun the wind. However, Nearctic's racing days were fraught with calamity and misadventure for it seems the horse became a pawn in a power struggle involving Windfields Farm's new publicist, an Argentine horse-trader, and McCann.

The publicist, Joe Thomas, arrived in Canada by a fairly circuitous route. In the summer of 1955 Taylor was in Kentucky for the sales. One evening at a dinner party he told the story of how he ended up with two farms, hence far too many horses and how that had led to his idea of holding his own yearling sale. He mentioned that he was looking for someone to take over the publicity and paper work. One of the group suggested Thomas.

As the story goes, Thomas arrived in Kentucky several years earlier in a boxcar with a half dozen horses headed to John (Trader) Clark. A prominent local horse trader, Clark was also publicity director at Keeneland racetrack and as such understood the value of favourable media coverage. The day the train carrying Thomas and the horses pulled into Lexington was the day the horse racing columnist for the local paper dropped dead.

Before anyone else applied for the job Clark met with the sports editor and assured him that he had just the person for the assignment — a young fellow who had just arrived from California by the name of Joe Thomas. That Thomas was not a writer did not seem to factor. Instead Clark began ghost-writing the column and then said it was by Thomas. Over the next few weeks Thomas mucked out stalls while Clark wrote the column. Finally Clark handed the assignment over to Thomas and eventually he gravitated to researching stallion pedigrees and farmdirectories for the *Daily Racing Form*.

It wasn't long after he arrived in Canada before Thomas assumed more and more authority, eventually awarding himself the title of Windfields Farm racing manager. And that's when everything started to unravel. Perhaps it was because Thomas had no experience training horses but he seemed unable to discern McCann's extraordinary ability with high-strung Thoroughbreds, nor of his value to Windfields Farm. Once Thomas donned his new title he declared that he, not McCann, was in charge of the racing stable. Before long Thomas could be seen in the walking ring, prior to a race, giving instructions to the jockey.

It was never difficult to spot the man. He was tall and had taken to wearing a wide variety of hats. The collection included everything from boaters to bowlers. Suffice to say, Thomas stood out in a crowd. By contrast, the bashful and diffident McCann was practically invisible. Thomas had developed an ersatz Kentucky drawl that could be heard from some distance; Pete barely spoke at all. Thomas was comfortable at the centre of a media scrum or among the owners and officials in the Trustee's rooms after a Windfields horse won a big race. McCann fairly blanched at the prospect and consistently refused to attend — much to the displeasure of Eddie Taylor.

When it came to the welfare or the training of his beloved horses, McCann simply refused to obey Thomas'orders. It wasn't long before the acrimony between the two men began to set in and Nearctic was caught in the middle of their ongoing dispute. Thomas' first volley was to take Nearctic from McCann and send him to the US to be trained by Charlie Shaw.

It was a disaster. The horse was handled badly and suffered bucked shins, a painful inflamation of the metacarpal (cannon) bone of the forelegs. Eventually Thomas brought Nearctic back to McCann. Indeed this would become a pattern: when things looked hopeless, Nearctic was returned to McCann; when Nearctic's health was restored, the horse was removed from McCann.

Somehow the Argentine horse trader, Horatio Luro, also joined the Nearctic bandwagon. Charming and flamboyant, Luro brought the first of many consignments of South American horses to the US in 1937. Along the way he teamed up with Charlie Whittingham who would one day be honoured as a Hall of Fame trainer. At the time, however, Whittingham was working as a jockey's agent, but dreamed of training. Luro had a few horses from Argentina he hadn't managed yet to sell. And so the deal was struck: Whittingham trained the horses and Luro trained the owners. Luro's friend and biographer, Joe Hirsch, summed up their adventures as "racing their stable up and down the West Coast, with a sense of timing that always kept them a step ahead of the sheriff."

During WW II Whittingham joined the US Marines. Luro moved to Florida with four unexceptional horses, no money, and no partner to train them. That first winter he met Harry Hatch, a wealthy Canadian with a small racing stable. Hatch suggested Luro bring his horses to Canada in the spring and promised that he would convince his fellow Jockey Club directors to defray Luro's expenses. Whittingham was still fighting in the war so Luro had to find someone to train the horses and convinced Reggie Cornell to take the job. Cornell, who would later be renowned as trainer of the great Silky Sullivan, traveled with the horses on the train to Canada; Luro traveled by automobile. Cornell attended to the horses; Luro attended the parties.

In 1956 Luro arrived at Woodbine racetrack with a mare named Eugenia II and a jockey named Juan Sanchez. The mare took most by surprise. She ran like a donkey in her first race and then several days later miraculously won the Canadian Championship. Somewhere between the purse and shrewd wagering Luro departed Canada far wealthier that when he arrived. Before the triumvirate of Eugenia II and Sanchez and Luro left town Luro made an appearance at the Championship post-race champagne party. There he was introduced to Eddie Taylor.

A month later Taylor was in New York where he and the Argentine met once again, quite by accident, according to Luro. The alleged *accident* occurred in the office of Dr. Cooper Person, husband of Liz Whitney, one of Luro's clients. There, in the waiting room, Luro was able to convince Taylor that he was the man to handle Nearctic. This too was a disaster.

While McCann was brilliant when it came to communicating with his horses, he was no match for those whose agendas were not in the best interests of Nearctic. Painfully shy and retiring, time after time McCann was over-ruled. Both the man and the horse suffered. Yet Nearctic somehow prevailed — carried no doubt by his courage, endurance and nobility and the fact that every time something went wrong, they brought the horse back to McCann who was able to calm and stabilize Nearctic.

Then in May 1959 McCann stopped working his magic on the horse. He refused to play the game any longer and he loaded Nearctic on a horse van and drove him to the National Stud Farm. It was probably the most assertive thing McCann did in his entire life.

As the van carrying Nearctic rolled along the long tree-lined lane towards the National Stud stallion barns it passed a band of mares and foals grazing the rich spring grass in a large meadow. Flaring Top, one of the five yearlings Taylor purchased in Kentucky when so very inspired by Citation, was now a broodmare. The dark bay filly with the small star beneath her forelock by her side had been born 24 April. She was her seventh foal. Flaring Top had been bred three times to Tournoi, a stallion Taylor had imported from France; once to Windfields; and twice to another French import, Menetrier. Then finally they got it right. After six detours on the road to Nijinsky, Flaring Top was bred with Bull Page. Their foal would grow up to be the dam of Nijinsky. Still there were a few more obstacles along the way.

By the spring of 1954 Taylor had a crop of nearly 40 yearlings roaming the paddocks. It was far too many horses for one racing stable. So he came up with another of his big ideas. Rather than sending the horses off to public auction, as most would do, Taylor decided to host his own sale. Lest he was accused of holding back the best horses for himself, he would offer all the yearlings. Each to carry a predetermined price tag. Optimistically he deemed that the sale would conclude when half the colts and fillies were sold. The rest would carry Windfields turquoise and gold silks. Then he drew up a list of friends, associates in horse racing and others he thought might be interested and invited them to his sale.

Of the thirty-five yearlings paraded before the buyers and spectators at the inaugural event five colts and three fillies were sold for a total of $51,500. Bill Beasley, the tall sandy-haired proprietor of an amusement company bought two of the youngsters. One was a smart-looking bay colt sired by Windfields. Beasley named him Canadian Champ. And indeed he was. At two Canadian Champ was in the money in eight of his nine starts. The following year he carried Beasley's scarlet silks to their first Queen's Plate victory. Beasley was ecstatic. Taylor could have had no better advertising. With every successive year the event had grown in prominence.

The sale in the fall of 1960 attracted even greater attention. Three years earlier Victoria Park had been among the Windfields-bred yearlings buyers had overlooked. On the first Saturday in May 1960 Victoria Park finished third in the Kentucky Derby. He was second in the Preakness and favoured to win the Belmont. The third leg of the US Triple Crown was held on the same day as the Queen's Plate and Taylor opted to bring him home for Canada's big race which the colt won in record time. With Victoria Park's achievements fresh in everyone's mind, prospective buyers and their trainers were scrutinizing each and every one of Taylor's yearlings.

Prior to the 1960 sale Taylor was invited to speak at the annual meeting of Canada's Thoroughbred breeders association where he shared his conviction that one day soon Canadian horses would grace the winner's circle of the world's classic races:

"If we use the right methods in Canada, that is proper feeding, proper exercising and constant effort to adjust to what horses suffer from there is no reason why, in time, Canadian horses should not rank right up there with the best in the world."

It is unlikely Taylor realized how close he was to fulfilling his prophecy. Yet, on the day of the Windfields sale, there was yet another detour on the road to Nijinsky. Ontario horse breeder, Frank Sherman, purchased the daughter of Flaring Top and Bull Page — the filly destined to be the dam of Nijinsky. But once again, the fates intervened.

When the filly arrived at Sherman's farm they discovered that she had a slightly inflamed fetlock in one hind leg. Since the filly was quite sound at the sale it is likely the injury occurred on the horse van en route to her new home. Nonetheless Sherman telephoned Taylor and complained that his purchase was faulty and requested a replacement. Ever anxious to please his customers Taylor immediately dispatched the Windfields Farm horse van to deliver a replacement and to collect the daughter of Flaring Top and Bull Page.

Winnie Taylor named the filly Flaming Page. That year McCann had close to a hundred horses of various stages and ages to train. Horatio Luro, who now operated out of New York's Belmont Park, was able to convince Taylor to send him several horses he believed had the best chance of succeeding in the US. Taylor chose Flaming Page and a colt named Choperion.

On 7 September 1961 Flaming Page was entered in her first race. It was late in the year for horses in North America to begin racing. There were fourteen fillies in the race and, with the exception of Flaming Page, all had been racing since the spring. Still, with all that time to get her ready Flaming Page was totally ill-prepared.

The bell clanged. The gates flew open. Jockeys hollered. Flaming Page freaked. She wanted nothing to do with this frightening experience so she decided to return to the relative safety of the starting gate stall. Her jockey was able to get her back on course and despite all this Flaming Page was second by a nose to the favourite, Darlin' Butchie.

Shortly thereafter Luro returned Flaming Page to Canada. Reggie Cornell was no longer training Luro's horses. Tom (Peaches) Fleming had taken his place as trainer. Luro continued training the owners, yet referred to Fleming as his assistant.

Flaming Page continued racing in Canada, but proved very difficult to handle. Naturally athletic, she possessed a great long stride and an extremely short temper. That winter Luro migrated to Florida and Flaming Page and Choperion were among the horses in his shedrow. Flaming Page was started in three races, but according to the *Daily Racing Form* she "was always outrun in a dull effort."

Luro's attention, it seems, was elsewhere. He had been sent a colt named Decidedly that was deemed good enough to qualify for the 1962 Kentucky Derby. In March Luro had Decidedly shipped to Keeneland, the last stop en route to the big race.

Flaming Page and Choperion went along for the ride.

One of the more bizarre traits of Luro's approach to horse races was his attitude towards jockeys. Ninety-nine percent of trainers understand the importance of a) attempting to hire the very best jockey for your horse b) one that suits the disposition of your horse and c) keeping said same jockey throughout the career of your horse. This is especially critical in classic races where the competition is fast and fierce. Experience and timing can make the difference between winner and also-ran.

Luro seemed to be totally oblivious to the logic behind hiring a top jockey. Perhaps he didn't actually understand. Until now Luro appeared content to spend his time in the Turf Club charming the owners and to leave the less glamourous behind-the-scenes horse training to the likes of Whittingham and Cornell and Flemming. The Kentucky Derby, however, changed all that. Matt Winn's schmoozing of reporters and columnists had paid off in spades. By the time Decidedly arrived in Kentucky for the Derby a legion of over 1000 news media types converged on Churchill Downs. All in search of the big story. Most of whom knew little, if anything, about horse racing.

It was a perfect stage for Horatio Luro. Back then the majority of trainers were rough and tumble horsemen. They were guys like Pete McCann who talked to his horses with much greater ease than with reporters. But Luro was different. He was exotic. He dated chorus girls and movie stars, danced the tango and played polo. He drove flashy sports cars and was always beautifully dressed. With his Latin good looks and charm he was soon the darling of the media and Luro appeared to radiate amid all the celebrity. The fact that he had scant, if any, experience training Thoroughbreds did not seem to bother him, nor enter the conversation.

Possibly because he was too busy for such trivial details, more often than not he didn't sign up a jockey until a day or two before a race. By then the top riders were frequently unavailable. Often he ended up hiring obscure jockeys and some with dubious credentials. Flaming Page's jockey in the Oaks Prep Stakes was a case in point. His name was Vincenzo Nodarse. A fairly thorough search of his experience in US classic races indicated that someone had given him a mount in the 1944 Kentucky Derby. The horse was called Brief Sigh and they finished fifth. In 1942 Nordarse made headlines when his horse dangerously plowed into the mount ridden by Eddie Arcaro who spent the remainder of the race seeking revenge. The opportunity arose in the stretch whereupon Arcaro slammed his horse into Nodarse's mount hard enough to catapult Nordase over the rail. Nodarse was not hurt, but when the stewards interrogated Arcaro instead of apologizing, Arcaro said, "What I really meant to do was kill that Cuban SOB." Arcaro was suspended for a year. Beyond this tidbit of infamy, Nordarse was never in the headlines as a rider of importance.

Conversely, the favourite in the race, a diminutive fireball named Cicada, was ridden by Bill Shoemaker. Considered the greatest US jockey, if not in the world, Shoemaker was known for his remarkably good hands and extraordinary communication with his mounts.

Cicada and Shoemaker won. Flaming Page finished fourth.

The day before the Derby Flaming Page was at Churchill Downs for the Kentucky Oaks. She continued to be ridden by Nordarse. Cicada, by Shoemaker. Still Flaming Page finished second, a testament, no doubt, to her ability. Her next race was the Black-Eyed Susan Stakes at Pimlico. This time she broke from the gate awkwardly and never really recovered. She was eighth in a field of nine. Decidedly, the horse that had won the Derby, was a distant eighth in the Preakness, thirteen lengths behind the winner. Undaunted Luro set out to Belmont Park with Decidedly. Flaming Page and Choperion were loaded on a horse van and shipped to Canada. His assistant, Peaches Fleming would be in charge of the pair.

On 9 June Flaming Page was entered in the Canadian Oaks at Woodbine. The talented filly with the fiery disposition now had a rider who was up to the challenge — Jim Fitzsimmons, the popular contract jockey for Windfields Farm. Flaming Page proved to be, by far, the best of this field of fifteen Canadian fillies.

Never fast out of the gate, Flaming Page cruised near the back of the pack in the early stages of the race. Fitzsimmons allowed her to settle into an easy stride for a bit before moving her to the outside allowing her a clear path. One by one Flaming Page bounded past the others. Coming into the final turn she shot past the leader and cruised across the finish almost five lengths ahead of the next horse.

Luro's trip to New York with Decidedly for the Belmont Stakes was in vain. The winner was Jaipur. The winning jockey, Bill Shoemaker. Luro managed to be in Canada for the Queen's Plate. Flaming Page and Choperion were running as a Windfields Farm entry. At a pre-race media scrum Luro pronounced that Choperion was his Queen's Plate selection and assured the admiring throng of reporters that Choperion would win. Furthermore he convinced Taylor to hire US jockey Bill Hartack to ride Choperion. Flaming Page continued to be ridden by Fitzsimmons.

A record crowd packed into Woodbine to witness this, the 103rd running of the race. The enthusiastic turnout was due in part to the beautiful sunny eighty degree weather. But many had come to Woodbine simply to see HRH Elizabeth the Queen Mother who would present the prize to the winners.

It was all quite grand. Silver trumpets heralded her arrival. The open carriage conveying the Queen Mother was drawn by four chestnut coach horses with a postilion on the lead horse. Two red-coated footmen stood at the rear of the landau which was escorted by a mounted guard of honour from the Governor-General's Horse Guards. Their lances bore the regiment's red, white and blue colours and the forty horsemen were resplendent in their silver helmets, topped with scarlet plumes and dark blue uniforms adorned with splashes of red and white.

When the landau eased to a stop in front of the grandstand the crowd was on its feet and people were clapping and cheering enthusiastically. In retrospect the royal ceremony would also serve to herald a soon-to-be equine monarch — Flaming Page, dam of Nijinsky. For the day surely belonged to this great filly.

The bell clanged to signal the start of the Queen's Plate, the stall doors flew open, and Flaming Page waltzed out of post position five. As was her wont she cantered leisurely along at the back of the field of thirteen horses until she was ready to run. At about the half-way mark Fitzsimmons steered Flaming Page to the outside to give her running room. And run she did. With each bounce her stride continued to lengthen. Soon she was sailing past the others as if they were standing still. At the top of the stretch Flaming Page had a commanding lead.

Just at that very moment on this warm and sunny afternoon a sun shower, a gentle mist of rain, sprinkled down upon Flaming Page as she bounded down the home stretch. An anointment, perhaps, by Epona the Celtic horse goddess, to the seventh foal of Flaring Top from the seventh crop of Bull Page.

Two days later Flaming Page was led into a horse van and driven back to Belmont Park. Located on the fringe of New York City, Belmont is about 600 miles south east of Toronto's Woodbine. Flaming Page arrived at Belmont early Tuesday morning.

Taylor had apparently left the decision whether or not to run Flaming Page in the Coaching Club Oaks up to Luro. He trusted Luro to make the right decision. Others did not. Cicada's trainer, Casey Hayes, in conversation with *Daily Racing Form* journalist Barney Nagler, was incredulous: "I hear talk of Flaming Page coming down (from Canada for the race) but that seems like a lot to ask her to do after the Queen's Plate.

Perhaps Luro had forgotten that the filly had shipped 600 miles to Canada on 5 June; ran and won the Canadian Oaks four days later; ran and won the Queen's Plate the following weekend; shipped back the 600 miles to New York; and was now being prepped to run a potentially tougher race five days after the Queen's Plate. According to Luro in an interview with Bob Horwood of the *Daily Racing Form*: "... She (Flaming Page) had a tough race in Canada and then she is tired from shipping, but she is a filly with a strong constitution. I think she will be up to the race Saturday."

Luro's estimation of the filly's constitution was not only inaccurate, but would result in dire consequences and once again render the road to Nijinsky in peril.

21 June 1962. The field for the Coaching Club American Oaks was confirmed and Flaming Page was listed among the eight starters. The favourite, Cicada, would be ridden by her regular jockey, Bill Shoemaker. Trainer Hayes was pleased: "We're lucky to have first call on Bill Shoemaker on her. They sort of go together, both are so quiet and nice."

Flaming Page was not so fortunate. Luro did not seem terribly concerned with these details. Two days before the race she did not have a jockey and for some odd reason Luro did not consider Fitzsimmons.

Cicada won the race. Flaming Page finished a very tired fourth, with a chipped sesamoid bone and ended up in a cast. Luro wanted to keep her in training. And did, once the cast came off. He planned to ship the filly to California to race. But somewhere along the line good sense prevailed and Flaming Page was retired to live out her days at the National Stud Farm.

On 19 July 1958 Nearctic won the Michigan Mile. It was the most prominent victory in his young life and the man in his corner that afternoon, appropriately, was Pete McCann. Two weeks later Eddie and Winnie Taylor were in Saratoga, New York for the races, the parties and the yearling sales. The winner's share of Nearctic's purse was $40,000, so they decided to invest winnings in a filly — with luck, a very special filly.

The exceptional yearling was a bay filly with one white stocking, a large star on her forehead and a white snip on her face that grew larger as it wrapped down and around her muzzle. Her sire, Native Dancer, was a hulking grey warrior. Vastly superior to every other racehorse of his generation, he was reputed to hate the whip and would swing his mighty head around, clamp his jaws around a boot, haul the offending rider out of the saddle and fling him on the ground. The female side of her pedigree was not nearly so rambunctious, but genetically powerful. She was also a granddaughter of Mother Goose, who astounded fans when she left twenty-nine of North America's top colts and fillies in the dust and screeched first past the wire in the 1924 Belmont Futurity. Mother Goose has passed on her mettle and blistering speed to generations of outstanding Thoroughbreds.

Winnie Taylor named their new filly Natalma and as her husband watched Natalma mature over the winter he decided Natalma was clearly good enough to race in the big US races so she was dispatched to Luro's operation at Belmont Park.

In the spring of 1959 Natalma won two races at Belmont and then vanned to Saratoga for the August race meet. There Natalma won the Spinaway Stakes by three-quarters of a length, but was disqualified. It seems she had inherited her sire's disdain for the whip. Coming out of the backstretch her jockey, Bob Ussery, had cracked her with his whip. In an effort to avoid the punishment Natalma had ducked to the inside and bumped the filly Warlike, causing her to hit the inside rail. Luro publicly castigated the jockey, then soon after the race he sailed to Paris, as he did annually, apparently to avoid the ragweed season.

In the meantime Natalma went on strike. It seems she equated racetracks with Ussery's whipping and wanted nothing more to do with racing. Eventually they were able to coerce her back into training, but then she pulled up lame. There was a bone chip in her right knee and so she was sent to the University of Pennsylvania veterinary hospital to have the chip removed. The operation was a success and Natalma was sent back to Canada to recuperate.

In the spring of 1960 Natalma was shipped to Kentucky to join Taylor's Victoria Park who was entered in the Derby and under the jurisdiction of Horatio Luro. Presumably Luro's allergies were on the mend as he was back in North America and holding court at Churchill Downs. With great authority he announced to the media hordes he had, with Victoria Park and Natalma, *the Kentucky Double* — winners of both the Kentucky Derby and Kentucky Oaks.

Six days prior to the Oaks Natalma was, once again, lame. Natalma accompanied Victoria Park through his challenge of the US classics. She was stabled next to him at Churchill Downs when he finished third in the Derby. She traveled to Baltimore with him for the Preakness and traveled back to Canada with him when Victoria Park returned for the Queen's Plate. After the horse van dropped Victoria Park off at Woodbine it continued down the highway to the National Stud Farm.

It was mid-June, considered late in the year to breed Thoroughbred racehorses since on January 1 all Thoroughbreds in the Northern Hemisphere are designated a year older. Hence a foal born in January and one born the following May are officially deemed the same age. In the early stages of a horse's development such an age gap can be significant in terms of physical and mental maturity. Nevertheless, it was decided to breed Natalma to Nearctic.

Natalma gave birth to their foal 27 May 1961. It was a tiny bay colt with three white socks. A narrow blaze, which began beneath his curly black forelock, ran down his face and across his left nostril. The angle of the marking gave him a cheeky impudent look. Which was appropriate, for he soon earned the reputation of being a bit of a devil. When it came time to bring him into the barn he'd careen around the paddock and come skidding to a halt at the gate — then he'd rear. No one wanted to bring him in on their own.

While the other yearlings grew taller, Natalma's son grew sideways. He was, of course, younger, still he did not look like the rest. He was short — standing 14 hands, two and one half inches high (4 feet 10 inches). He weighed 955 pounds, about 40 pounds less than the average. Unusually stocky, he looked more like a Quarter Horse than a streamlined Thoroughbred.

On 17 September 1962 the first crop of the offspring of Nearctic were among the 48 yearlings offered at the Taylor's ninth annual Windfields sale. When buyers received their catalogues in the mail they saw that the top price of $25,000 was placed on two of the colts. One of these was by the French stallion Menetrier. The other was the son of Nearctic and Natalma.

Several contemplated buying the later colt. Larkin Maloney was talked out of it by his trainer. Brothers Jim and Phil Boylen thought about it, but their trainer also advised them against it. "Who wants a midget?" he sneered.

Fifteen yearlings were sold that year. The remaining thirty-three would train and race for Windfields Farm. Among them was the stocky, feisty son of Natalma and Nearctic. Winnie Taylor had named him Northern Dancer and he would be renowned as Kentucky Derby winner, Canadian hero, and sire of Nijinsky.

Still, once again the fates were on full alert to ensure that this part of Nijinsky's gene pool actually made it to the winners' circle, much less the breeding arena. Northern Dancer's journey to the Kentucky Derby was surely fraught with countless obstacles and more highs and lows than a roller-coaster. In fact that the horse actually bounded out of the starting gate at Churchill Downs on that first Saturday in May 1964 is likely more remarkable than his record-setting victory.

When Bill Reeves arrived at the yearling barn the morning after the sale he noticed McCann's saddle was propped against the door to the stall housing Northern Dancer. Which was a good thing. Indeed the story might well have come to a grinding halt right at this very spot had it not been for McCann.

Not unlike his sire, Nearctic, Northern Dancer was an extremely wilful and volatile animal. The major difference was how they expressed their individual volatility. Nearctic preferred lunging and leaping skyward. Yet because he was a tall horse and he carried his head so high his rider was less likely to be tossed to the ground. The major challenges to riding Nearctic were 1) harnessing his energy, and 2) getting him to stop. Northern Dancer's explosiveness was more like riding a bucking bronco. Small and compact, he carried his head low and when he unleashed a buck few riders would not have found themselves being catapulted through the air.

Still McCann could sit a horse better than anyone. The fact that decades later, and well into his 'eighties, McCann was still galloping young racehorses, attests to his remarkable reflexes and abilities. This coupled with his experience with Northern Dancer's sire allowed McCann to help the volatile colt adjust to the early rigours of training. Still, when McCann was busy at the racetrack and not able to ride Northern Dancer no one else wanted the job. Sitting on Northern Dancer's back was akin to straddling a powder keg. When he trotted he didn't glide forward — he bounced from one foot to the next. When he broke into a canter he'd go a couple of strides then *boom*, he'd explode. Powerful and agile he could stop, turn on a dime, or fly off in the opposite direction.

Somehow, when it was time to send the yearlings to the track,

Northern Dancer ended up with Luro. Well, not exactly Luro. He was elsewhere. Instead he sent Peaches Fleming to Canada to train the colt.

Northern Dancer's racing debut was delayed due to a recurring cracked heel, a form of psoriasis in the hollow at the back of the pastern (the short bone just above the hoof). Once the infection sets in it is easily irritated by dirt or sand and causes the horse to go lame.

Northern Dancer's first race took place in August at Fort Erie. His partner was Ron Turcotte, the gifted young rider from New Brunswick It was a good partnership. In the right hands, the powerful colt's explosiveness could be channeled to acceleration. "The first time I rode Northern Dancer I knew he was something special," recalled Turcotte.

Turcotte rode him several times after that but was eventually dismissed because he apparently didn't ride the horse according to Luro's orders. In years to come Turcotte would partner the mighty Secretariat and be celebrated as one of the world's outstanding riders. Now instead of having one regular rider, and in the case of Turcotte, one excellent rider, Northern Dancer would endure a succession of different jockeys. Some of whom were up to the challenge, others were clearly not.

By the end of the year Northern Dancer was lame once again. This time with a quarter crack in the wall of his hoof. Theoretically the injury should have terminated his racing career, but an experimental vulcanized rubber patch was employed to hold his hoof together. The colt was rested for a bit and then returned to training and once again on the road to the US Triple Crown.

In February 1964 Luro hired Bob Ussery to ride Northern Dancer in a race at Hialeah Park. Ussery was the colt's fifth jockey. In the closing stages of the race Ussery clobbered Northern Dancer with his whip. Ussery, incidentally, was the jockey that hit Northern Dancer's dam, Natalma, five years earlier. The consequences were identical. Luro publicly berated the jockey.

And as in the case of Natalma, the colt refused to step a hoof back on to the track.

Strong, willful, athletic and agile, Northern Dancer colt had always been a handful, now, on top of everything else, he was angry. And when he wasn't angry he was on the lookout for fillies. Luro's solution was to have Northern Dancer gelded. And the story of Nijinsky would have ended on this page. Instead, this time the fates called upon Winnie Taylor to step into the fray. She and Northern Dancer shared a remarkable bond. Their kinship began when the colt was born and she visited him at every opportunity. It is safe to say that the only human this rascal actually liked was Winnie Taylor. They were kindred spirits, both small in stature and enormous in spirit.

Generally taciturn and gracious Winnie Taylor seldom voiced an opinion on the running of their racing stable, but during the 1960's her husband was frequently away on business. First she echoed her husband's wishes that Northern Dancer *not* be gelded. Furthermore she demanded that her horse have but one jockey and she insisted on the best — Bill Shoemaker.

Luro had no option but to obey her wishes, at least in the moment. Shoemaker was hired. The strategy worked. Northern Dancer responded willingly to his new rider. The following weekend Shoemaker was back in Northern Dancer's saddle for the Flamingo Stakes and the colt won with ease over a field of top Derby contenders.

The morning prior to the next big test, the Florida Derby, things fell apart once again. The story goes that Northern Dancer's regular exercise rider mysteriously vanished. According to Luro's biography: "... his regular rider, Ramon Hernandez, was not available. Hernandez had a commitment to ride in Toronto so a substitute boy was found." Which was odd, since there was no racing in Toronto at that time of the year.

The substitute rider was no match for the volatile colt. Feeling fit and strong, and ready to race, Northern Dancer grabbed the bit and bolted. Instead of an easy workout, Northern Dancer ended up running out of control around the training track. Both horse and rider could easily been hurt. Fortunately no terrible damage was done except that now, expecting him to run in the Florida Derby, was akin to asking the horse to race on two consecutive days.

Still, with Shoemaker sitting quietly on his back, Northern Dancer won. But the colt was tired. Shoemaker had to chose between riding Northern Dancer in the forthcoming Kentucky Derby or the California sensation, Hill Rise. A magnificent-looking animal, Hill Rise was on a seven-race winning streak, which included a six-length triumph in the premier West Coast Derby prep, the Santa Anita Derby.

In light of Northern Dancer's courageous, yet lethargic performance in the Florida Derby, Shoemaker chose Hill Rise. Luro then was able to give his friend Bill Hartack the ride on Northern Dancer. The antithesis of Shoemaker, Hartack was an aggressive rider. Arrogant, opinionated and sarcastic Hartack lashed out at trainers and spat insults at the media. He did, however, seem to like Luro.

Not everyone agreed that Hartack should be riding Northern Dancer. When Joe Thomas suggested in a newspaper interview that he thought Hartack was not the best rider for the horse, the controversy became public. "I am running the stable!" fumed Luro in the next edition. Luro's decision would also backfire — but the story had a few more furlongs to run.

Northern Dancer won the 1964 Kentucky Derby on sheer grit. In the final strides it seemed impossible that the little Canadian colt, straining with every short choppy stride could stave off the mighty Hill Rise. Mere yards from the finish Northern Dancer must have felt Hill Rise's hot breath on his shoulder, but he refused to yield to the much bigger horse. As they flew across the wire it was Northern Dancer by a neck. And in record time. In that instant Northern Dancer became "our" horse. Canadians poured into the streets to celebrate. His victory was our victory and we basked in the triumph he had given us.

Canada's horse went on to win the Preakness with relative ease and was back in his stall digging into his post-race meal when he was the subject of yet another storm of controversy. It seems that at the Preakness victory party Luro was holding court in the midst of a media scrum where he announced that Northern Dancer would not be running in the Belmont. Luro had not, however, consulted with his employers who were also in the room. Luro had also confided to his audience that Northern Dancer had "distance limitations."

Later, in private, Taylor explained to Luro that if Northern Dancer was physically fit the colt *would* run in the Belmont. And so he did. Apparently Luro's instructions were to keep Northern Dancer in check, behind the early leaders. The pace was exceptionally slow. Hartack maintained a strong grip on the reins as Northern Dancer strained at the bit and fought his rider every stride of the way. So much dirt was thrown up from the heels of the pace setters that for two hours after the race Northern Dancer spat and coughed up dirt.

Northern Dancer finished third behind horses he had sashayed past in previous races. Taylor was livid. An intensely private person, he publicly lambasted Hartack for misjudging the pace and not giving his horse the ride he deserved. The New York press said Northern Dancer couldn't go the distance. That he quit. Canadian reporters suggested Luro and Hartack, surely underestimated the capabilities of the horse. Others knew it was simply a very bad ride. At least one reporter mused if Luro's reputation as a shrewd gambler was a factor.

There were but two certainties: the tendon problem that would terminate Northern Dancer's brief career began at the Belmont; and after Northern Dancer's final race Eddie and Winnie Taylor ceased sending their horses to Luro.

When Northern Dancer returned to Toronto to run in the

Queen's Plate he was treated like a conquering hero. At city hall a civic reception was held in his honour and he was awarded a key to the city — this one carved from a carrot. Sacks of fan mail from across Canada, the US and Carribean began piling up at the entrance to the Windfields Farm office.

As Northern Dancer was led up the chute toward the saddling enclosure for the 105th running of the Queen's Plate hordes of fans clamoured the fence to catch a glimpse of him. Many had never been to Woodbine or even bet on a horse race, but they were here to cheer Northern Dancer. And cheer him they did.

Galloping around the clubhouse turn Northern Dancer was running dead last under a tight hold by Hartack. When the rider finally slackened his grip on the reins Northern Dancer began to fly. The entire crowd was screaming wildly, "Come on Dancer! Come on Dancer!" And did not stop until Northern Dancer sailed across the finish seven and a half lengths ahead of the second-place horse. There was no reason to ride the horse like that. Nor did he need to win by a large margin. Hartack was either grand-standing, or making a point. His reputation as a hot-head preceded him and there was speculation that this was Hartack's way of getting back at his detractors — and specifically Taylor for his public condemnation of his ride in the Belmont. The horse, however, would pay the price.

When Northern Dancer won the Queen's Plate the cheers of adulation were all but deafening — for the horse, and his owners. But now the colt was lame and at Winnie Taylor's insistence, he was retired shortly after the Queen's Plate. Several months later it was announced that Northern Dancer would enter stud in 1965 and stand at a fee of ten thousand dollars at the National Stud Farm. One day there were those willing to pay one million dollars for the opportunity. The reason: because he was the sire of Nijinsky. Still, that almost did not happen, at least, not right away.

February 1965. Windfields Farm's stallion manager, Harry Green, clipped the lead shank to Northern Dancer's halter and led him from his stall in the stallion barn and along the path to the breeding arena. Out in the cold, blustery air, Northern Dancer bounced and bucked happily. He was about to breed — or attempt to breed — his first mare, Flaming Page.

Once inside the breeding arena, Green could barely restrain the enthusiastic young stallion. Before long Green realized that there was a serious logistical problem. Try as he might, Northern Dancer was simply not tall enough to perform his mission. Eventually Flaming Page became so annoyed at Northern Dancer's antics that she kicked him smack in the ribs. The horses were returned to their respective barns.

After considerable head-scratching Windfields farm manager, Peter Poole, came up with what he called "a very scientific solution." He had the staff dig a shallow pit in the centre of the arena's dirt floor for the mare to stand in. They created a solid base and covered the area with non-slip matting. The following afternoon Northern Dancer was able to consummate his relationship with Flaming Page. Sadly the result of this mating was stillborn twins.

March 1966. Northern Dancer and Flaming Page met again in the breeding arena. This time their mating was surely blessed. On dark and cold winter night of 1967 Flaming Page gave birth to a magnificent-looking foal. A dark bay with long, long legs, three white socks, he had a distinctive white star in the shape of a heart in the centre of his forehead.

This son of Flaming Page and Northern Dancer grew and grew. He was weaned from Flaming Page at seventeen weeks at which point he and the other youngsters were moved from the National Stud Farm to the Taylor's Toronto farm. By the time he was a yearling this colt was so stunningly beautiful he took your breath away. His lofty carriage and regal presence were reminiscent of his aristocratic grandsire, Nearctic. Standing just a shade under 16 hands high, he possessed an unusually long stride, outstanding conformation and a reasonably easygoing disposition for a colt.

When Peter Winants, a leading US horse photographer, arrived at Windfields Farm to take publicity shots for a forthcoming advertising pamphlet, he was instantly transfixed by the elegance of this one horse. Indeed all the best pictures Winants took that summer were of the colt that would be named Nijinsky.

Another of the many to become enamored with the colt was Ireland's greatest horse trainer, Vincent O'Brien, who had been dispatched to Canada to look at another yearling in the Windfields group. The potential buyer was an American, Charles Engelhard. Inspiration for the villain Goldfinger in the James Bond 007 movie of the same name, Engelhard was chairman of a sprawling corporate empire that ranged from chemicals in Canada to diamond mines in Africa. With more money than Croesus, he spared no expense in getting what he wanted. And what he ultimately wanted was to have one of his horses win the English Derby at Epsom and meet the Queen. Since the victory came with an invitation to the Royal box his two wishes could be fulfilled on an afternoon at Epsom. All he needed was the horse that would take him there.

And he wanted that horse now. Did he know that his days on the planet were destined to be brief? He surely appeared to be a man in a hurry. Nine years earlier he began buying horses and collecting horse trainers all over the globe. He employed four trainers in England, one in France, one in the US and another in South Africa. In the summer of 1968, when Sir Ivor became the second O'Brien-trained horse to win the English Derby, Engelhard contemplated adding the Irish trainer to his roster.

This outing to Windfields would be a test. The yearling he sent the Irishman to appraise did not impress O'Brien. The son of Northern Dancer and Flaming Page, however, *spoke to him* so he commended Engelhard to buy the colt. Engelhard agreed and said he would instruct one of his executives to attend the sale and bid on the horse.

The year was 1968, the year Taylor decided to include his horses in the annual Canadian Thoroughbred yearling sale. Initially the announcement was met with a mixed reaction. Some of the local horse breeders saw it as a great boost to the sale while others moaned that Taylor would steal their buyers. In reality the inclusion of the beautifully-bred Windfields yearlings was a bit like inviting the National Ballet to a barn dance. The Windfields Farm Thoroughbreds and those raised by the rest of the Canadian breeders were surely worlds apart.

The atmosphere around the sales barns just prior to the event was charged with anticipation. The rumours that *big* buyers were coming from Ireland and the US were abounding, so consignors, spectators and journalists were ever on the lookout for these celebrities.

As in the past, Taylor put a reserve price on each of the yearlings. Should the price not be reached at the auction, the youngster would return to Windfields to run in the Taylor's turquoise and gold silks. Taylor set the highest reserve, $125,000, on a bay daughter of Northern Dancer and Windfields Farm's enduring racemare Canadiana. Despite her most curious conformation, which included a long swayback, Canadiana was an outstanding racehorse winning countless races including the Queen's Plate.

A big chestnut colt with a white blaze running the length of his face and over his nostrils was valued by Taylor at $100,000. He was a full-brother to Viceregal, the golden colt that turned a post parade into a pageant. Just prior to the sale Viceregal had won his seventh two year old race. The talk around the turf was that Viceregal would be headed for the Kentucky Derby and the following year. No doubt, Taylor wanted to keep his full-brother. Which indeed is what happened. Winnie Taylor named the colt Vice Regent.

Taylor also put a $100,000 ticket on the bay son of Ribot and Northern Queen that brought O'Brien to Windfields in the first place. The horse that spoke to O'Brien, this son of Flaming Page and Northern Dancer, carried a reserve of $60,000. The prices on the remaining forty-five Windfields yearlings ranged from $40,000 to $7,500.

The buzz of excitement and anticipation was palpable throughout the entire sales complex located at the southern end of the Woodbine racecourse property. Even those who had previously been opposed to the inclusion of the Windfields yearlings at *their* sale couldn't help but become caught up in the drama.

US Hall of Fame trainer, Elliot Burch, was there on behalf of his client Paul Mellon, one of the world's most distinguished art patrons and racing enthusiasts. Johnny Longden, former champion jockey and now a trainer, came by to inspect yearlings with his client Frank McMahon. The Calgary oil man was known to spend outrageous amounts on Kentucky yearlings.

Other major Canadian buyers included Quebec's most prominent entrepreneur, Jean-Louis Levesque and Garfield Weston, chairman of the Weston food empire, who now signed Barrettstown Castle, County Kildare, Ireland as his home address. Charles Engelhard had dispatched George S. Scott, president of Engelhard Industries of Canada, to the sale to bid on the son of Flaming Page and Nijinsky.

That Scott had never been to a horse auction, much less bid on a horse, was cause for some concern to O'Brien: "This man of Charlie's was entirely inexperienced where the buying of horses was concerned. And so I was worried what he might do. That he'd make some slip up ... and that I'd lose the horse." Little did O'Brien know that the numerous anxieties caused him by this horse had only just begun.

O'Brien wasn't the only person who wanted this grand looking son of Flaming Page and Northern Dancer. Taylor had invited his friend and former neighbour, Garfield Weston, to come to

Windfields and look at his yearlings before they went to the sale. Weston and his family had lived on an estate on Toronto's Bayview Avenue, a short distance from the Taylor's magnificent Windfields Farm.

Weston was immediately taken with the Flaming Page/Northern Dancer colt. When O'Brien heard Weston had flown Irish trainer Stuart Murless and a veterinarian to examine the colt O'Brien's anxiety over whether or not he would get the horse heightened. The Weston empire began at the turn of the century with a modest Toronto bakery. By the 1960's the multi-billion dollar conglomerate spanned several continents and covered a vast spectrum of food production and sales that included London's Fortnum and Mason.

Should Weston chose to buy the colt, money would not be a factor. Fortunately for O'Brien the fates stepped in once again and Weston's team decided that due to the colt's size he might take some considerable time to come to hand.

By the time the son of Northern Dancer and Flaming Page was led into the sales arena every seat in the place was filled. The rest of the onlookers crammed into the walkway at the top of the amphitheatre. When the colt walked boldly into the ring a hush descended throughout the cavernous building. The momentary trance shattered with the sound of auctioneer John Finney's voice commencing the sales patter. He spoke slowly, describing the racing highlights of Northern Dancer and Flaming Page. Then Finney's partner, Laddie Dance, gavel in hand took over, beginning with Taylor's reserve bid: "Who will give me $60,000?"

The magnificent colt stood stock still scanning the sea of faces. Never in his young life had he experienced anything like this. Until less than a week ago he had been grazing idly in his paddock, without a care in the world.

Bids bounced up from all corners of the arena and spectators strained to see who they were coming from. Eagle-eyed spotters dressed in black tie scanned the room on high alert for a flick of a wrist, an almost indiscernible nod, a slightly raised catalogue — all indicating interest and shouting "Yip!" every time they caught a sniff of a bid.

The bidding was brisk, and brief. The whole thing was over in a blink. The colt was sold for $84,000. Signing the chit was George S. Scott, president of Engelhard Industries of Canada. The majestic son of Northern Dancer was led out of the ring and back to his stall. After the sale the colt was returned to Windfields Farm to await the arrangements to ship him to Ireland

Had this tale been a fictional account of a magical horse that changed lives and made dreams come true, there could have been no more appropriate setting than Ireland. Reaching back and far beyond the mists of time, the horse shares an almost mystical kinship with the inhabitants of this small green island nation. To the early Celts the horse was their most valued possession. Spirit horses of Celtic religion carried dead heros to paradise and they worshiped Epona, the powerful Celtic goddess. Indeed, to honour Epona, Irish Kings were still symbolically united with a white mare right up and into the 11th Century in an ancient re-birthing ritual.

Historically horse racing has always been an enormously popular way to spend an Irish afternoon. On or beyond the fringe of civilization Ireland enjoyed, by far, the most horse racing of the Medieval Age. Earliest accounts suggest that in the year 1AD the Irish were hitching up their hardy little native horses to chariots and racing them full-tilt over turf courses at the Curragh of Kildare and sites of other annual fairs. By the mid 3rd Century the Irish had forsaken the carts. The famed regiment, the Fena of Erin, in County Kildare, honed their equestrian skills hunting on horseback from May until October.

The Book of Kells (AD 700), the most glorious of all ancient Irish manuscripts, is decorated throughout with images of horses and their riders. Clearly not warriors, the Irish equestrians are depicted riding bareback. This continued for centuries to be the Irish method of riding. After the Anglo-Norman invasion the English deemed riding without a saddle improper. Illegal, in fact. Hence the Irish were forbidden, by law, to ride in what the English considered the inappropriate manner of the Irish. Presumably the English felt more secure in a saddle.

The Irish also invented the sport of steeplechase. The first recorded event was held in County Cork in 1752 when Mr. O'Callaghan suggested that his horse was superior to the pride of Mr. Edmund Blake's stable. To settle the dispute the men agreed to a four-and-a-half mile gallop across open country which included splashing through a river and jumping over any number of obstacles. They decided upon two course markers: the steeple of the church in Buttevant, from whence this history-making event began, to the steeple St. Leger church in Doneraile.

The forerunner to the steeplechase was the *wild-goose chase*. Apparently a Tudor invention, it too was a cross country match, but with no particular objective, nor destination. Instead, whichever horse and rider commandeered the lead at 120 yards, got to stay in the lead for the duration. The other horse and rider were then obligated to follow wherever the first pair were inclined to go. A bevy of judges trotted along behind, also, it would appear, for no particular reason.

O'Callaghan and Blake's contribution of parameters was surely an improvement over the wild-goose chase. There is no record of who won the O'Callaghan/Blake match, but legend suggests that a solemn burial service was being conducted when the winner arrived at the front steps of the St. Leger church.

Since that fateful afternoon the Irish have proven the dominant force in the sport of steeplechase. Placing the magnificent Arkle on the top of a lengthy and distinguished list, the Irish have raised and trained so many of the world's greatest steeplechase horses. The Irish are also responsible for the sport of showjumping. And the first European polo match was held in 1868 in Limerick.

The Pooka, or magic spirit horse of Irish legend, is still sighted occasionally in remote and lonely places like dank and dark swamps and misty bogs. Only one person ever managed to ride the Pooka and that was Brian Boru, the mighty warrior king who drove the Vikings from Ireland in the Battle of Clontarf in 1714. By creating a special bridle using three hairs from the Pooka's tail, Brian Boru not only managed to control the magic horse, but convinced it to stop tormenting Christians and attacking Irishmen — except those that were drunk.

Laws and folklore demonstrate the importance of racing in ancient Irish society. According to the Brehon Laws (laws of the free farmers), an established 'fair-green' (fairgrounds) could be used for horse racing without fine or charge, by anyone, and regardless of anyone else's ownership or rights over the land. The laws also stated that no penalty or compensation was payable if someone happened to be inadvertently hit by a flying horseshoe. But perhaps most significantly, the pagan Irish heaven promised unlimited horse racing.

Still the dispatching of this Canadian colt to Ireland occurred in the 'Sixties. Horses were seldom flown anywhere back then, especially Canadian horses. Yet had the fates not whisked Nijinsky to Ireland, he would not have had the opportunity to excel as he did. As his grandsire depended upon the talents and instincts of Pete McCann for his very survival, it was imperative that horse named Nijinsky be in the hands of the world's greatest horse trainer — Michael Vincent O'Brien.

Michael Vincent O'Brien was born 9 April 1917 at home in Clashganniff House, a fifteen minute saunter along the road to the village of Churchtown in County Cork. From the moment O'Brien took his first breath there were always horses on the landscape of his life.

Looking east toward the Ballyhoura mountains visitors will catch a glimpse of the famed steeple of St. John's church in Buttevant and the starting point of a two-horse race that became the first recorded steeplechase. Almost two hundred years later young Vincent O'Brien would make his reputation as an extraordinary trainer of steeplechase horses.

The area is also home to the Dashing Duhallows, the oldest hunt in Ireland. It is also site of Cahirmee Fair which dates back to the days of Brian Boru and was renowned as one of the biggest gatherings of horses and horse-dealers in all of Europe.

O'Brien's father, Dan, was a horseman through and through. He kept a small racing stable and derived great pleasure from finding a horse, improving and schooling it, and of course, selling it. In *Vincent O'Brien*, Jimmy O'Sullivan described Dan O'Brien as "the best man I ever saw clip a horse. He would go off somewhere and come back with a horse that he had bought that you wouldn't give tuppence for, but when he had finished trimming it and pulling the mane and tail you could hardly believe it was the same animal."

As a child, while other children were reciting nursery rhymes, O'Brien was perched on his father's knee reciting bloodlines. When he got a little older O'Brien followed at the heels of his father, at every opportunity. They journeyed to the races and sales and across the countryside in search of young horses with potential.

While O'Brien clearly opted for the open spaces of a horse fair or race meet over the confines of a classroom, his early school experience was fraught with danger. County Cork was in the thick of guerilla warfare during Ireland's War for Independence.

"I remember on my way home from school, "recalls O'Brien in *Vincent O'Brien*, "we would hear the sound of one of the Crossley tenders carrying a unit of the Black and Tans and we would hide beneath some ditch until they had passed by; we would lie there in fear, our hearts stopping at the thought that if they spotted us they might begin firing indiscriminately."

By the time he was fourteen Vincent O'Brien had managed to persuade his father into releasing him from the schoolroom with the stipulation that his son spend a year at the racecourse with a trainer at Leopardstown. Following his apprenticeship O'Brien returned to assist his father on the family farm grooming, training, and riding in point-to-point meets. His responsibilities also included transporting the horses to the various racecourses.

In later years, when O'Brien built his magnificent Ballydoyle training centre, he installed a landing strip in order to facilitate flying his horses to England and the Continent. To ferry the man himself to racecourses, he had a helicopter pad built not far from his home. In the early days however, carrying his bicycle and gear, O'Brien led the horses along the road to the local train station. Once he had the horses safely aboard, he'd travel with them in the freight car. At the other end of the excursion O'Brien then walked the horses to the course. He fed them, bedded them down and then traveled back and forth from his lodgings on his bicycle.

Dan O'Brien died of pneumonia in 1943. It was the third time he had contracted the disease. A dedicated horse trader, his first two bouts were the aftermath being soaked to the skin while standing in the pouring rain at horse fairs.

Vincent O'Brien wanted to continue working with his beloved horses. The problem was he had neither money, nor clients. Nor a yard or training centre, for that matter. By Irish law the eldest O'Brien son, Donal, inherited Clashganniff House and Vincent O'Brien's future looked very bleak.

Even as a young man O'Brien was a remarkably gifted

horseman. Surely it would have been a terrible loss had he not found a way work his particular magic with horses, especially the exceptional horses, the ones that demand so much from their handlers. Horses like Nijinsky. Still, the fates had their work cut out to ensure this came about.

One afternoon during O'Brien's darkest hours he ended up at a local race-meet. Aimlessly wandering the grounds, he encountered a friend who raised sheep. The man, who's name was also O'Brien, had just procured a number of horses for one of his clients, Frank Vickerman. A wealthy British wool-merchant who had recently set up shop in Ireland, Vickerman had no interest in horse racing but thought the small stable of runners might make a splendid gift to his son when he returned home from serving with the British army in Africa. Now Vickerman would need a trainer. The fellow asked if O'Brien was interested.

At that moment the mists dissipated and course of O'Brien's life was revealed. A remarkably intuitive, passionate and compassionate horseman, he was about to embark upon a journey that would lead him to be the one chosen to meet the challenge of understanding and working with the brilliant, yet fragile and highly-spirited Nijinsky.

O'Brien's was a charmed life to be sure. It was as if he was dancing a jig along a path strewn with golden nuggets for at each crossroad all along the way, as in the case of Eddie Taylor, stood a remarkable, courageous horse ready to carry him to the next leg of the journey.

He didn't have to go far to meet with the first of these marvelous animals. Cottage Rake was living in the yard behind the surgery of the local doctor. The man had wanted to sell Cottage Rake so had sent the horse to the sales at Ballsbridge, but was forced to bring him back home when there were no offers. The following summer the doctor approached O'Brien and asked him if he would like to take Cottage Rake to train. On the condition, of course, that the horse would be sold.

Cottage Rake was a five year old and built like an equine greyhound. Tall and lean, he was lighter in bone than most steeplechase horses at the time. He looked every inch an athlete. His eye, bold and kind. Yet the animal had been languishing in a bog behind the surgery and would require time to be fit enough to face the rigours of steeple-chasing. The doctor, anxious to sell Cottage Rake, wanted the horse to start racing as soon as possible. Eventually O'Brien conceded and took Cottage Rake to Limerick on Boxing Day and entered him in a maiden (non-winners) hurdle.

While a rank beginner, Cottage Rake won with ease. His next race was in February and once again Cottage Rake bounded and galloped to victory. No sooner had the horse crossed the finish people were looking to buy him. O'Brien was about to lose his first good horse.

The initial offer came in at £3,500. The doctor was delighted. A veterinarian was called but found Cottage Rake had a wind problem and was not inclined to give him a clean bill of health. The following summer another purchaser, cheque-book in hand, arrived in Churchtown. Again Cottage Rake failed the veterinary test. The doctor, however, had become even more determined to sell the horse. Before long O'Brien heard through the grape-vine the doctor was thinking of sending Cottage Rake to England to be trained and sold.

O'Brien did not want to lose Cottage Rake. Still he really only had one client, the English wool-merchant, who was not interested in horse racing. The man did, however, enjoy a wager-or-two on the horses. Especially profitable wagers. With a little guidance from O'Brien he had indeed cashed a few lucrative tickets.

And so it was that O'Brien was able to convince his one-and-only client to purchase Cottage Rake for £3,500. Money, incidentally, that had come out of the winnings of a very profitable wager.

No sooner had O'Brien persuaded his client than Cottage Rake seemed a bit off. The horse was not exactly lame, but he was not moving fluidly. O'Brien immediately called in his own veterinarian. It was concluded that the horse was suffering from a touch of rheumatism in his shoulder. O'Brien now had to advise his client not to buy Cottage Rake.

It seems his client was clearly not accustomed to the fine art of Irish horse-dealing. The previous day he had issued a cheque to the doctor for £1000 as down payment *in good faith* to purchase Cottage Rake. When he returned to the doctor's office to retrieve his down payment he learned that the cheque had been cashed. He now owned the horse and the doctor wanted the rest of his money.

In March 1948 O'Brien and Cottage Rake boarded the boat that would ferry them to England and the heartland of Britain's National Hunt races, the Cheltenham Festival. Since the first meeting in 1902 Irish racing fans have been migrating to Cheltenham in droves. The mid-March timing of the race meet finds that St. Patrick's Day (17 March) generally falls during the Festival week. Currently about a quarter of the crowd are Irish and Ireland's renowned Guinness Brewery sponsors a tented area in the thick of the action. Thousands of pints of their black brew are consumed by enthusiastic Irish fans and all the rest who wish to be Irish on St. Patrick's Day.

It has been said that a number of Irish punters have asked that their ashes be strewn along the famed uphill finish. Tales of an Irish priest investing the parish collection on a *'sure thing'* in the third at Cheltenham might be slightly exaggerated. But part of the revelry or the *'craic'* is surely putting one over on the English bookies. According to BBC Sport: "Ireland is a great breeder of trainers and jockeys, as well as horses, and there has always been a huge incentive to get one over on the old English enemy on their own soil."

Cottage Rake won the coveted Cheltenham Gold Cup in March 1948. Vickerman was ecstatic. This, his first taste of horse racing glory, inspired him to sell Cottage Rake at a sizeable profit. Appealing to his client's entrepreneurial instincts, O'Brien explained that if Cottage Rake were to win the Gold Cup a second time, the value of the horse would escalate. Dramatically. Vickerman understood the strategy. And O'Brien continued to train the horse.

Then everything fell apart. A month before his second Cheltenham engagement Cottage Rake caught a virus. O'Brien had to take him out of training which meant there was no chance Cottage Rake could be fit and ready for the grueling Gold Cup. The wool-merchant would not understand. Nor would he be pleased. Once again O'Brien was on the brink of losing Cottage Rake.

This time he was saved by curious and unusual weather conditions. Suddenly, after the first two days of the Cheltenham race meet, severe frost came blasting into the area. The turf course was frozen rock-hard, thus impossible for horses to gallop and jump over. The feature race, the Gold Cup, was rescheduled for a month hence which gave the horse time to recover.

Fit and healthy, Cottage Rake battled on to win one of the most exciting Gold Cup's in history. The following year O'Brien, Cottage Rake and company returned to Cheltenham. Only four horses dared challenge Cottage Rake. The closest any of them got to him was when they all lined up at the start. On 9 March 1950 Cottage Rake won his third consecutive Gold Cup by a whopping ten lengths.

To this point O'Brien had been leasing his father's yard and facilities from his brother, but the time had come to set up his own training centre. After months of combing the countryside, the ideal locale materialized in County Tipperary just to the west

Slievenamon, or *the hill of the woman.* According to myth an Irish king sat atop Slievenamon while a collection of fleet and agile unmarried women scrambled up the mountain. The first to make it to the peak was crowned queen.

Ballydoyle, the farm that would become Nijinsky's Irish home, was located about 40 miles north-east of Churchtown and consisted of 285 acres over gently rolling countryside. A luxurious patchwork of fields were hemmed with stone walls and high banks topped with hedgerows. As he scanned the horizon, O'Brien surveyed the uphill rises and could envision grand gallops for his horses.

Every aspiring horse trainer needs a patron with huge financial resources, or a very good horse. Cottage Rake surely launched Vincent O'Brien. On all fronts. O'Brien had made a number of shrewd wagers on the horse that had paid handsomely enough for O'Brien to be in a position to set up his training centre. Winning the Cheltenham Gold Cup three consecutive years Cottage Rake was the best advertisement any young trainer could pray for and before long other owners were knocking on O'Brien's door.

Cottage Rake was immediately followed by two other very good horses — Hatton's Grace and Knock Hard. Hatton's Grace won the Champion Hurdle at Cheltenham three consecutive years (1949 - 1951). Knock Hard won the Gold Cup in 1953. The same year Britain's most demanding steeplechase, the Grand National, was conquered by O'Brien-trained Early Mist.

It seems that O'Brien and his horses frequently did things in threes. The following year O'Brien was back in the Grand National winners' circle, this time with Royal Tan. His third consecutive Grand National winner, Quare Times was named for a famous greyhound hailing from the same part of County Tipperary where the horse was foaled.

When Quare Times returned to Ireland he was treated like the conquering hero. First he was paraded along the main street of

Mullingar, hometown of his owner, Mrs. Welman. The spectacle was led by two bands and thousands stopped whatever they were doing to travel to Mullingar to join the celebrations. Next Quare Times was taken by horse box to Thurles, place of his birth, for another celebration and then on to a reception at Cashel. Eventually the well-feted horse arrived back at O'Brien's Ballydoyle training centre.

Quite possibly the greatest steeplechaser to gallop over Cheltenham's hallowed grounds was Arkle. And while not trained by O'Brien the horse was Irish from his fetlocks to his forelock. Arkle was bred by one Irish woman, Mrs. Mary Baker at Halahow House near Dublin and was purchased by another. Anne, Duchess of Westminister discovered three year old Arkle at the Ballsbridge Sales. Born in Country Cork, the Duchess was lauded as a skilled and compassionate horsewoman who refused to allow her horse to race in the Grand National: "I will never let my Arkle run in the Grand National, because I adore him, because he is one of the family, and because he is much too precious to me."

Arkle was, however, a fixture at Cheltenham. His race against Mill House in the 1964 Cheltenham Gold Cup is considered one of the greatest steeplechases of all time. Mill House was also an Irish-bred, but trained in England. Arkle was trained in Ireland. The Irish had their money on Arkle.

Mill House went to the post odds-on favourite. In the final mile and a half, Mill House was flying as he soared over the huge fences. At the second last fence Arkle had caught Mill House. Arkle was jumping like a greyhound, overlapping his forelegs with his hind legs. Coming into the final fence Arkle was in the lead. Up the hill he surged drawing away from the tiring Mill House with every determined stride. Arkle won his first of three consecutive Cheltenham Gold Cups by an astonishing five lengths. Arkle demolished the previous course record. The Irish in the stands went wild.

The charmed existence that seems to have permeated all aspects of O'Brien's life, included guiding him to the woman he would marry. This bit of magic happened not long after he moved into Ballydoyle: "That afternoon I had originally intended to turn right out of the gate and go south to Waterford. Something made me turn around and head north for Dublin."

Once in Dublin he planned to have an early meal so he could get some work done before going to the races the following day. O'Brien was enjoying a pre-dinner drink in the bar when two friends wandered in and invited him to join them. The two men were accompanied by Jacqueline Wittenoom, an attractive young woman from Perth Australia. Before long O'Brien found himself besotted with Jacqueline. At the end of the evening he invited her to join him at the races the following day at The Curragh. By the time the winner of the sixth race had galloped past the finish O'Brien realized he had met the woman he wanted to marry.

"That was May and she was going back to Australia on the fourth of July." O'Brien recalled. "I had to think pretty fast. I'd not much time."

Jacqueline left for England where she was to board the ship bound for Australia. O'Brien stopped thinking and hastened after her. By the time Jacqueline's ship was meant to sail O'Brien had proposed. Jacqueline accepted: "Vincent gave me an engagement ring in Jammet's Restaurant over strawberries and cream." She returned to Australia to say goodbye to family and friends. Six months later she and O'Brien were married in Dublin.

By 1955 O'Brien was clearly at the top of his game as a trainer of National Hunt horses. He had now saddled his third Grand National winner. His reputation as a trainer of steeplechase horses was stellar. His Ballydoyle was a magnificent training centre. And he was married to the woman of his dreams. He had it all.

As destiny appears factor in the sign posts all along the road that led to Nijinsky, it would appear that it also had a hand in guiding the man who would help the horse reach his fullest potential. If O'Brien was the man for the job then he would have to begin preparing for the challenges presented to him by this horse. The first step: he would have to forsake training National Hunt horses and concentrate on the flat runners.

It is unusual for a horse trainer to switch from steeplechase to flat racing. Especially if the trainer was as successful as O'Brien. The two disciplines are very different, as are the horses. Had O'Brien stayed with the steeplechase horses he would have had owners lining up at the front gates for the rest of his life.

But O'Brien was a gambler. In every sense of the word. Without a wealthy patron gambling was the only way for a trainer to make any money, especially in Ireland where the purses were sparse. Some of O'Brien's betting coups were legendary. Some failed. Others fairly lit up the sky. From time to time sizable profits were gleaned by those who listened to his sage advice.

This did not, of course, endear him to the bookmakers. In his authorized biography *Vincent O'Brien's Great Horses* he tells the tale of an encounter with bookmaker William Hill at the York races. Hill had been a member of the Black and Tans, the British military force charged with crushing the Irish in their War of Independence from Great Britain. O'Brien was standing with two British trainers when Hill walked up to O'Brien and said "It's a pity I didn't have you shot years ago."

When O'Brien made the move to focus on flat racing there were no new owners lining up at the gates of Ballydoyle. It was a huge gamble. Possibly the biggest of his life, but it was something he knew he had to do. A man of action O'Brien decided to travel to the Tattersalls' September Sales, which were then held at Doncaster. There was no reason for him to be there. He had no flat racing clients, no one to chose horses for. Again the fates stepped in.

Wandering about Doncaster O'Brien's path intersected with that of a solicitor from Yorkshire that he knew. The fellow enjoyed wager-or-two and his bets on the O'Brien horses at Cheltenham had proven quite profitable.

The solicitor was hosting a wealthy American who was interested in purchasing some yearlings at the sale. That evening he introduced O'Brien to John McShain. The son of Irish immigrants, McShain had assembled a massive construction business. His company built the Pentagon and was responsible for the restoration, brick by numbered brick, of the White House. His wealth was formidable. His influence, encompassing.

Before long he was convinced that he wanted O'Brien to select the yearlings he would purchase. There was, however, one snag. McShain wanted to take the horses back to the United States to be trained and raced. Which, since McShain lived in Philadelphia, made perfect sense.

O'Brien hadn't come this far by taking *no* for an answer. Over the next few days O'Brien introduced McShain to a variety of his friends, for the most part Irish horse breeders and horse traders. Each time McShain said he intended to take the horses back home to the United States, to a man they advised him to keep the horses in Ireland for a year or two. The unanimous theory was that they'd have a much better chance.

The strategy worked. Sort of. McShain agreed to allow O'Brien to take five of the yearlings with him back to Ballydoyle to be conditioned and trained. McShain would carefully monitor the experiment and decide at a later date when to ship them to the United States. In the meantime, McShain returned home to Philadelphia.

This long-distance arrangement taught O'Brien a very valuable lesson in running a training yard as a proper business. McShain was a huge asset to O'Brien's dream of training great

Thoroughbreds. He could not afford to lose this, his first real flat racing client. Still Mc Shain was an astute businessman. He once told O'Brien that when he was a child he did not spend his weekly allowance from his parents. Instead, when his siblings had spent theirs he loaned his money to them. With interest.

So O'Brien began writing detailed reports on the progress of McShain's yearlings and sending the reports by post: "He enjoyed getting the reports and he promptly replied to every one. He banged them back! He told me he would read my letters first in his office and then he'd take them home with him and read them all over again with his wife, Mary ... I've no doubt at all that our association would never have reached the heights it did, if I hadn't taken the trouble to correspond with him."

O'Brien's fastidious reporting resulted in McShain agreeing to leave the horses in Ireland for their two year old season. Then they would be shipped to the United States. The first of McShain's horses to win a race was named York Fair. The venue was a country track in the village of Mallow. It was not exactly success enough to justify the experiment. Nor the money invested in buying and training the small herd. O'Brien was going to need a miracle to keep these horses in Ireland.

The miracle came in the shape of a compact bay colt named Ballymoss. Initially, however, Ballymoss' brilliance was far from obvious — at least to the untrained eye.

Ballymoss began his road to glory in a maiden (non-winners) race at The Curragh in July and was soundly beaten so O'Brien took him down the road to the smaller track at Mallow. There Ballymoss was second to a filly called Bell Bird. Finally, at the end of September, Ballymoss won a race — minor event at Leopardstown. O'Brien's determination to keep McShain's horses at

Ballydoyle was unbridled. When he returned to Ballydoyle with Ballymoss that evening O'Brien sat down and wrote to McShain suggesting they set their sights on the English Derby at Epsom before sending Ballymoss to America.

To this point Ballymoss had given scant indication that he is driven to be a racehorse, much less a champion. Still no one can say that O'Brien did not think on a grand scale. The course of the Derby, one and a half miles of twists, turns, hills and dales, is the most demanding in the world. It requires great stamina, agility, speed, and courage of its contestants. Generally speaking there is a training strategy, complete with specific races, that give some indication of whether or not a horse is of the calibre to enter the Derby starting gate.

So far in Ballymoss' lead up to the Derby he was not even in the frame in his first race; then trounced by a filly at a country track; and finally won an insignificant race at Leopardstown. Now most might think this is hardly grounds to advise your client to book passage to England in June and to pack his top hat.

In his first three year old test, the Madrid Free Handicap, Ballymoss "Ran deplorably ... He finished right out of the back door," according to O'Brien. His jockey put this latest loss to the heavy footing and that Ballymoss seemed more interested in the charming the fillies than in beating them in a race.

In the meantime all the other Derby candidates were competing in considerably more taxing events. And for the most part, in England. Still O'Brien assured McShain that Ballymoss would run in the Derby. Then, following the Madrid, it was discovered that Ballymoss had bruised his foot, which meant that his training would be impeded.

In May O'Brien sent Ballymoss off to Leopardstown with a filly named Gladness to run in the Trigo Stakes. The grand rangy filly was odds-on favourite to win. Few took notice of her traveling companion. Yet Ballymoss won the Trigo. Apparently the ground was hard and fast, conditions disliked by Gladness, but obviously pleased Ballymoss. Indeed the entire concept of racing must have pleased Ballymoss for the next date on his card was the English Derby and he ran his heart out and placed second.

Three weeks later Ballymoss easily won the Irish Derby. Next he prevailed over damp turf at Doncaster to win the almost two mile St. Leger, the third leg of the British Triple Crown races. Then in September O'Brien and the Irish troop invaded France. Their target was the country's most prestigious horse race, Prix de l'Arc de Triomphe. When it began to rain on the day of the competition O'Brien's hopes were dashed. Yet the remarkable Ballymoss overcame his disdain, once again, for soft turf and won the great French race and his owner sang the praises of O'Brien for all to hear and for ever more.

McShain not only played a role in O'Brien's reputation as the world's most accomplished horse trainer, he helped set the stage for the first Celtic Tiger, for it was McShain who brought O'Brien to the US and introduced him to Kentucky and the Keeneland Yearling Sale. Not unlike Ireland's horse fairs, Keeneland is also festival of horse traders — buyers, sellers, crowds of spectators and beautiful horses. While they wandered from stable to stable housing the glossy young Thoroughbreds McShain introduced his Irish trainer to any and all. Among O'Brien's new acquaintances was Raymond Guest, US Ambassador to Ireland.

Guest was an enthusiastic steeplechase fan and his dream was to have one of his horses win the Grand National and of course O'Brien had trained winners of the famous race. Guest asked if he could send O'Brien one of his steeplechase horses. While O'Brien had walked away from that part of his life and set his sights on learning to train horses to win the English Derby, he agreed to take Guest's horse. Before long Guest had his best steeplechase horse, Virginus, flown to Ireland to train with O'Brien at Ballydoyle.

Virginus was not an especially inspired racehorse. According to O'Brien, "he was awfully slow and I think we won just one race with him." No doubt O'Brien's enchantment with the English Derby was contagious for in time Guest's dream of winning the Grand National had altered slightly: "... the notion now came to Raymond Guest that it would be pleasant to win the Epsom Derby."

O'Brien contacted Tom Cooper, director of the Irish branch of the British Bloodstock Agency and off to Ballsbridge Sales they went, looking for a Derby winner for Guest. The year was 1960. The horse that won the Derby that year was named St. Paddy — a portent of things to come.

O'Brien and Cooper purchased a small chestnut yearling colt with a wide white blaze running the length of his young face. O'Brien was concerned about the colt's size: "... the was definitely a question as to whether he was going to grow big enough ... His height was the one thing against him."

Nonetheless they paid 12,200 guineas for the little colt and brought the him to Ballydoyle to train for the Derby. Guest named the colt Larkspur and his initiation to the rigours of horse racing was inauspicious. According to O'Brien Larkspur "was quite a useful two year old." Which translated from horse trader lingo, meant Larkspur was not exactly a world-beater. Although O'Brien did say that Larkspur ran a "good race" in the Timeform Gold Cup and offered that Larkspur's jockey was convinced that had the colt more running room he would have been close. Larkspur, incidentally, finished seventh.

Larkspur finally won a race, the Wills Gold Flake Stakes at Leopardstown. While O'Brien kept the colt on the trail to the Derby, the British racing press were less than effusive over the small, pricy colt. The *Timeform Annual* was kind: "... (Larkspur) was not everybody's idea of a classic winner." Furthermore, O'Brien's stable jockey opted against riding Larkspur and chose another horse O'Brien was saddling for the Derby.

Nine days before the Derby a swelling appeared below the hock on Larkspur's near-hind leg. Veterinarian, Bob Griffin, was summoned from his clinic at The Curragh. Griffin prescribed "fomentations and two days rest."

O'Brien decided to inform the racing press there was every likelihood Larkspur would not run in the Derby. O'Brien's rationale was that as a betting man himself he did not want the public to place their wagers on his horse only to enrich the bookmakers if the horse didn't run.

The week before the Derby the veterinarian returned to Ballydoyle and as the swelling was no worse gave O'Brien the 'okay' to ship Larkspur to England for the Derby. Upon hearing the news apparently Guest began making some very large wagers on his horse.

The year was 1962. Remembered as the year of the 'disaster Derby.' An accident at the front of the field of twenty-six horses caused seven to fall. Horses and riders went down like bowling pins. Three jockeys were hurried to the hospital; one horse suffered a broken leg. Larkspur was well back in the pack and out of harms way when the horses fell. He actually jumped over the favourite, Hethersett, as the colt was sliding to the turf.

Amid all the confusion and chaos, loose horses and ambulances, little Larkspur won the Derby. O'Brien's euphoria was short-lived. He was immediately called up in front of the stewards. Lord Derby, who's ancestor won the coin-toss to have the race named after him, was among those questioning the Irish trainer. The fact that Raymond Guest had wagered so much money, and at very long odds, coupled with O'Brien announcing to the press the horse might not run, gave them cause for some suspicion. Still, they accepted O'Brien's account of the events leading up to the Derby.

Larkspur was entered in the Irish Derby and St. Leger, but the horse had no more races in him. Guest sold him to Japanese horse breeders and Larkspur stood at stud in Japan. O'Brien had his first English Derby.

Six years passed before another horse marched O'Brien into the English Derby winners circle. Where Larkspurs Derby victory was a fluke, the next horse to bring honours to the Irish trainer clearly belonged among Thoroughbred elite.

This horse was named Sir Ivor. He was a lanky, good-looking bay colt with a generous disposition. Beautifully-bred, his sire, Sir Gaylord, was a half-brother to Secretariat. His dam, Attica, descended from a line of stalwart racemares and was a gift to Kentucky horse breeder Alice Chandler from her father who predicted that one day Attica might give her an exceptional racehorse.

It took many years, however, before the prophesy came true. Attica's first three foals all won races, but it wasn't until Chandler sent Attica off to the court of Sir Gaylord that things clicked. Still in the beginning no one could of predicted that the result of this mating would prove spectacular. Quite the opposite, in fact. He seemed to grow taller and taller by the day. Like a gangly teenager he grew so rapidly he appeared lopsided — one end out of sync with the other end. Yet as much as Chandler despaired over her ill-proportioned colt, she believed him quite intelligent: "... Some people say horses have no sense, but that's not true. We have some terrible storms here. Well one night when he was a yearling I could hear him nickering over top of the lightening and the thunder, so I went out to him with my raincoat flapping and with no shank, no lead rope. I called him. He flew up to me and slid the brakes on and I just reached up and grabbed him and took him into the barn."

Chandler's frightened, yet trusting yearling grew into a courageous champion, winning some of the most prestigious races in England, France, Ireland and the United States. Yet initially little was expected from him because of his immaturity. When he arrived at Ballydoyle in the fall of 1966 the lads in the yard recalled him as so big and backward that it was unlikely Sir Ivor would run as a two year old. When he was ridden out on O'Brien's all-weather gallop the leggy colt galumphed about more like a giraffe than a sleek Thoroughbred. But the following spring he began to grow into himself and by May O'Brien began to think he might be ready to race.

At the end of June Sir Ivor was vanned to The Curragh. He finished fourth, but his rider, Liam Ward was impressed with the way the colt handled himself. A month later Sir Ivor justified Ward's faith by winning at The Curragh and was back in September to win the National Stakes quite brilliantly. Then Sir Ivor was flown to France when he set about trouncing the country's top two year olds in the Grand Criterium.

That winter O'Brien opted to send eight of his horses to Pisa, Italy for the winter. The small racecourse and training grounds were sheltered by a parkland of woods on three sides. The stable area with its red-tiled roofs was situated on the other side of the small forest. While the Mediterranean climate agreed with horses and staff alike, the soil was quite sandy and before long Sir Ivor was suffering from an abscess in his hoof caused by sand making its way up through the hoof. Finally Sir Ivor's leg became painfully swollen.

O'Brien's Irish veterinarian was flown to Italy and he was able to relieve the abscess. He advised the staff to hand-walk the colt and bath the foot daily to help draw out the poisons. In the meantime Sir Ivor had other ideas. Fit and feeling full of himself, the colt was aching to run, so O'Brien decided to let Sir Ivor's lad ride him out with the others.

One morning as the horses were en route from the stable area to the track Sir Ivor jumped straight up off all fours, lashed out a fierce buck and a kick and his lad went hurtling to the ground. The pathway ran alongside a fairly busy road used by everything from clattering lorries to herds of sheep. A long water-filled dyke bordered the other side of the road. O'Brien was in a car following his procession of horses when Sir Ivor dumped his lad. O'Brien was out of the vehicle and on the run the moment he realized what had happened. Fortunately the fellow had landed on his feet and kept a hold on the reins.

"We almost died of fright," O'Brien recalled years later. "We jumped out of the car and we got our hands wide out round him ... If he'd got away from us he'd have toppled over into that dyke."

Sir Ivor's first three year old race was at Ascot in the Two Thousand Guineas Trial. The turf was desperately heavy, still Sir Ivor won — but only just. He then went on to Newmarket and won the Guineas handily. Sir Ivor appeared to be maturing rapidly. By the time he arrived at Epsom for the Derby he looked superb and stood out head and shoulders above the rest of the field.

Sir Ivor had Lester Piggott on his back and half-way through the big race it didn't look as if Sir Ivor had a hope and it appeared as if the leader, Connaught, had the event sewn up. A hundreds yards out Piggott had Sir Ivor tucked in on the rails. Then suddenly he moved the colt to the outside and took aim at Connaught.

Alice Chandler was in the stands: "A hundred yards out he had no shot at winning. Then you've never seen a horse run so fast in your life. We didn't believe he'd won. I've seen that film many, many times and I'll still give you 6 to 5 he got beat."

Sir Ivor's herculean effort took a toll and he lost his next three races in England and Ireland. Sir Ivor was then dispatched to France for the Prix de l'Arc de Triomphe but had to settle for second behind yet another very good horse, Vaguely Noble. Sir Ivor went on to win the Champion Stakes at Newmarket after which he was flown to the United States where he won the Washington DC International before retiring to stud at Kentucky's Claiborne Farm.

Where Sir Ivor was a truly extraordinary animal, the next horse on O'Brien's horizon was magic. The stage was now set for the horse named Nijinsky.

No sooner had Nijinsky arrived at Ballydoyle than his highly-strung temperament became evident. For starters he spurned O'Brien's finest Irish oats. As hungry as he must have been, Nijinsky sniffed at his feed tub each mealtime and turned away to nibble on his hay. After several days O'Brien telephoned Windfields Farm and discovered that Nijinsky had been raised on a diet of crunch — compressed cubes of oats, bran, molasses, and supplements.

Several bags of the mixture were immediately shipped to Ireland. The day the bags arrived, the mercurial Nijinsky decided to start eating the Irish oats. Still he continued to give O'Brien no end of anxious moments.

There were mornings when Nijinsky refused to come out of his stall. Most horses leave their stalls willingly. Not Nijinsky. Some mornings it would take forever to coax him out. He'd rear straight up and fight every inch of the way.

Perhaps if O'Brien had been familiar with Nijinsky's grandsire, Nearctic, he might have been better prepared for the extreme nature of his Canadian colt. From Nijinsky's regal head carriage to his disposition — his volatility to his brilliance — all were inherited from Nearctic. Because Nearctic's racing days were fraught with such calamity little was known about him, which is quite remarkable since he is the patriarch of the most dominant Thoroughbred sire line in history. That O'Brien, without knowledge of Nearctic, was able to bring out the best in his grandson, is clearly testament to his title as the world's greatest horse trainer.

At Ballydoyle horses went in sets to train over the gallops. Initially Nijinsky was relegated to the second group. As soon as the first lot of horses were tacked up and in the yard, their riders on their backs, ready to for their morning work, Nijinsky started to fret and pace anxiously back and forth in his stall. It seems that he wanted to go out with every set. He did not want to stay confined in his stall when there was action elsewhere.

One of the keys to O'Brien's great success was his uncanny

ability to understand and adjust to the foibles of his equine charges. After pondering Nijinsky's accelerating anxiety O'Brien had his staff convert an old covered drive shed on the property into a kind of walking ring. Then in the company of a companion horse, Nijinsky would stroll around and around and around, until the others returned and it was his turn to be worked.

When they rode Nijinsky out on the gallops, he wasn't keen to work with the other horses. He was a force unto himself. Eventually his rider got him to start to settle down and cooperate. Yet, if for some reason the group came to a stop, even briefly, Nijinsky would rear and cause a fuss. He didn't like to be still. Like his grandsire, Nearctic, this high nervous energy was often difficult, sometimes impossible to contain. It did, however, fuel his instinct to race beyond the wind.

"Most good horses take it easy at home" explained O'Brien. "Sir Ivor, for instance, just worked with whatever horse he was working with. No matter how bad the latter was, Sir Ivor would just head him, and that was that, no more.

"Nijinsky, once he hit the front, pricked his ears and went on from there, galloping away from the other horses — which was quite remarkable and most unusual ... He didn't require a lot of work ... He was active all the time. He wasn't just ambling about, but always alert and using himself. Therefore he was a horse that was at his best when lightly trained."

O'Brien also credited his residence riders with helping Nijinsky contain his high nervous energy by keeping him settled and relaxed: "Nijinsky could easily have been spoiled. They had the strength to handle him and the patience not to knock him about."

Still, O'Brien was concerned over Nijinsky's volatility and felt it prudent to write a note to Engelhard: "I am somewhat concerned about Nijinsky's temperament and that he is inclined to resent getting on with his work. My best boys are riding him and we can only hope he will go the right way."

As with his spurning of O'Brien's finest oats, Nijinsky waited until O'Brien posted the letter then, almost immediately, the colt settled into the training routine. Nijinsky did, however, continue to be anxious and easily excitable and his handlers continued to adapt to his idiosyncracies and volatility.

No sooner had Nijinsky galloped over the hallowed turf of The Curragh of Kildare the word began to spread throughout this land of the horse. The Canadian colt epitomized the consummate Thoroughbred racehorse; his conformation perfect in every way; his stride as fluid and powerful as an eagle in flight. Young and old followed his every move with interest and authority of people who knew horses.

The first time Nijinsky entered the starting stalls the Irish flocked to the ancient course. Fathers stood with their sons by the parade ring, in awe at the majesty of Nijinsky as the great horse danced and pranced. Bringing the next generation to witness the perfect horse was like rites of passage to Irish horse-loving men and women.

Nijinsky was, in all ways, the anointed one. The sum of his mighty ancestors, he embodied the very finest traits of the greatest, bravest, boldest horses in the history of the Thoroughbred. It is hard to imagine a more dynamic pedigree. Inspired by the intrepid Citation, his bloodlines offered a kaleidoscope of grandeur: elegant English Derby winners; rugged Kentucky Derby winners; the indomitable Nearco and his noble son Nearctic; and an elite collection of the most important matriarchs tracing back to the origins of the breed.

For those blessed with a passion for horses, Nijinsky was as much inspiring as he was breathtaking.

Nijinsky went to the post five times as a two year old and barely had to move beyond a canter to win all five races. The first four were run in Ireland and the final race of 1969 was the Dewhurst Stakes at Newmarket, considered a preview of the main contenders for England's classic races. Nijinsky won the Dewhurst with such ease:

"Only a horse right out of the top drawer could have treated his opponents in such an off-hand manner ... a horse of the highest class. Everything about him is impressive ... Small wonder he is looked upon as an exciting prospect for the Classics." *Timeform: Racehorses of 1969.*

Liam Ward, the jockey who rode Nijinsky in his Irish races was exuberant in his praise of the horse: "You could ride him on a silver thread ... He just did everything. You could sit and wait all day because he had this terrific speed.

"He was such a good ride that you could drop him in behind horses anywhere at all, just where you felt like it. Pull him out and say "Go" and that was it. He went into another gear immediately ... It was just a matter of whenever you wanted to win on him, that was it."

Nijinsky was declared Champion Two Year Old in England and Ireland in 1969. There were those, however, who saw his breeding as suspect. He was, after all, born in Canada, at the time, a country known for producing great hockey players — not great Thoroughbreds. Not yet.

Nijinsky made his three year old debut at The Curragh in the Gladness Stakes and once again coasted to an easy victory. He then was shipped to England for the Two Thousand Guineas. Among those skeptical of Nijinsky's breeding were many of England's bookmakers. Rumour was that it would cost them close to $1 million if Nijinsky won the Guineas. O'Brien hired a private security force to guard the horse.

While the bookmakers may have had their misgivings over Nijinsky, there seemed no doubt at *Sporting Life* over what horse would win. On the morning of the race the headline read: **Who's going to be second to Nijinsky?**

Nijinsky went to the front of the field early in the race and there he stayed winning this, the first race in the English Triple Crown, by two-and-one-half lengths. The horse was still in the winners' enclosure when bookmaker William Hill jumped up and was offering 5 to 2 odds on Nijinsky for the English Derby. Presumably Hill, generally considered an astute judge of horses, for some reason was not impressed.

The next day Hill reinforced his opinion with a series of advertisements that continued to offer odds of 5 to 2 while on the other side of town rival firm Ladbrokes had Nijinsky at odds of 9 to 4. Two days later Hill followed suit, but as the Derby neared both firms settled down and into the reality that Nijinsky might very well win their biggest race and offered reduced odds. In the meantime thousands had taken up the bookmakers on their early odds and Hill and Ladbrokes stood to lose a king's ransom should prevail in the Derby. To be on the safe side, instead of stabling Nijinsky at Epsom with the other horses, O'Brien sequestered the colt at nearby Sandown Park.

"The Thoroughbred exists because its selection depended not on experts, technicians or zoologists, but on a piece of wood: the winning post of the Epsom Derby. If you base your criteria on anything else you will get something else, not the Thoroughbred ... the conditions of the Derby have remained unchanged and its validity unquestioned; it is the Epsom Derby which has made the Thoroughbred what it is today."

— Federico Tesio

The day before the Derby, Nijinsky was driven to Epsom to become accustomed to the course and the footing. Nijinsky galloped easily over the famous turf and was then driven back to Sandown. Upon arrival, disaster struck. Nijinsky was sick. He broke into a sweat and began pawing the ground. He was showing all the signs of colic which includes severe abdominal pain caused by spasms in the intestinal walls. Normally a trainer would give the horse a drug to help relax the intestinal walls and allow the pain-causing gases to escape. But the rules of horse racing dictate no drugs within 24 hours of a race. Fortunately someone recalled an ancient remedy. They gathered fresh grass and mixed it with bicarbonate of soda and bran. It worked.

Nijinsky's Epsom Derby was quite possibly the most beautiful, the most brilliant horse race ever contested. The ease in which Nijinsky won this, the race that defines the Thoroughbred, was astounding. The horses he left behind in this eleven horse field included some superior racehorses like the French sensation, Gyr. In fact the distinguished French trainer, Etienne Pollet, was so convinced that his monstrous chestnut colt would not only win the Derby, but sweep the Classics, he postponed his retirement for a year in order to run him.

It was at this time, in the walking ring prior to the Derby, that it became noticeable Nijinsky's fragile nervous disposition was becoming unhinged. He was sweating and appeared anxious, but once in the starting stalls he calmed down.

The bell clanged and Nijinsky leapt smartly from the gate and settled into the middle of the pack. And there he remained around the slight turn to the left, the sharper turn to the right; around the curve to the left; down the hill to Tattenham Corner. Now, with three-and-a-half furlongs to go, the race started taking shape. Horses began vying for position. Still no action from Nijinsky. With two furlongs remaining, the hulking Gyr powered into the lead.

Then suddenly Nijinsky began to accelerate — his ears perked, his eyes focused beyond the horizon. Ordinary horses have four gaits, but Nijinsky had a fifth, magical gait that grew longer and longer each time his hooves brushed the soft turf. His entire being, a powerful symphony of perfect rhythm and harmony, transcended the limits of his earthbound companions.

The final furlong is uphill. The decisive test. Yet Nijinsky cruised to the front of the pack with ease and grace. It was as if for most of the race he had simply been taxiing along the runway. Now, in the closing seconds of the Derby, he moved into liftoff. And then, into full flight.

It was so astonishing. No one who witnessed Nijinsky's Derby will never forget the majesty and the elegance of that horse. Eddie and Winnie Taylor were among the cheering crowd. As was Romola Nijinsky. Widow of the late Vaslav Nijinsky was among the guests of Charles Engelhard. A year earlier, when Mme Nijinsky initially heard of the colt named for her husband who had believed he would be reincarnated as a horse she instructed her secretary to "always back him."

When Nijinsky floated past the famed finish post, Eddie Taylor was already on the run and burrowing through the ringside crowds to shake the trembling hand of Engelhard. Red and white Canadian flags billowed from buses parked opposite the grandstand. When the usually poker-faced Piggott rode Nijinsky into the winner's circle he was beaming from ear to ear. A rare sight indeed. Charlie Engelhard was positively euphoric and confessed he is too nervous to watch his horses, instead he observes the face of his racing manager, David McCall: "I must admit I started off looking down, but I saw the smile on David's face and I watched it all."

In a rare act of courtesy from horse owner to breeder, Engelhard invited Eddie Taylor to join him in leading Nijinsky into the winner's circle. According to long-held tradition, the owner of the winning horse was invited to the Royal Box. "This is the greatest day of my life." enthused Engelhard. "Two marvellous things have happened: I won the Derby; and met the Queen."

Nijinsky was shipped back to Ireland for the Irish Derby, which he also won, and by three lengths over a boggy course. Nijinsky was, however, becoming increasingly distressed and prior to the race was in a white lather.

A month later he was in the stalls for the King George VI and Queen Elizabeth Stakes at Ascot. And won. "Probably Nijinsky's best race ever," exclaimed Piggott, "because he was up against good older horses and he still won in a canter ... I have never been more impressed with a horse."

A week later Nijinsky was back in Ireland and suddenly broke out in a severe case of ringworm, a fungus that creates inflamation of the skin and hair follicles. He could not be ridden, so was hand-walked around O'Brien's yard. His conditioning obviously suffered.

Nijinsky's next, and final, race was scheduled to be the Prix de l'Arc de Triomphe, but his itinerary was changed to include the St. Leger, third race in England's Triple Crown. On 12 September 1970 Nijinsky won the nearly two-mile St. Leger. No horse had won all three races — the Guineas, the Derby, and the St. Leger — since Bahram in 1935. It is unlikely that any horse will ever again. The British Triple Crown belongs to Nijinsky.

Somewhere between the ringworm, his lack of race conditioning, his fragile nerves and the length of the race, Nijinsky lost a total of thirty pounds from the time he walked into the starting stalls and crossed the finish.

"The Leger was too far for him," offered Piggott, "He had been off the track for quite some time and he had this skin disease. Actually he had a very easy race, but the distance, I think, took that much more out of him that it had done in any previous race."

Three weeks later Nijinsky was in France for the Prix de l'Arc de Triomphe. When he was led into the walking ring he was mobbed by photographers and camera crews. The crowd outside the ring clapped and shouted loudly. By the time Nijinsky walked on to the course he was, once again, coated in a white lather.

In the early stages of the Arc Piggott appeared to be riding a waiting race keeping Nijinsky well back in the fourteen-horse field. Entering the straight Sassafras and Blakeney set off to the front of the pack. Finally Piggott moved Nijinsky to the outside but the horse now had a lot of ground to cover before reaching the leaders. In the final seconds of the race Nijinsky was in a duel to the finish for the first time in his life. He was neck and neck with the French horse Sassafras. Piggott cracked Nijinsky with his whip. Nijinsky had never been hit before and tried to duck away from the punishment at the very moment the horses flashed across the wire. In a photo finish Sassafras won by a scant nostril.

No race in the history of horse racing has been more debated and analyzed than this one. Everyone agrees that Nijinsky was vastly superior to Sassafras. So what happened? Probably a number of factors that included the effect of the ringworm, the physical toll taken by the St. Leger, and the mental stress of the whole thing. Many believed that Piggott was at fault, or at least guilty of misreading both the pace of the race and the condition of the horse.

Nijinsky was exhausted. His nerves were shattered. Still, two weeks later, they ran him one more time — the Champion Stakes at Newmarket. The largest crowd in the history of the historic race course turned out to cheer on Nijinsky. But Nijinsky could no longer take the pressure and once again finished second to a vastly inferior horse.

"I think that the number and type of races that this horse was asked to win," said Engelhard, "is perhaps more that one normally can ask any animal. This is one of the reasons that in my opinion, we as humans let him down."

In March 1971, ten months after Nijinsky fulfilled his dream of owning the winner of the Epsom Derby, and meeting the Queen, Charles Engelhard died. He was fifty-four.

The Tiger

When it was announced that Nijinsky would be retired from racing at the end of his three year old season, there was an hullabaloo like none other. The first waves of outrage came from the Irish media and the fans. The average Irish farmer knew far more about horses than most of the wealthy racehorse owners. For starters they knew that horses are not fully mature until their fifth year. Thus it would seem reasonable that Nijinsky had his best years ahead of him.

Possibly the most eloquent of those beseeching Engelhard to keep Nijinsky in training was Irish racing correspondent, Sean Murphy, in *The People* (5 July 1970):

> "... a cloud covered the sun when you remarked you would not run the horse as a 4-year-old ... The demeaning facts of commerce have compelled owners of many good horses to whip them off to stud after they have won a Derby or other big race ... These owners do so, some because they feel that the horse at such a moment is at his peak as a commercial proposition for stud. This isn't sport; this is business ... I am told, however, that you have a few hundred millions. So these considerations need not apply to you ... but no doubt you are pressured very much by your accountants and lawyers to take this great-hearted Nijinsky and turn him into a valuable asset on the right side of some balance sheet ...
>
> "... Remember that great volley of a cheer of triumph that shook The Curragh stands when Liam Ward slipped Nijinsky loose and he began that super-powered run through the [Irish] Sweeps Derby field? ... they rose like one man to the greatness of Nijinsky and were grateful and happy to be there to see it ...
>
> "Accountants have no place in that world, it is the world of heros and poetry ..."

As the roar of protests swelled groups of racehorse breeders on both sides of the Atlantic were quickly and quietly gathering. Speculating that Engelhard would not be swayed by Nijinsky's legions of fans, nor loyalty to O'Brien and his Irish horse-handlers, they began raising money for the inevitable syndication of this remarkable animal.

In the UK Lord Wigg was striving toward securing permission from the Treasury to offer as much as £2,000,000 in US dollars. He and Engelhard's English racing manager, David McCall, were eager to have Nijinsky stand at the National Stud in Newmarket. They had drawn a list of sixteen English horse breeders who they believed would pay £40,000 a share in Nijinsky and were preparing to turn themselves inside out in attempt to convince Engelhard to accept their offer.

Across the Irish Sea, Captain Tim Rogers, longtime friend of Vincent O'Brien and Chair of the Irish Breeders Association, plunged into the fray with the speed and agility of a stag in full flight. While Lord Wigg was carefully negotiating his way through the proper channels and red tape of currency exchange controls, Rogers, one of Ireland's most accomplished horse-traders, rapidly marshaled commitments for £2,000,000. At the time it was a staggering amount for the Irish. Rogers immediately fired off his proposition to Engelhard.

The Irish didn't have a hope. No matter what they offered the Americans could, and would, up the ante. Furthermore, Engelhard was an American. He had no allegiance to the Irish. He got what he wanted. His dream to lead his horse into the English Derby winners circle and be invited to the Royal Box had been fulfilled. The game was over.

In mid-August Engelhard proclaimed that Nijinsky had been syndicated for a record $5,440,000. Syndicate members paid $170,000 per share in the horse. After his final three year old race, Ireland's great champion would be flown back across the Atlantic and he would live out his days standing at stud at Claiborne Farm in Paris, Kentucky.

Losing Nijinsky was a bitter pill. Had it not been for O'Brien its unlikely the horse would have come out of his stall, much less won the English Triple Crown. A horse of Nijinsky's tremendous scope and volatile nature clearly would have not excelled in North America with the oval dirt tracks. What he needed, and received, to prepare him physically and mentally for the challenges ahead, was long slow gallops over the soft Irish turf of O'Brien's Ballydoyle gallops. He also needed O'Brien's quiet genius. So the Irish had every right to be angry.

What happened next was quite extraordinary. After several millennia of losing their land and their horses and whatever else, they determined to fight back. Not that they hadn't gone to battle before, they surely had, time and again. But this was a contest they could win. Down, but not defeated, a group of Irish horse traders decided that if there ever was going to be another Nijinsky, they would find him and bring him home to Ireland. And there, he would stay. They didn't know how they were going to achieve this mission. The odds against success were astronomical, if not entirely off the board.

They did, however, have several things going for them. The Irish had been practicing the fine art of horse trading since God was a boy. At one time all of Europe ventured to Ireland to buy their horses.

Cahirmee, in County Cork and not far from the birthplace of Michael Vincent O'Brien was renowned as one of the biggest gatherings of horses and horse-dealers in all of Europe:"the town fills with newcomers, whiskey-faced men with breeches and crops, ladies who have the sound as well as the look of horses, shabby copers (horse dealers) with a reputation of being worth 'gallons of gold,' escapologists, wheel-of-fortune operators, sellers of web halters, and the vagrant horse-dealers whose caravans are parked in a line along the verge of the Limerick Road."

Hundreds of horses were herded along the dusty roads, their

drovers whooping and chanting Irish phrases contrived to keep the procession moving. The parade included sulkies and carts and traps. The vast spectrum of horses ranged from elegant Thoroughbreds to hardy Connemara ponies.

All around the little green at the crossroads on the edge of town groups of individuals congregated. Some men sprawled lazily on the soft grass. Several leaned up against the wooden sign-post pointing the way to Mallow. Others stood back from the crowd. Their attitude as casual as a lazy day by the sea shore. Their eyes as sharp and keen as an eagle in hunt. These Irish horse traders would confide that the 600 brave chargers of Light Brigade trotted down this very same dusty trail to be sold at the Cahirmee Fair. As did the Duke of Wellington's horse Copenhagen, and the most famous charger of all, Marengo, the oft-painted white steed that carried Napoleon Bonaparte to battle against Wellington.

Another thing the Irish horse traders had going for them was Charles J. Haughey who, one day, would reign as Taoiseach (Prime Minister). Haughey, whose surname in Irish, Eachaidhe, means horseman, was a passionate racing man and when Nijinsky entered the starting stalls at The Curragh of Kildare, Haughey was among the crowds of Irish that flocked to the ancient course and was among those to fall beneath the spell of this magnificent animal.

In 1969, the same year Nijinsky began racing in Ireland, Haughey, then Ireland's minister of finance, introduced legislation releasing Irish stud farms from the nuisance of having to pay taxes.

The first to grab to golden ring was John Magnier. Reputed to be the most astute and shrewd horse trader of them all, Magnier wanted to stand Nijinsky at stud on the family farm near the village of Fermoy in County Cork where his family had been breeding horses since the 1850s. The dream was dampened by the reality that he did not have the necessary millions. Not then.

To purchase a horse in the league of Nijinsky Magnier was going to have to trap a leprechaun with several very large pots of gold. The miracle curiously materialized, not at the end of a rainbow in an Irish bog, but in England of all places. The year was 1971, the year following Nijinsky's races. The locale was Haydock Park, a small racecourse on the outskirts of Manchester and a far cry from the glamour and prestige of Ascot or Epsom, places graced by the noble Nijinsky when he raced in England.

The pots of gold were provided by Robert Sangster, sole heir to the family coffers — a tidy bonanza gleaned from Vernons, the football pools operation. Started by his grandfather and father in 1923, Vernons was a lottery designed to induce football fans into gambling a bob or two of their weekly wages on the however-remote possibility of winning a fortune. There is no record of how many ticket holders ever became rich, but the Sangster family surely profited from the football pools.

At the outset Sangster, the thirty-one year old Englishman, and Magnier, the twenty-three year old Irishman, shared absolutely nothing in common. An only child, Sangster was born in Liverpool and at 14 was despatched to the public school, Repton. At 19 he did a two-year stint in the National Service and eventually joined the family firm, simultaneously developing a flair for the finer things in life which included a succession of high-performance sports cars.

While vacationing on the Cote d'Azur he met his first wife, nineteen year old Christine Street, a tall dark-haired fashion model from Manchester. Two months prior to their wedding in May 1960 he was introduced to Nick Robinson, grandson of Sir Foster Robinson, a well-respected racehorse owner, breeder and member of the British Jockey Club. Over lunch Robinson encouraged Sangster to wager on Chalk Stream a horse his grandfather had bred at his Wicken Park Stud in Buckinghamshire. Between the time Sangster laid down his £25 on the horse and the actual race, he and Robinson met frequently and their conversations invariably drifted to the world of horse racing.

On the day of the race Chalk Stream ambled home at the back of the pack of 31 runners. Nonetheless after the race Sangster asked Robinson if his grandfather would sell him the horse, which he then presented to his bride-to-be as a wedding gift.

John Magnier was not shipped off to boarding school. Instead he stayed home and mucked out stalls. One of three sons, he was15 when his father died and Magnier opted to assist his mother in the running of the family farm, Grange Stud. Magnier's inheritance was not money, but of horses. Specifically stallions. And more specifically, National Hunt stallions.

His grandfather, Thomas Magnier, owned the good Irish stallion Edlington winner of fourteen races in the 1880s and then as a "traveling stallion" was ridden across the Irish countryside to cover the mares of the local farmers and horse breeders. Magnier's father, Michael, stood the stallion Cottage, sire of three Grand National winners and Vincent O'Brien's intrepid Cottage Rake.

Not long after finance minister Charles Haughey introduced legislation sparing Irish stud farms the bother of taxes Magnier convinced several partners to join him in purchasing Castle Hyde Stud, not far from the village of Fermoy in County Cork, the home of his ancestors. His ambition was to build Castle Hyde into a financially successful operation.

The means to this prosperity would be derived from the syndication of stallions, a risky business at the best of times. In the days prior to this tale and back in the time of Edlington and Cottage stallions were simply trotted from farm to farm. Generally, but not always, the stallion had already proven to be a stellar racehorse, hence the theory was that he would pass his exceptional genes on to his descendants. Should the results of the matings live up to these expectations, the stallion and his handler were invited back in ensuing years. A fee was paid and that was that.

In the late 1960s the notion of syndicating Thoroughbred stallions started to become popular. The British deemed that the number of shares, or coverings per year, would be forty. Possession of a share in a stallion gave the owner the right to send a mare to the horse every year for its lifetime.

The tricky part is that not all great racehorses become great sires. In the wild which stallions will, or will not breed, is determined by the horses themselves. Generally by the time the young males have reached their second birthday they are banished from the herd and form their own group. There they will scuffle and play-fight amongst themselves in preparation for the day one of them will have the opportunity to engage a herd stallion in battle. Its all about survival of the species and to that end horses innately understand that only the very strongest males are meant to breed.

Sadly humans lack equine intuition. For example, the great US champion Cigar was a brilliant and enduring racehorse. Amid great hoopla Cigar was syndicated for a whopping $60 million, but the horse was impotent. Conversely there is the long list of Thoroughbreds that did *not* have particularly distinguished racing careers, that became outstanding sires. Horses like Danzig and Vice Regent. And then there are those horses that share the same parents, thus identical genetic makeup. One is a pre-potent sire, the other isn't. Northern Dancer and his brother, Northern Native, are but one example.

Possibly the biggest variable in all this is that it takes years to discover whether or not a stallion selected by human standards can live up to the investment of time and money and ego. Furthermore, the most important part of the equation is the mare. Her genes dominate the genetic pool. So you will want to have your stallion bred to the very finest mares.

The equine gestation period is eleven months. Thoroughbreds often begin racing as two year olds, but the major races are scheduled for three year olds hence it will take five years before anyone knows if the stallion's progeny destined to be runners, much less champions.

When Magnier and Sangster met in 1971 at Haydock Park the Englishman was there to present the trophy, the Vernons Sprint Cup, sponsored by the family betting operation. The Irishman was there to spirit away what he considered the real prize, a horse named Green God, that was running in the race.

Considered to be the fastest horse in England at the time, Green God had won five consecutive races that season only to be left flatfooted at the start in his previous effort in France and lost out to Fireside Chat. Green God's challengers for the Vernons trophy included Sweet Revenge winner of several major French races, beating Fireside Chat both times and Apollo Nine winner of the Stewards Cup at Goodwood (England) in August, bearing a colossal 131 pound handicap.

Sangster was among the crowd gathered in Haydock Park's members' bar prior to the race and found himself ensconced among a group of Irish horse traders. One of whom pointed out a tall dark-haired young Irishman across the room and explained that he had just concluded an agreement with Green God's owner, David Robinson.

Green God would be sold on this the eve of the big race for £160,000 to an Irish syndicate. No matter what the outcome of the race, the deal would stand. Green God would be leased back to Robinson for the race to run in Robinson's silks one last time. Following the race Green God would be shipped to Ireland and begin his career as a stallion at Castle Hyde Stud.

Sangster's companion went on to explain the ins and outs of stallion syndication along with the various financial scenarios based on whether or not Green God won the race. No matter how you cut it, this added up to a huge gamble for the young Irishman.

The following afternoon Green God got off to a nail-biting start but rallied to win the race a length ahead of Sweet Revenge. Sangster presented the Vernons Cup to David Robinson and after the ceremonies returned to the members' bar and made his way through the crowd to the Irish horse trader he had been speaking with the previous day. The fellow was now in deep conversation with the young Irish purchaser of Green God. Sangster was introduced to John Magnier and the two men talked long into the evening.

One aspect of the conversation that, in later years, Sangster said he would never forget was twenty-three year old Magnier's conviction that *he should have bought* Nijinsky and stood him at stud in Ireland.

Magnier reasoned that while, based on 40 shares, each syndicate member paid £55,000, he predicted that yearlings sired by Nijinsky would fetch that much, maybe even more and that would cover the initial investment. After that the investor would breed his mares to Nijinsky every year for the rest of his life at no cost.

Perhaps he had overlooked that Charles Engelhard had more money that Croesus and had no intention of standing the horse in Ireland. Still, it was a good theory. Magnier also apparently predicted that Thoroughbred prices would rise substantially because of a recent run of truly exceptional racehorses. Besides Nijinsky there were English Derby winners Mill Reef and Sir Ivor. Brigadier Gerard had not yet been beaten. In North America yearling prices for offspring of Northern Dancer and other top stallions were nearing the $200,000 mark.

The following spring the talk of the turf in the UK was whether or not Vincent O'Brien had yet another English Derby winner in his stable. So far there had been lucky Larkspur, then Sir Ivor had won this, the race that defines the Thoroughbred in 1968, followed by Nijinsky two years later. Now in 1972, O'Brien had Roberto, the mercurial bay colt with a white blaze running the length of his face. Roberto was fast, although occasionally unpredictable. This inconsistency, coupled with last minute juggling of jockeys fueled controversy among the British racing press.

As a two year old Roberto won his first three races in Ireland so brilliantly that people began speculating that he might be as good as Sir Ivor. Maybe even Nijinsky. Everyone, it seemed, wanted to have their money on him. The best price a punter could get on Roberto in the Two Thousand Guineas and Derby was three-to-one. Then Roberto was sent to France where he was considered the hot favourite in the Grand Criterium only to finish fourth. Before long the bookmakers were offering odds of eight-to-one

Roberto had matured considerably over his winter at Ballydoyle and returned to the races appearing ready to resume his position at the head of the pack. His first test was the Two Thousand Guineas which turned into a two-horse race between Roberto and High Top. High Top won, but Roberto had fought gallantly and was at High Top's girth as they flew past the post. The rest of the horses straggled in much later.

Ten days before the Derby Roberto's jockey took a spill in a race at Kempton. On the Monday prior to Epsom his doctor declared him fit to ride, but Roberto's American owner, John Galbreath, devised a new plan. He wanted Lester Piggott to ride Roberto.

In the final stages of the Derby the race had distilled to contest between Roberto and Rheingold. First one in the lead, then the other, and then back again. Both horses were tiring and the battle was desperate. In the final twenty yards "receiving four more severe cracks of the whip on top of the many he had suffered from the distance, Roberto struggled forward to gain first prize by a short head." A lengthy inquiry ensued. Not into Piggott's continued horse abuse, instead into possible interference. Eventually Roberto was awarded the trophy and Galbreath and company were invited to the Royal box to meet the Queen.

After the race John Magnier telephoned Robert Sangster and during the conversation suggested the Englishman meet up with Magnier and his Irish friends in Kentucky for the Keeneland Yearling Sales in July. It would mark Sangster's first foray into the heart of Kentucky's renowned 'bluegrass country.' A field trip, so to speak, to gain a first-hand perspective of the business of buying and selling Thoroughbred yearlings.

In May Sangster received the second installment of his inheritance. Although he had borrowed millions to pay capital gains taxes, its likely he had enough left over to purchase a horse or two.

Some of the bits and pieces of schemes and dreams that ultimately coalesced into the initial Celtic Tiger phenomenon appear to have been drifting and floating about for centuries. Other aspects were more recent, inspired by yet another Irishman, Jack Mulcahy.

O'Brien credits Mulcahy with giving him the best advice he ever received which was that O'Brien should insist on part ownership of every horse at Ballydoyle. The strategy no doubt was a factor in how Mulcahy left Ireland pennyless and returned to Ireland a very wealthy man.

Mulcahy emigrated to the US in the mid-1920s to escape Ireland's impoverishment. He had heard the streets were paved with gold. Instead, not long after he arrived the country was devastated by the spiraling depression following the Crash of 1929. By day Mulcahy took whatever work was available and by night studied accounting. He eventually landed a job with Quigley Steel. Before long he became confidant to the owner, and upon the owner's death Mulcahy ran the company for Quigley's widow. Ultimately Mulcahy emerged the major shareholder of Quigley Steel.

Mulcahy's brother Dan remained in Ireland and worked as a cashier at the Munster and Leinster Bank in Cork when O'Brien opened his first bank account in 1943. Over the years Dan Mulcahy and O'Brien became friends.

Jack Mulcahy frequently returned to Ireland. Initially he purchased several grand homes, including Ashford Castle, which he turned into a hotel. When he began thinking about horses, he turned to Vincent O'Brien.

At the time, Claiborne Farm, under the guidance of Bull Hancock, was the leading breeder of Thoroughbreds in the US. So Mulcahy suggested that O'Brien approach Hancock to see if he was amenable to a partnership arrangement. Hancock liked the idea. In 1971 the first group of Claiborne yearlings arrived at Ballydoyle. Among them was Thatch, who would be distinguished as Europe's top miler.

The partnership arrangement with Claiborne continued through to 1981. The concept, however, would be expanded upon and find its way into the philosophy of the first Celtic Tiger.

When Sangster arrived in Kentucky in the summer of 1972 no one on the rambling Keeneland stable area recognized the Englishman, nor had heard of him. This soon would change. Upon catching up with Magnier's group of Irish friends he was at once introduced to the famous Vincent O'Brien.

Magnier's relationship with O'Brien was more than casual. The Magnier family and the O'Brien's had been friends for generations. Magnier's mother was the matron-of-honour at Vincent and Jacqueline O'Brien's wedding. Now her son John was courting Susan O'Brien, one of their three daughters. Soon he would propose marriage. Susan would accept.

During the course of Sangster's first day at Keeneland he struck up a conversation with the only other Englishman in their group, Charles St. George, a wealthy Lloyds of London insurance broker. O'Brien was bent on buying a particular yearling for St. George and on having this colt in his yard. He wasn't alone. Leading French trainer, Alec Head, also saw something special in the colt. As did British trainer Bernard Van Cutsem.

Back and forth across the arena the bids flew. The auctioneer and his spotters scanning the room on high alert and spotting almost indiscernible signals. A nod here. "Do you have $100,000?"droned the auctioneer. "Yip!" Hollered the spotter. A flick of the wrist there. A slight nod over there. And the bid rocketed to $150,000. Another nod. A raised catalogue. The auctioneer's hammer finally fell at $240,000. O'Brien had won the duel.

At the conclusion of this, his inaugural trip to Keeneland and the high stakes world of horse auctions, Sangster was apparently hooked. Wagering at the track surely paled in the light of the action and excitement of the sales ring.

That fall John Magnier set his sights on yet another sprinter owned by David Robinson. Deep River, a chestnut colt that, as a two year old, had proven a dazzling winner at Royal Ascot, but had not yet, proven terribly brilliant at three. Magnier was convinced the horse would not only improve with time but be an excellent stallion prospect. Thus Magnier set out to buy the horse. There was only one flaw in Magnier's plan — Robinson, did not want to sell Deep River. At least, not yet.

Deep River finally found his running legs in the Nunthorpe Stakes at the York course in north-east England. Deep River not only won the race by two lengths over the good filly Stilvi, he set a track record. Again Magnier approached Robinson. Again he said 'No.'

Robinson planned on running Deep River in the Prix de l'Abbaye, the top sprint race run at Longchamp outside Paris in early October. There Deep River would encounter current champion sprinter, Home Guard. On the day Deep River blasted out of the starting stalls, opened up a huge early lead, and scorched across the finish four lengths ahead of Home Guard.

Now Magnier was even more determined to buy Deep River, so he phoned Sangster. They might have to go as high as £400,000, but according to the Magnier stallion syndication theory the horse was still a bargain. If, of course, his offspring deigned to be exceptional racehorses. A month later, Magnier's negotiating skills and Sangster's £400,000 brought Deep River to Castle Hyde Stud. It was approximately a year after these two met and would mark the first time the Irishman's vision and the Englishman's money would join forces. But far from the last.

The first Celtic Tiger had begun to stir

Meanwhile on the other side of the Atlantic, as if scripted, the golden age of Thoroughbred racing in North America was about to unfold. Leading a parade of absolutely brilliant and exciting horses was a grand golden colt named Secretariat.

In the spring of 1973 Secretariat did what no other horse had been able to achieve for the past twenty-five years in the United

States. He won all three US Triple Crown races. He not only won the races, he shattered the track records in all three classics and in the process Secretariat had become a folk hero.

The timing couldn't have been better, for this was the era of Watergate — a dark time in the annals of US political history. Agents employed by the re-election committee of Richard Nixon during the 1972 Presidential campaign were caught breaking into the Democratic headquarters in the Watergate building. The scandal was exacerbated by attempts to conceal the fact that White House officials had approved the burglary.

Against this bleak and dismal horizon the golden Secretariat galloped into the hearts of the US public. Within the span of a week Secretariat's picture was featured on the front covers of the country's top national magazines — *Time, Newsweek,* and *Sports Illustrated.*

The night before the Belmont Stakes an army of young people were camped out along the parkway leading to Belmont Park. They had traveled from all across North America to see their champion 'Big Red,' and wanted to be assured of a good vantage point during the race. The horse would reward them with the memory of a lifetime.

9 June 9 1973. The day broke clear and sunny. When the gates to Belmont Park opened at 8:00 a.m. thousands of Secretariat fans surged into the racetrack, many positioning themselves along the paddock rail in order to get a glimpse of their hero when he was walked to the saddling enclosure. They waited nine long hours. The moment Secretariat appeared the cheers and applause was deafening.

The starting gate for Belmont Stakes was directly in front of the grandstand. There were only five horses in the race. Secretariat had drawn the inside post position. Sham, who had finished second to Secretariat in the Kentucky Derby and Preakness, drew the outside post.

The bell clanged and Secretariat bounded out of the gate and was instantly in the lead. Laffit Pincay quickly drove Sham up to challenge. Secretariat's partner in this gallop into history, jockey Ron Turcotte, had not intended on being in front, but with Sham dogging them on the turn and then gaining a fractional lead he was forced to make a crucial and tactical decision. While bearing in mind the mile-and-a-half length of the race, he opted to allow Secretariat to go to the lead. Secretariat surged forward.

Instantly the two horses were in a speed duel and one far too fast, it appeared, for a race this long. Turcotte, of course, had a bit different vantage point. He knew exactly what he was doing.

"We were going easy," he said later, "I never worried about what other people were going to say to me. If you win, they are all going to say nice things. If you lose, they are going to say bad things anyway. So I can't worry every time I go out on the racetrack.

"Had Secretariat not been fit for the race, had he not won his last two races so easily, had he not worked two seconds faster than Riva (Ridge) did a year before, I might have ridden more conservatively."

Around the first turn Secretariat was in front by about a neck and then Turcotte eased him back and let Sham take over. Briefly. At the half-way mark Secretariat was well in control of the race. There was still three quarters of a mile to go. For the next eighth of a mile Sham bravely battled to hold on to second place. Then Secretariat started to fly.

At the mile pole Secretariat was clocked at a blistering 1:34 1/5 and as he entered Belmont's long homestretch there wasn't another horse in sight. Trainer Lucien Laurin was standing in the owner's box, yelling: "Oh my God, Ronnie, don't fall off! Just don't fall off!"

Turcotte could hear the tremendous roar from the stands, but it wasn't until he looked back under his left arm that he began to understand what all the noise was about. At first he didn't see any other horses, so he looked a second time. This time the rest of the field were just now coming into the stretch.

"It seemed they were a mile away," recalled Turcotte, "Then I looked up and saw 2:20 on the tele-timer and I didn't have far to go. I was an incredible feeling. He was just whistling through the air."

Not only had Secretariat become the first US Triple Crown winner since Citation twenty-five years earlier, he won the race by an astonishing thirty-one lengths! In fact, when Secretariat blasted across the finish, Turcotte was unable to pull him up. The horse was galloping at such a pace that he appeared to want to soar yet another lap of Belmont's oval track — just for good measure.

By the time Turcotte got Secretariat slowed down and steered over to the winner's circle, there was so much screaming and yelling and jumping up and down by the huge crowd, it felt as if Belmont's massive grandstand would be shaken from its foundation.

"I rode him back into the winner's circle," recalled Ron Turcotte, "and the crowd went wild. They loved Secretariat. He was the people's horse."

The last race of Secretariat's brilliant racing career was the Canadian International Stakes at Woodbine. Penny Tweedy, daughter of the colt's owner, Christopher Chenery, chose the Canadian venue for any number of reasons, not the least of which was that both Secretariat's trainer and jockey were Canadian. Every major US turf club wanted to host Secretariat's final performance, so going to Canada was a clever political move. Needless to say, some of the US tracks were displeased. So displeased, in fact, that just prior to the race the New York Racing Association suspended Turcotte for a trivial infraction, which meant he was disallowed from riding Secretariat this one last time. In light of this, the Canadian officials arranged for Turcotte to ride Secretariat in a work-out early one morning several days before the big race.

The event was scheduled for 7:00 a.m. A crowd of over 4000 who had driven to Woodbine to witness this farewell ride waited patiently for the dense fog that had descended over the turf course to lift. After at least an hour, the bright autumn sun had turned the thick blanket of fog into a heavy mist, which lent a mystical aura to the occasion. Turcotte borrowed a bright red nylon jacket from one of the youngsters in the crowd so people could see them coming through the mist. It wasn't necessary.

When Secretariat and Turcotte trotted off into the distance and virtually disappeared from view, the crowd became dead quiet. No one even coughed, much less spoke. It was like being in a sacred place, a cathedral or a temple.

Suddenly a distant noise caught the attention of the congregation. From somewhere out in the mist, there was 'whoosh, whoosh, whoosh.' It was the sound of air exhaling from Secretariat's massive lungs. Jockeys who rode against Secretariat said he sounded like a train coming down the track. As the volume of the intermittent whooshing sound increased, it was joined by the rhythmic pounding of his hooves as he bounded along the soft turf and the ground began to shudder.

Suddenly the grand red colt came bounding out of the mist. Pegasus, soaring out of a cloud, landing briefly to bless the earth beneath his feet and touch mortals with the magic of his powerful aura. Only to vanish into the mist. And Pegasus soared back to the heavens.

Scant few North Americans had even seen Nijinsky, much less were cognizant of his brilliance. Only those Canadians, somehow connected to the horse, had followed the meteoric trail Nijinsky scorched across the turf of British and Irish race courses. But now North America had its own equine hero.

When the buyers convened at Keeneland in the summer of 1973 its hard to imagine that there was anyone there who still wasn't awestruck by Secretariat's astonishing 31-length triumph in the Belmont Stakes a mere seven weeks earlier. So there can be little doubt that almost everyone (the North Americans) in the crowd were desperately searching for another Secretariat. And all the rest (the Irish, English and Europeans) were looking for another Nijinsky.

When O'Brien, Magnier and company convened at Keeneland they found themselves in the midst of what was considered at the time 'the bull market to end all bull markets.' Prices for Thoroughbred yearlings were spiraling upward at a brisk clip.

Much of the frenzy was due to Secretariat. He was so popular there were those who believed that he not only could run for president of the US, but would win. Secretariat was not only a national hero, but he had surely ignited a passion for horses and horse racing never seen before or since in North America. Like Nijinsky, he too was adulated like a rock star and his fans were legion.

Now in the Keeneland sales pavilion owners, bloodstock agents, trainers battled it out for the next Secretariat. The prices began to reflect the intensity of the search. Several of Nijinsky's yearlings sold in the $200,000 range. One Northern Dancer yearling colt went for $200,000 and another four for over $100,000.

But the colt many considered to be the *next Secretariat*, the colt that almost everyone desired to own, was one of the last sons of Secretariat's sire, the now deceased Bold Ruler, out of the French mare Iskra. Tom Cooper the Irish bloodstock agent who helped O'Brien pick out Larkspur, considered this Bold Ruler/Iskra colt the finest looking animal in the Keeneland sale. O'Brien solemnly concurred.

After counsel from Magnier, Sangster advised O'Brien that they could go to $500,000 for the colt. He would do the bidding. It was, after all, his money. Furthermore, the Englishman had an idea that he thought would intimidate anyone else interested in the colt. Lamentably for Sangster his idea didn't work.

Generally the auctioneers at horse sales begin off their patter with a high evaluation and then drift downwards until someone enters the bidding game. After they have delivered the animals pedigree they will say: "So who will give me half a million for this good looking colt? ... okay, how about $300,000 ... $200,000 ... $100,00000 ... all right do I have $50,000? ... Yes I have $50,000 ... Who'll give me $75,000?" And thus, the game begins.

On that particular evening, Sangster's idea was to cut to the chase. No sooner had the auctioneer asked "Who will give me $500,000?" The Englishman casually raised his hand. The auctioneer was clearly dumbfounded. It never happened like this. Still, he cleared his throat and announced: "I have $500,000."

The bid was but $10,000 short of the all-time record price paid at Keeneland. Seemingly pleased with his coup, Sangster sat and waited for the shock waves to subside. Nonetheless, the auctioneer carried on asking for a higher bid. Much to almost everyone's surprise, it happened. Lexington bloodstock agent, Jim Scully, bidding on behalf of a Japanese syndicate headed by Zenya Yoshida, answered Sangster's challenge by offering $600,000.

Now the Englishman didn't know what to do. This was, after-all, his first real foray into the high stakes Thoroughbred yearling market. His cavalier plan had failed and he sat with his head down, saying nothing as the auctioneer called for further bids, and eventually said: "Going once, going twice, sold for $600,000!"

Over the next twenty-four months Sangster had many opportunities to ruminate over the Bold Ruler/Iskra colt, *the one that got away*. He was named Wajima after a famous Sumo wrestler. He wasn't the next Secretariat, but Wajima was an exceptional and fearless animal.

Wajima won nine races, vanquishing Kentucky Derby winner

Foolish Pleasure twice, but his finest hour was in the Marlboro Cup at Belmont Park, where in an exciting, head-to-head stretch battle Wajima prevailed over Forgo, the formidable three-time US Horse of the Year. Wajima ran the ten furlong Marlboro Cup in 2:00 flat, 1/5 of a second off the record.

Along the way Wajima won back close to what Yoshida and his syndicate had paid for him, was voted champion three year old in the United States and was syndicated as a stallion in 1975 for $7.2 million.

In 1973 Vincent O'Brien bought 50% of the nearby Coolmore Stud owned by his friend Tim Vigors a former Battle of Britain ace fighter pilot and now a horse dealer. Two years later Vigors agreed to O'Brien's suggestion that they bring in his soon-to-be son-in-law, John Magnier, to manage the operation.

Shortly thereafter Magnier took up residence at Coolmore and began building the stud farm of his dreams. Facilitated by Sangster's injection of capital the Irishman was orchestrating a program of improvements for Coolmore, the likes of which had never been seen in Ireland.

Stallion boxes were renovated, a network of new drainage systems were incorporated, great beech hedges were planted, paths were laid and fences rebuilt. A state-of-the-art telephone system was installed. Staff were hired. Once ready for business all they needed were the all-important, eye-catching, money-making stallions.

Magnier named the enterprise Coolmore, Castle Hyde and Associated Stud farms (incorporating Magnier's Grange and Castel Hyde and several other smaller studs such as the nearby Longfield, Dunmahon and Beeches studs). Magnier ruled as managing director and according to Patrick Robinson the young

Irishman "quickly adjusted to the role of Master of Coolmore. Tall, handsome with a thick mane of hair and a misty shroud of the black Irish, his persona was charming, yet surely enigmatic. And Magnier dressed the part sporting tailored tweed jackets, cravats and expensive cigars."

Five stallions were housed in the newly renovated barns — horses that were decent racehorses and theoretically, at least, would make decent stallions. Still Magnier, with the help of his English money-man, appeared bent of turning Coolmore into a commercial operation like none other. That, thanks to Charles Haughey, they didn't have to pay taxes, would help. But what they needed were really top stallions. Horses in the league of Nijinsky.

Now with a cache of serious money at his disposal Magnier was able to dream on a far grander scale. The plan he devised was fairly straightforward and based on his limited knowledge of Nijinsky. There were, however, aspects to the story of Nijinsky he failed to factor into his scheme, but Magnier was young, ambitious and in a hurry. He saw what he wanted to see. He saw that Nijinsky was purchased for $84,000 at the Canadian Thoroughbred auction.

All they had to do, Magnier reasoned, was fly to North America. Go to the horse sales. Buy all the horses with top bloodlines — bloodlines similar to Nijinsky — and trust one of them will be the next Nijinsky. Keep the horse in Ireland. Stand it at Magnier's farm. Sell shares. Make money. Repeat this formula over and over until all the objectives were met.

The grand scheme might not have gone much further than chats over drinks in the Members Bar at Haydock Park had Magnier not convinced his father-in-law, Michael Vincent O'Brien, to join their mission. O'Brien surely brought the most to the table, not the least of which was credibility and contacts. People trusted the man with their money and their horses. From O'Brien's perspective, even the slightest opportunity to work with another Nijinsky in his yard was enticement enough.

The men approached their mission with the zeal and meticulous planning of a military maneuver and agreed to make their first collective assault on Kentucky's Keeneland Select Sale in July 1975. Each of these men had their priorities, but it was O'Brien who insisted: "We must buy the Northern Dancers. We must buy them at all costs. And the same goes for yearlings by Nijinsky. We must have them. I am very certain of that."

To fulfill this mandate they were going to need several pots of gold — far more money than Sangster's inheritance. Hence, the Englishman was awarded title of Syndicate Chief and dispatched to the hinterlands of the United Kingdom to raise more money for the Irish mission.

Charles St.George, the wealthy British Lloyds of London insurance broker, needed little encouragement to join the syndicate. Then came Alan Clore, son of one of England's leading financiers, Sir Charles Clore, and as such was the beneficiary of a very large inheritance. Sir Charles Clore was an enthusiastic horse racing man and had owned the good filly Valoris, winner of the English Oaks in 1966 and trained by Vincent O'Brien. Alan Clore was not inclined to follow his father in the world of finance, instead he was considering going into the Thoroughbred bloodstock business and the concept of ownership in world-class stallions would further his ambitions — especially if the horse turned out to be the next Nijinsky. Clore was also confident that if anyone could get them there, it was Vincent O'Brien.

Next Sangster journeyed north to Beaufort Castle in the Scottish Highlands and to the west of Inverness, home of the Barons Lovat, a ruling Scottish clan since the fifteenth Century. The reigning Lord and Chief of the Clan Fraser served with great distinction as a commando in the Second World War, fighting fearlessly in Dieppe and the Normandy landings. Wounded, he was awarded the Military Cross for bravery and leadership. While he certainly would have qualified for the planned assault on Keeneland, it was his son, thirty-five year old Simon Fraser, Master of Lovat, that Sangster was after. Simon Fraser loved horse racing and like Charles St. George, and Alan Clore, he was yet another client of Vincent O'Brien.

The fourth syndicate member was the wealthy expatriate, Jack Mulchay, who would become a stalwart in the syndicate, both financially, and in his absolute, conviction in O'Brien's talents with horses.

The final member, other than Sangster himself, of the team that would be charged with keeping the war chest brimming with money was Walter Haefner, a Swiss, who had several years earlier bought Moyglare, the 440 acre Irish stud in County Kildare. He too had ambitions to breed and raise the finest champion Thoroughbreds.

Two Englishmen, a Scot, an expatriate Irishman, and a Swiss. They would provide thirty per cent of the financial artillery required for the pending raid on the Keeneland Select Summer yearling sale. Sangster would put up forty per cent. O'Brien and Magnier would ante in fifteen per cent each. When all the calculations were determined, they would arrive in Kentucky armed with $3 million dollars.

In 1974, the previous year, the average price for yearlings at Keeneland's Select sale was in the neighbourhood of $50,000. With their war chest brimming, they were surely in a position to take whatever horses they wanted, and however many horses they wanted.

In May O'Brien secured the services of Tom Cooper. Each year Cooper, on behalf of the British Bloodstock Agency, toured all the top Thoroughbred breeding farms in North America offering yearlings for sale. His tour took him from Canada, through

Maryland, Pennsylvania, Virginia, and Kentucky. Armed with a tape recorder and a shrewd eye, Cooper made meticulous and detailed notes on every well-bred, good-looking youngster that caught his attention.

Possibly because he was gambling a piece of his inheritance Sangster opted to have his own Irish horse trader, Patrick 'PP' Hogan, close by his side. Born in County Limerick, Hogan was a former amateur rider who had ridden occasionally for O'Brien. During one afternoon at Ireland's Punchestown Racecourse in the 1940's Hogan rode six races, had five winners and one second. It is said his nickname 'PP' was born of that day and stands for 'Punchestown Pat.'

In *Horsetrader*, Patrick Robinson describes Hogan as: "A small wiry little man with the smile and charm of a leprechaun, (who) could beguile any man alive with his stories of hunting and racing deep in the green heart of southern Ireland. He could also sell you anything. After a few glasses of stout you would be well advised to check your wallet."

Sangster had known Hogan for a few years and during that time the Irishman had purchased fourteen yearlings for Sangster. Ten were winners and another two had finished second. Sangster had reason to trust Hogan's judgement.

The Kentucky-bound troop would also include Bob Griffin, O'Brien's veterinarian and O'Brien's brother, Phonsie, who, like Hogan, at one time enjoyed the reputation as a fearless amateur rider. The final member of the party, and sole woman in the invasion force, was O'Brien's wife, Jacqueline.

When Cooper completed his rounds of the major North American farms and their yearlings he provided a report of his findings to O'Brien. The moment the document arrived the game was afoot. O'Brien and Magnier studied every pedigree. O'Brien would be looking for the next Nijinsky. As would Magnier, but just as important, baby stallions that would grow into great race-horses and ultimately fill the stalls at Coolmore.

Then the sales catalogues arrived from Keeneland. With the dedication of prospectors searching for gold nuggets in the shallows of a Klondike river, the two men sifted through the data, and sifted, and sifted through again. Often long into the night.

On Wednesday morning 16 July 1975 John Magnier drove up Ballydoyle's drive and came to a stop at the front door of the O'Brien's rambling old stone house. O'Brien, his wife, Jacqueline, and his brother, Phonsie, were waiting, their suitcases by the door. The four downed a hasty cup of coffee and then headed out to Shannon Airport where they rode a commuter plane to Dublin Airport. When they arrived veterinarian Bob Griffin was settled on the airplane that would fly them to North America. Tom Cooper and Patrick Hogan had gone ahead and were already in Kentucky.

In London Sangster boarded a British Airways flight scheduled to land in New York City at approximately the same time as the Irish contingent. A private jet would fly the group to Kentucky. The Englishman had made all the necessary banking arrangements to give them access to $3 million. O'Brien and Magnier had ear-marked fifty yearlings that most interested them. Of these, they would probably purchase twelve.

They were embarking upon a huge gamble — but then, they were gamblers. In his early days as a trainer, O'Brien gained the reputation as a very canny and frequently successful punter. According to jockey Lester Piggott in *Vincent O'Brien: The Master of Ballydoyle*: "... I know there are those who would say he was a 'gambler' in those days. I would prefer to describe him as 'an investor' ... they didn't all win, of course. That is the law of averages in this game — a great leveler of persons and reputations. In Vincent's case, however, if he got beat, you could rest assured that the average of winners over losers was far, far higher and so at the end of each year the ledger invariably showed a profit and a substantial one at that."

Sangster, of course, was no stranger to gambling, it was after all the family business. And while not in the same league as the other two men, Magnier had already gambled on his instincts with a number of racehorses he believed would become successful stallions.

Nonetheless, Thoroughbred horses, no matter how regal their breeding, no matter how beautiful their conformation, no matter how much you pay for them, simply do not come with guarantees. Furthermore, this had to be a long-term project. It would be years — at least six or seven — before they would know if they had succeeded. What they really needed from their first group of yearlings was a horse that was both an outstanding racehorse, and an outstanding stallion. Another Nijinsky.

Akin to finding a needle in a haystack, the most predictable aspect of Thoroughbred racing and breeding is it's inherent *unpredictability.* "I've never known a business that relies so much on luck as horse racing," confessed Alan Paulson, Chairman of Gulfstream Aerospace Technologies and owner of the international champion Cigar, "In other businesses you can reduce the risk and anticipate things with a lot more precision. With horse racing you never know quite what can happen next." This Irish crew plus one Brit was going to need all the *luck of the Irish* they could muster in order to pull off this coup.

At 8:23 p.m. the tires of the Gulfstream jet touched down on the tarmac runway of Lexington's Blue Grass Field airport. Keeneland, their ultimate destination, was directly across the road.

By this time the yearlings were all bedded down for the evening. Most of the local Kentucky horse owners had departed to their farms. The out-of-town owners and buyers had returned to their hotels. Almost everyone involved with the sale was either dining at one of Lexington's many fine restaurants, or relaxing in their homes over a pre-dinner drink. Little did any of them know that very shortly their world would be turned upside-down.

Keeneland seemed an unlikely locale for the carnival atmosphere that soon would begin to permeate the yearling sales. In many ways it stood as the epitome of Thoroughbred horse racing tradition. A rural track it is the most visually appealing of all of North America's racecourses.

Located six miles west of Lexington, Keeneland lies in the heart of Kentucky's famed 'bluegrass country.' Driving along the nearby country roads, visitors are awed by the host of magnificent Thoroughbred farms. The panorama of these farms — their stately mansions, often opulent stables, thousands of paddocks housing even more thousands of Thoroughbreds bespeaks that the state of Kentucky surely is horse country.

Horse racing in Kentucky is said to date back to 1787. The races were often spontaneous events — one horse owner boasting that his horse was faster than that of another. These contests generally began on Lexington's Main Street and careened on up the hill to Ashland, home of US statesman Henry Clay. At the turn of the Century, and no doubt with the safety of unsuspecting citizens in mind, they constructed a modest racetrack in order to confine the races to an area where pedestrians would not be imperiled. Known as Williams' Track it was located in Lee's Woods which is now part of the Lexington cemetery. Several decades later the newly-formed Kentucky Association, a group of local Thoroughbred breeders and horse racing enthusiasts, built a track right in the centre of the town.

The stock market crash of 1929 and the ensuing Great Depression devastated the lives of the vast majority of North Americans.

By 1933 the sport of horse racing had hit rock bottom. Average purses in the United States had plummeted to a meagre $672, which was shared among the first, second, third, and fourth (if there was a fourth horse in the race). Some racing stables simply tightened their belts, others folded. Many race tracks were hard-pressed to stay afloat and Lexington's track was one that was unable to weather the storm.

So in 1933, after over a century of operation, the Lexington track was shut down and the Thoroughbred breeding capital of the United States was left without a place to race and showcase its treasured horses.

In 1935 Major Louie A. Beard, manager of the Whitney Thoroughbred racing and breeding interests, called upon all those interested in the welfare of the sport to a meeting at the Lafayette Hotel in Lexington. The upshot of this gathering was the formation of a non-profit organization dedicated to creating a centre of Thoroughbred sport, for the sake of the sport.

Their first move was to purchase 147.5 acres of land to the north of Lexington on Versailles Pike from the estate of John Oliver "Jack" Keene who had coincidently died 1935. The group could not have found a more appropriate site to build their Thoroughbred centre, which they would ultimately name in honour of Jack Keene.

A horse racing legend in the United States, Jack Keene loved Thoroughbreds. He saddled his first winner at Nashville, Tennessee in 1897 and his numerous horse racing adventures included a trip to Japan and another to Russia, where, as the story goes, his horses won many races because his were the only ones wearing light aluminum shoes.

When Keene eventually settled down on the family homestead he dreamed of developing the place into a haven for horses and horsemen and horsewomen. He envisioned an elaborate stable and living quarters which would serve as a sort of perpetual open house for like-minded Thoroughbred lovers and their horses.

Apparently Keene was very particular about the size and shape of the stones that went into the gates at the entrance to his property. By the time he had finished scouring the countryside for precisely the perfect stones for his gates, there were enough stones left over to construct the enormous structure of his dreams. It took twenty years to build and cost $400,000.

This unique structure, which was converted into the clubhouse, became the nucleus of Keeneland Race Course. The other features included a 1-1/16 mile track, a sand-based infield training track, and a grandstand. The entire complex was laid out in a natural, country style.

On 15 October 1936 Keeneland staged its inaugural nine-day race meet. The star of the show was the lightning-quick filly, Myrtlewood. In fact, in a two day period, Myrtlewood first won the Keeneland Handicap and then a mere forty-eight hours later she won the Ashland Handicap. Myrtlewood finished the 1936 season winning eight of ten starts and was voted champion sprinter. Myrtlewood's presence at the fledgling track's first race meet surely helped to establish Keeneland's solid credibility.

Nearby Churchill Downs had an entirely different agenda. Where Keeneland's managers were bent on creating a dignified, traditional setting, Churchill Down's publicist, Matt Winn, was busy creating a carnival atmosphere for his track and its most famous horse race, the Kentucky Derby. Winn had set his sights on emulating England's Epsom Derby. Not the race, but the party aspects. He had witnessed first hand as Epsom's grounds were transformed into a gigantic fairground, with Sanger's Circus occupying a large area between Tattenham Corner and the winning post. For many who had traveled to Epsom, it's famous race was secondary to the fun and merriment of the event. Dancing and partying continued far into the night.

Conversely, the conservative directors of Keeneland would see Ascot, England's only racecourse that belongs to the Crown, as their role model. Ascot got it's beginning when, driving out one day from Windsor Castle, Queen Anne was struck with the notion that Ascot Common was an ideal site for horse racing. That was in the very early 1700's and the racecourse has been connected to the Royal Family ever since. The annual Royal Meeting is a significant social occasion combining horse racing of the very highest quality and a touch of royal pageantry. The Royal Procession, introduced by George IV in 1820, still rolls down the course before the first race and experienced punters boast that they are able to detect the condition of the turf by the amount the carriage horses are blowing when they pull up in front of the Royal Enclosure Stand.

To a great extent both Churchill Downs and Keeneland achieved their respective and surely divergent goals. The Kentucky Derby climaxes a fortnight of parties and parties and more parties dubbed the Derby Festival. The race day itself — from the thousands of merrymakers that cram into the infield to the box-holders, owners and their often famous guests — is one grand and raucous party.

Keeneland, on the other hand, created an aura of decorum and dignity. And while the stately and regal Keeneland does not enjoy royal patronage on 11 October 1984 Her Royal Highness, Queen Elizabeth II, Queen of England and proprietress of Ascot spent an afternoon enjoying the races at Keeneland during a private visit to Kentucky. On that day and in honour of this royal visit to their version of Ascot, Keeneland management created the Queen Elizabeth II Stakes race.

The quiet charm of Keeneland is readily apparent upon entering its front gates. Giant trees form a canopy along the lane leading to Keeneland's ivy-covered buildings, radiant flower gardens and tree-shaded walking ring. Beyond it's boundaries horses graze lazily among the miles of white board fences that crisscross rolling green hills and meadows. It is said, in the United States, that only at Keeneland can a horse be seen thundering down the stretch to victory, just minutes from where it was born and raised.

The cornerstone of Keeneland's philosophy was echoed in its slogans and advertisements: "Racing as it was meant to be." In fact, such was Keeneland's devotion to tradition that for the first sixty-two years of Keeneland's existence there was no public address system. No blaring sound of a racetrack announcer calling a race. Instead there was only the rhythmic sound of hooves pounding on the dirt and the ever-intensifying din of the crowd as the horses thundered closer and closer to the finish. The rationale was that Keeneland's racing crowds were sufficiently sophisticated to identify the horses by the racing silks. Binoculars were, however, a necessity.

Only in 1997 did Keeneland install a public address system and a racetrack announcer. The change was met with chagrin by horse racing traditionalists who enjoyed the unique atmosphere that not having an announcer created.

The allure and beauty of Keeneland and its adherence to a horse racing tradition of days- gone-by was found in subtle touches. Wandering around the complex, there were, for example, no photographs of people. The only portraits hanging on the walls at Keeneland were of horses.

The public were not allowed in the in-field, as they were at nearby Churchill Downs, because it was believed that it would take away from the natural beauty of the course and its horses. Keeneland's basic colours were green and white and there was a dress code for track employees so as not to de-emphasize the horse.

Keeneland hosted its first horse sale 25 April 1938. Local farmers and horse breeders congregated with their animals in Keeneland's paddock. Prospective buyers wove in and out among the horses — checking their limbs, their height, their teeth. They slapped the horse's necks, shoulders, rumps. It was a fairly casual affair. The auctioneer stood on a raised platform and one by one the horses were led by their owners to a cleared space in front of the auctioneer. When the sale was over thirty-one horses had sold for a total of $24,885 or an average of $802.74. The top price, $3,500, was paid for the nine year old mare Marmitina and the foal by her side.

Long before the horses and buyers arrived for the 1975 July sale Keeneland's staff added the track's traditional touches to the rows of stalls that would house the yearlings. In front of each barn they erected green-and-white tents to shade the buyers from Kentucky's hot summer sun. Along with each tent came six green park benches, a large green container containing flowers, a water fountain, a good supply of drinking cups, and a huge metal tub to hold ice.

Keeneland's traditional, subtle stage had been set and now awaited the arrival of the actors and actresses — the yearling colts and fillies. Soon a fleet of horse vans would be ferrying the select Thoroughbred yearlings to their allotted stable areas. Once the young horses were bedded down and settled into their stalls, crews from each of the individual consigners began adding their own, and often colourful touches.

Some of the big outfits, like Claiborne, sent people over to Keeneland in advance of the horses to dress up their stable area. One year the Claiborne crew used rolls of bright yellow leg bandages — the same colour as its racing silks — and covered all of the posts and doors in their stable area.

The Windfields operation was a study in turquoise and gold — the Taylor's racing colours. The signs were turquoise with gold lettering. The staff were dressed in gold polo shirts with turquoise lettering. The hospitality tent outside the stables was turquoise with gold lettering.

On the morning of 17 July 1975 the Irish brigade and lone Englishman drove the sort distance from their hotel to Keeneland

Racecourse. Once they arrived and disembarked from their automobiles, with O'Brien in the lead, they headed toward the sales barns. Each person carried a catalogue — the pages showing the pedigrees of the yearlings they planned to look at were marked. The time had come to put their plan into action.

Like a Field Marshall leading his troops into battle, O'Brien marched purposefully toward his first quarry — the turquoise and gold Windfields consignment barns. There were other farms offering Northern Dancer yearlings, but since this is the farm that not only spawned Nijinsky, but his sire Northern Dancer and his grandsire, Nearctic, and Nijinsky's dam, Flaming Page, this seemed a good place to start their search.

Windfields Farm was selling two Northern Dancer yearlings along with one by Nearctic and another by Nijinsky. The colt that had drawn O'Brien here on this the first morning of their mission was a son of Northern Dancer and the mare Fleur. A daughter of Victoria Park, Taylor's first Kentucky Derby contender, Fleur's dam was Flaming Page. In horse lingo this made the number one prospect on their list a three-quarter brother to Nijinsky.

In the spring of 1969 Flaming Page had given birth to another colt sired by Northern Dancer, hence a full-brother to Nijinsky. He was a grand, very big and very flashy chestnut. Taylor owned him in partnership with Charles Engelhard and they sent the colt to Ireland to be trained by O'Brien. They named the big colt Minsky and began hoping for the impossible — he would be the next Nijinsky.

He wasn't. Minsky was a good horse. He didn't follow in the hoofprints of Nijinsky. He was, however, named Ireland's champion two year old colt in1970. The following year Minsky was fourth in the Two Thousand Guineas and was eventually shipped back to Canada. The first yearling O'Brien wanted to see, this three-quarter brother to Nijinsky, in no way resembled Nijinsky. Nijinsky was a deep, rich bay. This colt was a golden chestnut. Nijinsky was tall and elegant. This colt was short and stocky. Nijinsky's markings were subtle — white sox capping his two hind and right fore coronet bands, and a white star in the shape of a heart, beneath his black forelock. His three-quarter brother's markings were flashy — four white stocking stretching up to his knees, and a wide white blaze running the length of his face, over his nose, and like Northern Dancer, wrapping around his left nostril.

"I was definately concerned about his height," recalled O'Brien, "I remember going back to his box more than once to see if I could make myself feel any easier about it. But he was certainly small. He did grow in the end. He finished just short of 15.3 hands, which was big enough. But again, this Northern Dancer breed was something new in the racehorse world. They don't have to be big to be good."

O'Brien had learned this lesson the hard way. Five years earlier he was in England at the Newmarket yearling sales and he saw a bay colt by Northern Dancer out of the mare Goofed. The colt was small, almost a clone of his sire — the same size, same colour and the same long white blaze down his face. Except where his sire's veered off over his left nostril, the colt's stayed the course and tumbled straight over his muzzle. Because of the colt's size, O'Brien didn't bid on him.

Leading French trainer Alec Head purchased the little colt on behalf of Madame Germaine Wertheimer, widow of Pierre Wertheimer, prominent French horseman and owner of the famed House of Chanel. Madame Wertheimer named the colt Lyphard in honor of the Ukrainian-born French ballet dancer and choreographer Serge Lifar.

Lyphard raced in France, Ireland and England, winning six of his twelve starts including the Group One Prix Jacques Le Marois and Prix de la Forêt. However it was as a sire that Lyphard would best be remembered. Where Northern Dancer was the preeminent Thoroughbred sire of the 20th Century, his son Lyphard ranked in the top five. No doubt O'Brien, who incidentally was not particularly tall, did not wish to allow the size of a horse to obscure his judgement this time around.

Now everyone — the Irish crew and Windfields staff were standing back watching the famous trainer look at the flashy little chestnut son of Fleur and Northern Dancer. O'Brien did not speak a word. He simply stood quietly looking into the eye of the colt. The colt stood absolutely still, staring back at O'Brien.

O'Brien slowly moved to the colt's shoulder, gently tugged his ear, patted his neck, and ran his hand along the colt's flanks. The proud little colt still did not move.

"He's more than 14 hands," said O'Brien to no one and everyone, "But not much. He could be big enough, but only just."

O'Brien asked the Windfields groom to walk the colt along the pathway and stood silently watching as the colt was led away from him. He watched the rhythmic swaying of the colt's powerful hind quarters, his flaxen tail flicking back and forth, ever so slightly.

The groom then turned the colt around and led him back toward O'Brien. The colt moved well — straight and boldly. Yet he appeared to have nothing in common, other than bloodlines, with Nijinsky. Instead he looked a bit like a miniature version of Minsky. And as this was 1975, O'Brien would not, of course, known that Minsky would reign, posthumously, as Japan's leading sire in 1980. He would only remember the hope there had been for Minsky to be another Nijinsky and how disappointed they were when he wasn't.

O'Brien stood for another minute or so just looking at the colt. Finally he asked the Windfields yearling manager, André Blaetler, if he could see their other Northern Dancer yearling. This one was a filly. He also asked to see the Nearctic and Nijinsky yearlings.

O'Brien and his troop spent close to an hour at the Windfields consignment. When it was time to move on to the next stable destination on their list O'Brien asked his veterinarian to stay behind and to check out the little flashy chestnut. Every inch — from his forelock to his fetlocks.

Over the following two days O'Brien and his troop patrolled the barns, checking and double-checking the flesh and blood young horses against their pedigree pages. When O'Brien arrived in Kentucky he came with a list of approximately fifty horses he wanted to see, based on their pedigrees and Tom Cooper's reports. By the afternoon prior to the opening day of the sale O'Brien had distilled the list down to about a dozen that he felt good about. The one, however, that would cause him the most anxiety was the little Northern Dancer/Fleur colt. They returned to the turquoise and gold Windfields barns again and again.

Beyond the fact that the colt was small and stocky and looked absolutely nothing like Nijinsky, the flashy chestnut had four white legs and feet. There are a number of variations of this maxim about white markings on a horse:

One white foot, buy a horse;
two white feet, try a horse;
three white feet, look well about him;
four white feet, do without him.

On the first day of the sale, with Tom Cooper doing the bidding, they bought a Round Table colt for $110,000 and a son of Northern Dancer for $45,000. That evening they sat back and watched as the bidding escalated rapidly on the full-brother to Majestic Prince. There had been rumours around the sales barns that this son of Raise A Native would top the sale.

Not only was the colt a fine-looking animal, but there was a great deal of emotional sentiment surrounding Majestic Prince.

A golden chestnut, he truly had a majestic presence, but it was in the US Triple Crown races that mere mortals had to bow to this supremely courageous animal. Just when it looked as if the 1969 Kentucky Derby was going to end in a three-way dead-heat Majestic Prince summoned the strength and the will, in the final two strides, to hurl himself across the wire and win by a neck over Arts and Letters.

Again in the Preakness Stakes Majestic Prince fought another titanic battle with Arts and Letters. This time he won by a head. The races had exacted a terrific toll on the intrepid horse. His trainer, Johnny Longden, didn't want Majestic Prince to run in the Belmont Stakes. He was over-ruled by the colt's owner. In the Belmont, locked in yet another speed duel with Arts and Letters, Majestic Prince faltered and broke down in the stretch. Still Majestic Prince continued and limped across the finish in second place. The ligaments behind the knee of one of his forelegs were so badly torn he would never run again.

Majestic Prince's full brother, by Raise A Native out of the mare Gay Hostess, was beautifully bred and on paper had attracted the attention of O'Brien when he began pouring over the Keeneland catalogue at home in Ireland. When he went to see the colt O'Brien apparently quite liked him, but the colt 'did not speak to him.' He was not, at least for O'Brien, the next Nijinsky.

When the bidding began on this full-brother to Majestic Prince O'Brien and his troop were like most of the of the people in the sales arena — mere spectators. After electrifying bidding from all corners of the pavilion the auctioneer's hammer finally fell at $715,000. People were stunned. It was a gargantuan amount to pay for a Thoroughbred yearling. A world record bid. This too would change.

The following afternoon, not long before Windfields Farm's flashy chestnut colt was about to be auctioned, O'Brien disappeared. When he returned O'Brien was with the veterinarian.

He had gone, once again, to see the colt. The veterinarian had pronounced the colt to be 'sound as a brass bell.'

O'Brien was running out of time. Finally he summonsed Tom Cooper and instructed him to bid on the colt. The agent reminded O'Brien that there were other Europeans at the sale, many of whom would be thinking about Lyphard, the son of Northern Dancer they let slip away because they thought him too small.

O'Brien lapsed in silent thought. Obviously wondering whether he could be wrong about this three-quarter brother to Nijinsky who was too small, too chestnut, with far too many white stockings. Finally O'Brien emerged from his reverie, looked up at Cooper and said: "No limit Tom. Buy him." And so they did, for $200,000. Yet O'Brien continued to have his doubts." D i d we, or did we not, make a good buy?" recalled O'Brien, "He was small and compact, with not much scope. Chestnuts with a lot of white are not usually attributed with the greatest complement of courage either."

This is one of the many myths and preconceptions that this flashy little chestnut colt would dispel. For he surely was courageous beyond measure.

Not long after Vincent O'Brien returned home to Ballydoyle, an Aer Tura DC8 cargo plane eased slowly out of the sky and landed gently on the tarmac of Ireland's Shannon airport. The plane's passengers were twelve Thoroughbred yearlings.

Nine of the twelve young horses being walked off the cargo plane and up the ramp into the waiting Ballydoyle horse van traced their direct ancestors to Ireland. Four of them descended from the stallion Princequillo who was born in County Tipperary. Three of them traced to County Kildare's Turn-To. One was the son of County Meath-born Vaguely Noble. Another was a grandson of County Kildare's Nasrullah and if you looked back far enough, the two Northen Dancer colts had a bit of the Irish in them. Northern Dancer's dam, Natalma was a daughter of Almahmoud. Her sire, English Derby winner Mahmoud, was out of the Irish mare Mah Mahal, daughter of the Irish matriarch Mumtaz Mahal.

Their shopping trip had cost $1,796,000. The most expensive of the lot was a Round Table colt. They had to go to $500,000 for him. They paid $375,000 for another. It seemed, at the time, outrageously high prices to pay for Thoroughbred yearlings. Yet, within the next decade, these amounts would seem like pocket change.

When the yearlings arrived in Ireland Ballydoyle took on the dimensions of the Óenach Colamin — the market fair of ancient times. The moment had come to allocate the horses among the shareholders and the long Irish history of horse dealing surely came into play. For a horse trader, a spit on the palm followed by a handshake, was contract enough. Deals were struck. Shares distributed. Sangster was a major shareholder in almost every animal. O'Brien and his son-in-law were in on every horse. The other shareholders selected the animals that appealed to them.

Once the details were sorted out and the yearlings bedded down in their new Irish surroundings, O'Brien and his troop were back on a plane to the US. This time their destination was the Saratoga Yearling Sale in Upper New York State. They had set their sights on a full-brother to Sham, the brilliant racehorse that had the misfortune to be foaled the same year as Secretariat. Sent out time and again to compete against Secretariat, as fast as Sham ran, Secretariat simply ran faster.

Sham's full-brother was the only horse that interested them and they paid $127,000. Yet another grandson of Princequillo was on his way to Country Tipperary and not far from where his grandsire had been born.

Presumably committed to Magnier's vision of making their fortune by amassing a stable of brilliant young stallions, Sangster was busy assembling a herd of mates for the stallions. To that end he had paid $300,000 for two blue-blood mares from the estate of Charles Engelhard. Both mares were in foal to Nijinsky. Both mares gave birth to twins. The likelihood of one mare producing twins was remote. For both to have produced twins was highly unusual.

The Englishman approached the executors of Engelhard's estate suggesting that under the circumstances he felt justified in requesting one free stallion service to Nijinsky to make up for his bad fortune. The executors declined his request. Apparently, according to Patrick Robinson in *Horsetrader*, this single event, this sole rejection, disturbed Sangster irrevocably: "Robert never got over that. It hardened him. Some people think it really changed his entire attitude to what had become a serious business."

The two sets of twins were but a few of Sangster's personal and financial difficulties. On one of his trips to Australia it seems he fell in love which would have been glorious had he not already been married. The new object of his affection was Susan Peacock, wife of politician Andrew Peacock and mother of three.

Then there was the tax issue. In 1966, on the eve of his 30th birthday, Sangster was handed the first third of his Vernons Pools inheritance. The capital gains tax: £1.5 million. Five years later he received the second third. The capital gains tax: £2 million. Each time he borrowed money to pay the tax. Soon, upon his 40th birthday, Sangster would receive the final installment. Still he was apparently displeased with having to pay the enormous taxes on his even more enormous inheritance. In order to raise additional funds Sangster attempted to merge the family business, Vernons Pools, with other bookmakers, but in the end his father blackballed the deal.

Unable to borrow, unable to sell, Sangster abandoned England. Initially his 'tax exile' took him to Marabella. The Spanish playgrounds of the jet set, luxurious yachts lolled patiently awaiting their passengers to disembark from the parade of Bentleys and Ferraris. Eventually, and appropriately, he moved closer to Ireland and his new Irish friends when he purchased a home on the tax haven Isle of Mann.

In June1976 the catalogues for the Keeneland and Saratoga yearling sales arrived at Ballydoyle. Once again O'Brien and Magnier studied the pedigree pages. Over and over. Looking for the next Nijinsky and those juvenile stallions that would provide shareholders substantial return on investment. They were, of course, making up the rules as they went along, but before long they realized that to keep going they were going to need more money. So once again Sangster was dispatched to re-fill their war chest. Two of the syndicate members — Alan Clore and Simon Fraser — had already taken their leave. They were disinclined to throw more money into the pot.

Sangster was going to have to move quickly so he contacted yet another Irish horse trader, Billy MacDonald from Ballynahinch. The son of the Irish Showjumping Association chairman, MacDonald gained his fifteen minutes of fame not from horses, but from plowing a sailboat into the island of Alcatraz in San Franscisco Bay. This brief notoriety occurred when MacDonald was living in California and had, for the moment, forsaken selling horses, for selling Rolls Royces.

It seems MacDonald and another Irishman, Michael O'Sullivan, contrived to impress their girlfriends by implying they were totally at home on the sea. To that end they leased a forty-foot single-masted sailboat and off they went. The problem was they may have overstated their prowess and when the wind came up in the San Francisco Bay they were dumbfounded.

Within moments the boat was flying over the bay's reputed shark-infested waters and across the dangerous currents. Eventually they crashed into the rocks skirting the island of Alcatraz, the site of the former penitentiary, from which, it is said, no man ever escaped. With the help of the US Coast Guard rescue crew all four lived to tell the tale, which made the front pages of the *San Francisco Examiner*.

Shortly thereafter MacDonald returned to the business of horses and established a stud farm in England for Kjell Qvale, his former employer in the Rolls Royce dealership and major shareholder in the Golden Gate Fields racetrack.

By the time Sangster went looking for money MacDonald was back in California and dealing horses and was able to convince Bob Fluor and Danny Schwartz to join the syndicate. The war chest was topped up and once again the Irish troop, led by Vincent O'Brien, swept into Lexington, Kentucky for the 1976 July Yearling Sales at Keeneland.

Billy MacDonald was among the troop one afternoon when they were touring Kentucky farms to view the yearlings before the animals were shipped off to the auction. One of their stops was Claiborne Farm, a short distance from the town of Paris, Kentucky. Apparently MacDonald gestured Claiborne's yearling manager aside; pressed a hundred dollar bill into his palm and asked him which of the yearlings he preferred. Without hesitation the yearling manager pointed to a diminutive filly. His assessment was based on a number of factors, not the least of which was her disposition. She was disposed to outrace the others.

Claiborne spans over 2000 acres of rolling countryside. The horses roam large and sprawling paddocks. The yearling manager pointed to a nearby gate and explained to MacDonald that at mealtime the yearlings will race to this point from far across the field. The first one to the gate invariably was this little filly.

The endorsement was good enough for MacDonald so he went back to report his findings. The Irish troop, of course, were looking for colts, so the filly, especially such a small one, was of absolutely no interest. Nevertheless, MacDonald soldiered on and announced that he was going to buy her and wanted to know if any of them wanted in as partners.

While O'Brien considered her too small, and she surely didn't fulfill Magnier's juvenile stallion mandate, they, along with Sangster, bought into MacDonald's discovery. The filly went to the Keeneland sale and they purchased her for $40,000. It was the best investment of the entire mission — start to finish.

After reconnoitering the sales barns, O'Brien had selected twelve yearlings. Again, with Tom Cooper doing the bidding, they bought them all. They paid $1 million for a pair of colts by the Irish stallion Vaguely Noble and $330,000 for two sons of Northern Dancer. They also went to Saratoga where they picked up a colt and a daughter of Sir Ivor for $75,000 each.

The pattern had now taken shape. The rules of the hunt established. They came to North America. They saw what they wanted. They bought them. No matter what the cost.

So far, in these past two years, the mission to find the next Nijinsky and in the process, potential stallions, resulted in the purchase of 30 yearlings. It had cost the syndicate almost $5 million dollars and that didn't include all the other related expenses: air transportation, insurance, upkeep and training, fees to Tom Cooper, and all the additional costs incurred by the human contingent in their raids on Keeneland and Saratoga.

"Basically, you could say we were getting a bit jumpy at this stage," recalled Sangster.

Spending $5 million on several dozen Thoroughbred yearlings was a huge, and in the opinion of most, an outrageous gamble. That year, 1976, about 8,700 Thoroughbred foals were born in

Ireland and England. Thirty-three percent were sold as yearlings. Yet, even getting these youngsters to the track is fraught with a multitude of complications and variables. The list is long. Young Thoroughbreds are susceptible to injury, virus infection, unsoundness, even premature death. Then there are those who are simply not fast enough and others not inclined to race at all. Approximately half the annual crop of Thoroughbreds may never manage to achieve the purpose for which they were bred. Of the 8,700 foals in Ireland and England, 2,900 would run as two year olds and another 1,000 might be expected to make their racing debut at three, or even four. A majority of these older horses will have been 'put away' and allowed time to mature to follow a steeple-chasing career.

Of the 2,900 two year old flat racers, only twenty-five percent would win a race in their first season. Less than 2% could be expected to place in the frame of a classic race, much less win one. At the time the odds against a horse even paying for its keep in one racing season were about 10-1, or 20-1 if it was a jumper.

The odds of finding the next Nijinsky were off the board and even if *one* of the colts they had chosen won a classic race, what were the chances of him becoming a great sire? Again — no guarantees. One only has to look at the long list of Thoroughbreds that were outstanding as racehorses, but were not disposed, for one reason or another to be prolific sires. How and why it happens is a mystery — fundamentally unpredictable. So while a myriad of educated guesses are offered, in the end the whole thing is determined at the whim of Mother Nature.

In his ballad "Run For the Roses," the journey of a foal to the Kentucky Derby, Dan Fogelberg sums up the whole mystery quite splendidly: " ... it's the breeding and the training and the something unknown, that drives you and carries you home."

It's the something unknown. And no one. Not Vincent O'Brien, not Federico Tesio, not Eddie Taylor, not John Magnier, nor all the horse traders on the planet can know, or see, that illusive *something unknown*. It will not, however, stop them from trying.

In less than thirteen months, the Irish had wagered $5 million dollars, and their reputations, on a scheme that was fundamentally unpredictable. It was a gamble, of course. Using the money of others. Yet already two syndicate members had dropped out.

At this point in the saga, it's entirely likely that if something quite remarkable didn't happen in the not too distant future, they might well have folded their tents. What they needed was a small miracle.

Curiously, that's what happened.

The *small miracle* was The Minstrel, the flashy little chestnut son of Northern Dancer and Fleur that O'Brien was agonized over because of the colt's size and his four white socks. The colt that they looked at, over and over, and over again. The colt that O'Brien instructed Tom Cooper to purchase at the very last moment. The colt that O'Brien had doubts about, even after they purchased him.

Upon his return to Ireland after their second foray to the US yearling sales, O'Brien started the first of their prospective stallion purchases. Named Brahms, O'Brien suffered no indecision over this racy-looking colt. His dam, Moccasin, had been outstanding. O'Brien had trained his full-brother, Appalache, voted 1973 champion two year old in Ireland and England. O'Brien had no difficulty in telling Tom Cooper to buy Brahms at any cost. At $500,000 he was their most expensive purchase in 1975.

Running his first race at Leopardstown Brahms came from well off the pace to win by two-and-a half lengths. Things were looking good. The punters backed Brahms the odds-on favourite to win his second start, the Railway Stakes at The Curragh.

Straining every inch of the final few yards, Brahms managed to win the race in the bob of a head. It was a courageous performance, but Brahms lacked the classic brilliance for which they were hoping.

Nonetheless, shortly thereafter, they were able to sell new shares in Brahms and thus, in the process, re-syndicate the horse for $1.4 million. They banked the profit and focused their attention on the next of their herd to enter the starting gate, The Minstrel. This one was fast and tough. At The Curragh, in his introductory race, the Moy Stakes on 8 September 1976, The Minstrel was stellar. He won by five lengths and set a record for six furlongs. Then, partnered for the first time with Lester Piggott, easily won the Larkspur Stakes at Leopardstown. Three weeks later The Minstrel was shipped to England where he completed the year winning the Dewhurst Stakes at Newmarket by a decisive four lengths.

In the meantime another great champion had arrived in O'Brien's Ballydoyle yard, albeit, by a somewhat circuitous route. His name was Alleged and he was one of the yearlings O'Brien dismissed at the 1975 Keeneland yearling sale.

Indeed O'Brien and the rest of the troop were in the audience when this colt was led out of the arena 'unsold.' The bidding reached only $34,000, which was below the breeder's reserve price. The colt eventually ended up with 'pin-hookers' Monty and Pat Roberts who shipped him to their farm. Another form of horse trader, pin-hookers aspire to make their money buying low, selling high. They too comb the horse sales, but are focused on finding foals and yearlings at auction they hope will sell at a better advantage at a later date.

Billy MacDonald was a friend of the Roberts and visited them frequently on their farm. He had watched the colt mature over the winter and knowing he would soon be off to the California auction ring MacDonald telephoned Sangster. The colt, he reported, had grown into a big solid horse with good shoulder.

He had, however, weak knees — not a desirable attribute in a runner of any stripe.

Still MacDonald convinced Sangster to put up the money. Presumably to cover all the bases MacDonald was also singing the praises of the colt to Californian, Bob Fluor. He too was swayed by MacDonald. Now MacDonald had two prospective purchasers.

Roberts had bought the yearling after the Keeneland sale from his breeder for $40,000. In March 1976, less than seven months later, Roberts had him galloping and entered in the Two Year Old In Training Sale. The mere thought of young horses whizzing around California's dirt tracks at this stage of their development horrifies most Europeans. In England at that time of the year the norm for most horses is a regime of quiet canters over Newmarket's cushy downs. After all horses are not fully developed until they are five.

There are several versions of who actually did the bidding and bought the colt. Nevertheless, MacDonald and company did buy him for $175,000 and Pat and Monty Roberts, with the help of their Irish friend, banked a tidy bonanza of $135,000 in less than seven months.

Later that day MacDonald was approached by a trainer from Arkansas who had also wanted the horse. He offered him yet another profit on the horse. MacDonald checked with Sangster who agreed to 'flipping' the horse, and set the price at $200,000. Still MacDonald reckoned he could acquire a bit more money, so he returned to the Arkansas trainer and told him they would not take less than $225,000.

The Arkansas trainer thought MacDonald was asking far too much money for a horse with vulnerable knees. So they were forced to keep the horse. It was, no doubt, an error of greed, but one that would work out in their favour. The horse was named Alleged and he was brilliant.

As the situation unfolded it seems that Bob Fluor, the wealthy

California businessman, had the impression that he was the major shareholder. In the meantime, now that they had the horse, they had to decide what to do with him. Alleged's knees would not likely stand up to training on the unforgiving, hard dirt US surfaces. The soft Irish turf seemed a more appropriate ground for the colt and and so it was that Alleged ended up with O'Brien at Ballydoyle.

"When he arrived I did see that his legs were already showing signs of trouble," recalled O'Brien, "So I'd decided that I'd take my time with him. They'd prepared him for what they call their Horses in Training Sale. So they get two year olds ready and they ask them to find some speed — which is a bit unusual for that time of the year."

In the closing days of the 1976 Irish racing season, O'Brien entered Alleged in a race at The Curragh for horses that were yet to win. Alleged was joined by a field of fourteen others. This soft Irish turf was indeed easy on the colt's delicate knees and Alleged romped to victory by an decisive eight lengths.

"Well, if The Minstrel is the nicest two year old I've seen all season," said O'Brien after the race, "this fellow would be very nearly the second best."

Interestingly, the star of Ballydoyle, The Minstrel, was the horse O'Brien agonized over, and almost did not buy. The co-star, was a horse O'Brien rejected entirely. Yet here both were in his yard. There are those who believe that the gods and goddesses created horses to teach we humans humility.

The Minstrel was shipped to England's Ascot course for the Two Thousand Guineas Trial, the first race of his three year old year. The Minstrel's mettle would surely be tested. Incessant rain in the London area had turned the course into a bog. The ground was so soft and deep that the organizers were unable to get the starting gate through the mire.

Many questioned the logic, much less the integrity, of even considering to run the race. If the ground were unpassable to humans and machines, why would they ask these eager young horses to risk their limbs? Nevertheless, that is what they did. The officials had the horses line up and gallop off at the sound of a starter's pistol and at the drop of a flag. The Minstrel slogged through the mushy, slippery turf and emerged, as was his wont, at the head of the pack. The Minstrel won the race by a length and a half but clearly hated every difficult stride of the race. In the winners circle he was heaving with exhaustion.

The race should not have been run. The ground was atrocious. Some of the horses were ruined for life as a result of the experience. The Minstrel was the only horse to have prevailed and endured, relatively unscathed. Still the race exacted a terrible toll from The Minstrel as well.

His herculean effort installed The Minstrel as betting favourite at Newmarket for the English Two Thousand Guineas. Considering the toll the Trial must have taken, a poor post position, and a slow start, it was not surprising that The Minstrel did not win. Instead, he was third, remarkably though, just two lengths back of the winner.

Next The Minstrel was shipped back to Ireland for a two-day fixture at The Curragh, beginning the evening of Friday, 13 May. O'Brien had contracted Lester Piggott to ride five three year olds for him that weekend.

O'Brien had The Minstrel entered in the Irish Two Thousand Guineas, in what was perceived to be The Minstrel's last chance at winning a classic race. He did not think the tough, and flashy chestnut colt could handle the mile and a half distance of the English Derby.

Tenacious to the end, The Minstrel ran his heart out in the Irish Two Thousand Guineas. He surpassed English Two Thousand

Guineas winner, Nebbiolo, who crashed into The Minstrel in the final furlong, but lost the contest to Pampapaul, by a short head and had to settle for second place.

It proved a discouraging development, no doubt for O'Brien, but worse for those syndicate members looking for return on investment. The Minstrel was not the next Nijinsky. For the colt to fulfill their baby stallion mandate he had to have at least one classic win under his girth. To add to their collective gloom that weekend, Valinsky, the horse O'Brien considered his English Derby prospect had gone down to defeat in the Group 3 Royal Whip Stakes at The Curragh. The winner, at 33-to-one, was Alleged, ridden by one of the Ballydoyle work-riders.

How Alleged went to the post at 33-1 is a mystery. He had won his only two year old race quite smartly by eight lengths. While not quite so impressively, he won his first three year old race, the ten furlong Ballydoyle Stakes at Leopardstown at the end of April. The Royal Whip Stakes was Alleged's third start. More than a few members of the crowd at The Curragh that day were taken aback when they watched Alleged move up alongside the favoured leader, Valinsky, cruise past him, and win the race quite handily.

The English Derby was little more than a fortnight away. Their hopes in Valinsky had been dashed. Alleged, with his vulnerable knees, could not possibly be ready in time. O'Brien had another three year old son of Northern Dancer in his Ballydoyle collection, Be My Guest. His dam was the 1965 US champion What A Treat and he was the first Northen Dancer yearling since Lyphard to be offered for sale at a public auction in Europe. The site of this event was Goff's brand-new sales arena at Kill, County Kildare and it was expected that the good-looking chestnut colt would surpass the record of 55,000 Guineas set the previous year for a son of Habitat. And so he did. After persuading the agent for Greek shipping magnate, Stavros Niarchos, to back out of the bidding, O'Brien finally got the colt for 127,000 Guineas.

Be My Guest raced in the colours of Diana Manning, sister of US Ambassador Raymond Guest, yet like so most of the horses currently in the Ballydoyle yard, the horse was now owned by a partnership that included O'Brien, Magnier and Sangster.

Be My Guest started just twice at two and won the second of these races, a six-furlong maiden event at The Curragh. So far this record price-setting colt had won £690. In the spring of his three year old year, Be My Guest won the Blue Riband Trial Stakes and it was thought that his forte would be as a middle-distance runner. His loss to Orchestra in the ten-furlong Nijinsky Stakes caused his handlers to rethink this strategy. Of one thing they were certain, Be My Guest did not look like an English Derby contender.

At the conclusion of the final day of the brief race meet at The Curragh in May that began Friday 13th a gloomy Vincent O'Brien, his son-in-law, and company had to face the fact that after spending $5 million on thirty yearlings, they did not have a horse for the English Derby. Their scheme appeared doomed.

It was then that Lester Piggott uttered his soon-to-be-infamous line, "If you run The Minstrel, I'll ride him."

It seemed a formidable task for The Minstrel. He would be going up against the Aga Khan's Blushing Groom, winner of the French Two Thousand Guineas and currently the 9-4 favourite for the English Derby. Based in France, Blushing Groom was considered by the French to be the fastest miler since his great-grandsire, Tudor Minstrel, back in the 1940's.

O'Brien and company were taking a terrific risk running The Minstrel in the Derby. A third loss in a classic race would clearly diminish The Minstrel's prestige as a stallion prospect. The terrible bog The Minstrel was forced to slog through in the Two

Thousand Guineas Trial and his tenacious battle in the Irish Two Thousand Guineas would all be forgotten. Instead he would be tarred with the reputation as a horse that couldn't win a classic — that he lacked the necessary courage. None of this would, of course, bother the horse, but his owners were looking for an injection of cash. A loss in the Derby surely would hit them in their bank balance.

The 1977 English Derby at Epsom was off at a quick pace. The Minstrel and Blushing Groom settled in behind the early leaders as the horses entered Tattenham Corner. Swinging into the steep part of the left-hand downhill turn Piggott maneuvered The Minstrel to the outside and into third position. Flying past the three furlong pole Willie Carson, riding the extremely tough Hot Grove, grabbed the lead and began kicking for home. Piggott sent The Minstrel in pursuit.

The Minstrel was giving everything he had but could not catch Hot Grove. At the quarter-pole Piggott went to his whip. He hit The Minstrel twice, and with such fierceness that people well back in the stands said that it sounded like the crack of a rifle shot. Piggott was also aware that another horse was coming up behind them and rapidly gaining ground. A quick check over his shoulder confirmed that it was Blushing Groom.

With less than two furlongs to go up Epsom's rise to the finish The Minstrel still was unable to lessen the distance between him and the leader Hot Grove. Blushing Groom was tiring and starting to drop back.

Again Piggott went to his whip, reaching back and cracking The Minstrel's hind quarters with two sharp slaps, and then five more times in rapid succession. Where Nijinsky no doubt would have gone berserk with this kind of abuse, The Minstrel just dug in and kept trying. By the time they reached the final furlong one length separated Hot Grove and The Minstrel.

The Minstrel was running as if his very life depended on it. His four white legs pounding the turf, his lungs searing. And again Piggott began flailing The Minstrel with his whip. Four more violent slashes.

In the final hundred yards the two horses strained up the rise to the finish. Hot Grove still had a slight edge over The Minstrel. Just when it seemed that he was destined to be the runner-up, The Minstrel dug in even deeper. It seemed impossible, but inch by inch, stride by painful stride, he was gaining. His head, with its wide white blaze was now next to Hot Grove's saddle cloth. In two strides the horses were even. Piggott slashed him again. And again. A stride from the finish The Minstrel's head was in front. At the wire, The Minstrel won the English Derby at Epsom by a neck.

In the winners' circle The Minstrel was wringing wet, and lathered in sweat He was shaking from his ordeal, and his sides heaved as he struggled to regain his breath through his red, flaring nostrils. O'Brien confessed that as he witnessed the horses flying past Epsom's famed finish post, he was trembling with emotion. His wife, Jacqueline, had tears teeming from her eyes. Long after the race had ended, some members of the crowd had not moved. Instead, were standing, glued to the spot where they had witnessed the race, their hands still gripping the rail.

There are those who believed that Piggott should have been censured, if not incarcerated for the beating he gave The Minstrel. Piggott did eventually go to jail, not for abuse however, but income tax evasion.

They took The Minstrel back to Ireland and entered him in the Irish Derby. He won by a length and a half. It was his fifth race in twelve weeks. Then late in July he was shipped back to Ascot, site of the English Two Thousand Guineas Trial. This time there was no bog for him to plow through, instead The Minstrel faced more mature horses in the King George VI and Queen Elizabeth Stakes.

Once again running for all he was worth, under the sting of Piggott's whip, and in a struggle no less excruciating than the

English Derby, The Minstrel prevailed by a head over Orange Bay, the great champion Exceller was third and French Derby winner, Crystal Palace, was fourth.

Meanwhile back in Canada, the colt's breeder, Eddie Taylor, was following The Minstrel's career with more than passing interest. Convinced The Minstrel was the 'heir apparent' to Northern Dancer, he wanted the colt back in North America to stand at stud at his Windfields Farm. Taylor was, however, going to have to work quickly. There had been an outbreak of Contagious Equine Metritus in the United States and an embargo on shipping European horses to the United States would go into effect in September.

Taylor had offered $7.2 million for The Minstrel after he won the Derby — $7 million more than Windfields Farm had received for the colt at the 1975 Keeneland sale. But the Irish syndicate were not prepared to sell The Minstrel. Not yet.

Following the King George VI and Queen Elizabeth Stakes, Taylor upped the ante. He was suggesting a $9 million syndication of The Minstrel. He offered to pay $4.5 million for half the 36 shares in the horse on the grounds that there would be no more races for The Minstrel (there had been talk of running him in the Prix de l'Arc de Triomphe). Taylor's terms stated that The Minstrel would stand at stud at Windfields Farm and the horse would be despatched to North America immediately to avoid the embargo.

Since the Irish syndicate would retain the other half of the shares they had the choice of either sending some of their own mares to The Minstrel or of selling the remaining shares which were valued at $250,000 each. Try as he might, there was no way Magnier could come up with enough money to counter this proposition. Eddie Taylor's holdings were vast and international. His financial well was far deeper than that of Sangster's inherited wealth.

In the summer of 1977 O'Brien, his wife, son-in-law, brother, veterinarian, Sangster, and the rest of the Irish troop returned once again to Keeneland. They set a new record purchase price for a yearling when they paid $725,000 for a son of Secretariat from the Windfields consignment. They spent $290,000 for a pair of Windfields-bred colts — one by Northern Dancer and the other by Graustark. When the sale had ended the Irish had bought nine yearlings for a sum of $2,272,000. They were, by far, the biggest spenders at Keeneland and had succeeded in raising the average yearling price up almost thirty percent over the previous year.

Then they went on to Saratoga. They bought one Northern Dancer colt for $375,000 and another for $340,000. They ended up spending $1,271,000, and again, vastly more than any other buyers. When all the chits from the two sales were added up after this latest buying spree the total was just over $3.5 million. In three years they had spent over $8 million. So when Taylor offered them $4.5 million in cash for The Minstrel, plus 18 (half) of the shares in the horse, it was an offer they could not refuse.

Simon Fraser and Alan Clore were originally listed as co-owners of The Minstrel, but they had bailed out of the syndicate after the first year. It is unclear, if not unlikely, they would have a say in the fate of the horse or a share in the profits.

It seems the horse trading rituals and rules of yore — when a spit on the palm followed by the shaking of hands was a binding contract — began gaining a certain elasticity. It would also appear at this stage of the tale that the mission to find the next Nijinsky was becoming less and less about horses — at least judging from the actions of some of the main players. Furthermore, before long a number of clients and syndicate members would find themselves mauled by this the original Celtic Tiger.

From all accounts and with the counsel of Sangster this Irish group was taking the art of horse trading to a whole new level. According to one Kentucky reporter the horses had become secondary to the money game which he dubbed 'the battle of wills and wallets.' Had risking enormous amounts of money in the sales arena become so intoxicating? Whatever was occurring, Taylor's money would go a long way in replenishing their war chest, which ultimately meant they could keep playing the game. Whatever game that might be.

The consequences of The Minstrel and his sizable syndication would reverberate throughout the world of the Thoroughbred for years to come. Interestingly, however, this would not have happened today. Britain now has a stringent whipping rule in effect. In July 1993 the British Horse Racing Board decreed that in any race, only five cracks of a whip are allowed in a finish, none of which can begin from a position above the shoulder. Jockeys are no longer permitted to apply the whip in a forehand position down on a horse's shoulder, nor to raise the whip above their own shoulder height.

Had Piggott not flailed The Minstrel as he did the horse would not have won the English Derby, nor the King George VI and Queen Elizabeth Stakes for that matter. Today if a British jockey beat a horse as severely as Piggott beat The Minstrel, the horse would have been disqualified. The jockey would be fined and suspended from race riding — and if activists had their way, he or she would go to jail.

Had The Minstrel not won the English Derby he probably would not have even been syndicated, much less for millions. The history of Thoroughbred racing over the past few decades would be quite different.

Around the time of the syndication of The Minstrel Robert Sangster experienced a kind of an epiphany: "I came up with an idea that is so simple I'm surprised no one thought of it before — turn breeding into a strictly commercial venture." An epiphany, incidentally, that ran contrary to the entire fabric of Thoroughbred racing and breeding.

Three of the most successful breeders of Thoroughbred horses in the 20th Century were Federico Tesio, Eddie Taylor and Christopher Chenery. All three devoted the major portion of their energy and resources in pursuit of developing the finest Thoroughbreds. Tesio, an Italian, bred Nearco and Ribot. Both great champions, there are scant few Thoroughbreds, the world over, that do not trace their lineage to one of these animals. Virginian Christopher Chenery's life-long love-affair with horses bestowed the world with the great Secretariat. Among Eddie Taylor's gifts were, of course, Nijinsky, Nearctic, Northern Dancer and The Minstrel.

The men had much in common. Foremost, they were horsemen. An enthusiastic polo player and fox hunter, Christopher Chenery rode almost daily until his health failed him in 1966. From Argentina's Pampas to the Canadian prairies, Federico Tesio viewed great expanses of the world from the back of the horse. In the mid-Fifties Eddie Taylor's riding horse stumbled and Taylor was catapulted. He had fractured his pelvic bone and his doctor warned him never to ride again. Taylor ignored the warning and only stopped riding when felled by a debilitating stroke. He was but a few months short of his eightieth birthday.

Taylor and Chenery were self-made men who spent millions building their farms and investing in the finest mares available. Conversely Tesio was not a wealthy man, hence he spent his limited funds carefully and methodically. His band of broodmares was a little more than a dozen, yet the calibre of great horses that hailed from his Dormello Stud is staggering. Tesio was simply a genius. His book, *Breeding the Racehorse*, published in 1958, has been reprinted dozens of times and continues, in the 21st Century, to be read by students of the Thoroughbred.

Sangster could not be accused of being a horseman. Instead, according to biographer Roy David in *Robert Sangster: Tycoon of the Turf*, Sangster was "a figures man. His life was ruled by profit and loss ... the horses themselves would, however, be kept at a safe distance." David also mentioned that Sangster did not lead his horses into the winners circle. "... much too shy, much too nervous, much too English."

Perhaps the thing that distinguished Sangster was that instead of spending a fortune on horses, Sangster set out to make a fortune from them. One of his schemes to maximize profits was to go global. He already had a sort of base in Australia. He had negotiated interest in several Australian stallions and owned a number of broodmares. His fascination with Australia was not confined to horses. It was while attending the 1975 Melbourne Cup that he was introduced to Susan Peacock, wife of Australian politician Andrew Peacock. Down the road she would become Sangster's second wife.

Sangster apparently wanted an even greater Australian profile. And money. Which, of course, the horses would provide, according to his epiphany to turn breeding horses "into a strictly commercial venture."

His idea was to sell foals to the Australians. So in the spring of 1977 he rounded up a prodigious herd of 35 Thoroughbred mares for his experiment. The mares were to be bred in Ireland to stallions at Coolmore, of which he had equity — in both horses and the farm. Once the foals were weaned from their mothers he planned have them flown by cargo plane to Australia. There were several technical glitches, not the least of which — different hemispheres. In the Northern Hemisphere Thoroughbred foals are generally born between mid-February to the end of June. No matter the actual date of the animal's birth, according to the rules of The Jockey Club all Northern Hemisphere Thoroughbreds share January first birth-date. In the Southern Hemisphere foals are born from late August to November. Their official Jockey Club birth-date is August first.

In order to have his herd of foals in sync with his Australian market, he devised a scheme that ultimately would shake the foundations of the Thoroughbred breed. Sangster's initial idea was simply to breed these 35 mares in the off-season. After all the breeding season happened in the spring so the rest of the time the stallions were just lolling about out in their paddocks eating grass, costing money. So in the fall of 1977 the Coolmore stallions were back in the breeding arena. As were the 35 mares for Sangster's experiment.

Few animals are more highly-tuned to their environment than horses. Flight animals, they are exquisitely designed to sense danger from considerable distances. Their constantly shifting ears operate like radar, detecting the slightest sounds. Their feet are acutely receptive sensors that pick up vibrations from the earth, which are then amplified and fed to their inner ears and brains via their nervous systems, bones, and body cavities. Indeed the horse's entire body is one great sound receiver and allows them to detect earthquakes and other environmental changes long before their human caretakers.

This affinity with the world around them is a powerful driving force within the psyche of the horse. In either hemisphere the greatest concern for the mare is the well-being of its offspring. Thus the cycles of the horse, both stallion and mare are in sync with their environment, and the seasons. Their prime mating season is designed so that the foals will be born in the spring with its abundant fresh sweet grass and soft footing.

Sangster's experiment ran contrary to the laws of nature. The equine mating period corresponds to increased daylight following winter months. In the Northern Hemisphere the first cycle begins in April when the sun is overhead and the days noticeably longer. As with many mammals, the biological rhythm is determined by the alternation of a short period of darkness and a long period of light in the course of twenty-four hours.

If for some reason the mare is not covered by the end of August she will not be receptive again until the following year. The natural world dictates that a late birth date would surely hamper the foal's chance of survival. The gestation period is eleven months. Foaling in the spring when young tender grass is brimming with nutrients is the ideal.

Sangster's experimental foals were born the following autumn. Now he was faced with a dilemma he perhaps had not considered. With winter coming and these animals entirely attuned to their environment, they began growing thick winter coats. This, he believed, would be bad for business. Where their Southern Hemisphere counterparts would brandish sleek summer coats, his lot would surely be looking a bit scruffy.

So he decided to trick them. Well actually, trick Mother Nature. He decided that the foal's coats were growing because of the declining daylight hours. Thus to compensate he had the staff leave the overhead lights in the barn on 24 hours a day. Mother Nature was not that easily duped. The artificial light had no effect.

There were other problems. Winter grass holds none of the nutritional value of the rich spring grass. Thus the pasture mares would graze upon while nursing lacked any real benefit. As with any young animal, the first few months are critical to their growth and these poor foals were clearly suffering. So Sangster had his staff start feeding a high-protein supplement to the mares hoping this would be passed on through their milk to their foals. That, of course, did not work either.

Eventually several poorly-developed yearlings with shaggy coats were dispatched to Australia. They were the best of the lot. There is no record of what happened to the majority of these animals.

Sangster's experiment was a dismal failure. Down, but not defeated, he came up with a revised money-making scheme. While he gave up on the mares and foals idea, he focused on the stallions. Sangster calculated that the stallions could be bringing in twice as much money if they were to stand them in the Northern Hemisphere half the year, then load them on to a plane and ship them off to Australia for the second half of the year.

As with the mares, the stallion is also affected by nature and the changing season. The onset of sunlight will trigger his sexuality. In the wild he lives and roams in the company of a band of mares. He has battled other stallions to win this right and he will continue to battle as the younger stallions continually challenge his supremacy.

With the advent of spring and thus the mating season the herd stallion becomes super-charged. His job, after all, is to breed and to pass on his superior genes. The survival of his herd, and ultimately, his species, depends on his stamina and his ability to identify the appropriate time to cover each and every mare.

Horses possess extraordinary senses, not the least of which are their highly developed olfactory senses. Its long face houses extensive and complex nasal cavities. Within the system are vomeronasal organs that enable the stallion to detect the scent signals or pheromones of the mare. Most stallions are able to detect a sexually receptive mare for at least a half mile off in the distance. Some, like Northern Dancer, miles away.

To facilitate his ability to determine the precise moment to breed, the stallion employs its flehmen action whereby he will inhale the scent of the mare, then curl his upper lip over his nostrils so that it shuts out any other scents. He then will store and analyze the information. Needless to say he will stay on high alert until his role in the herd is completed.

The increase in sexual hormones translates in the development of larger neck, chest and shoulder muscles. This macho look is most evident by the manner in which he arches his neck when he approaches the mare. In the wild he will raise his tail like a great banner and dance and prance around the mare like a peacock. The dance has two purposes: 1) to impress and 2) to be on the move should his enthusiasm find him courting a mare who is not quite ready. If that is the case, she is very likely to lash out with her hind feet. Older stallions are, no doubt, more savvy than a young inexperienced one.

The quality of the stallion's semen and his sexual vigour are better in late spring and early summer than during the winter months. In the wild the stallion has a 95% to 98% success rate. While potency of some Thoroughbred stallions is high, the average success rate ranges between 40% and 70%. There are any number of mitigating factors, not the least of which is that it is the human handlers, and not the stallion, that must determine the appropriate mating times.

Sangster would have had to convince Magnier and the other Coolmore shareholders of the merit of this latest strategy. No one at the time knew what effect this would have on the stallions.

While The Minstrel was running for all he was worth over Epsom's turf and Sangster was attempting to dupe Mother Nature, on the other side of the Atlantic Ocean there was yet another US Triple Crown winner — Seattle Slew. He was an awesome racehorse and later on, a respectable stallion. O'Brien and Magnier would not have had any interest in him. Not on his pedigree and certainly not on his looks.

As a foal Seattle Slew had a presence, but not a particularly graceful one. He was tall, big-boned and gangly. His off-fore turned out at almost 90 degrees. He had an avaricious appetite. The only early indication of his determination and speed was that Seattle Slew was always first to the feed tub.

His breeder applied to enter the big dark brown colt in the July sale at Keeneland, but when the inspectors came out to look at the colt they rejected him. So his breeder took the colt down the road to the Fasig-Tipton Summer Sale just outside Lexington. The sale was only in its second year and was perceived to be the place for people with champagne dreams and beer budgets. The yearlings were, for the most part, the ones that had not qualified for the Keeneland Sale. The left-overs.

The word that there was potential gold at the Kentucky Sales was spreading far and wide. In this case as far as a logging camp in the woods outside a small town in Washington State called White Swan, which was where Mickey and Karen Taylor parked their mobile home. Both thirty years old, Mickey was a logger. Karen worked as a stewardess.

The previous year, on their third wedding anniversary, Mickey bought his wife a racehorse. The horse won a few races, so they purchased another. It too had done well. Presumably buoyed by this instant good fortune they had decided to forsake their careers and to try their luck with Thoroughbred yearlings.

Their plan was to buy yearlings as cheaply as possible and ship them to Sunland Park, an obscure track in New Mexico. Next they'd crank the youngsters up to race early in their two year old year. Then sell them at a rosy profit. So off they went to Kentucky and booked into a modest Lexington motel. As the story goes, once settled Mickey walked down the hall to purchase a soft drink from a vending machine. He deposited coins into the dispenser, but the tins of soda pop refused to roll out. He thwacked the machine but still nothing happened.

At that moment the young veterinarian Jim Hill and his wife Sally entered the corridor. The trio struck up a conversation. In the twenty-four hours between the vending machine incident and the Fasig-Tipton Sale the Hills and the Taylors had forged a business relationship. The Taylors to provide the seed-money and Hill would act as their their horse advisor.

The first horse they bought, on the advice of Hill, was the big-boned gangly colt — Seattle Slew. The price: $17,500. The Taylors continued buying horses and before long had amassed a small herd of thirteen. Next they hired a horse van to transport the animals to New Mexico. Unfortunately the van only accommodated nine horses. Perhaps they had erred in their addition, still it was a miscalculation that clearly worked in their favour.

Hill suggested they ship the four yearlings least likely to develop into their 'quick turn-over' scheme to the East Coast. He also recommended a young trainer, ex-steeplechase jockey, Billy Turner. Seattle Slew was among the four that were sent east. It didn't take Turner and his wife, Paula, long to understand they were going to have to take their time with the big gangly brown colt. Paula nicknamed him 'Baby Huey' after the lumbering, rolly-poly duck in the Walt Disney cartoons.

As the colt began to mature they realized that his awkward physique belied a hugely aggressive disposition. The Turners would devote months to trying to calm the demons that drove this horse to run at almost blinding speeds. Their slow careful conditioning paid off. Coming up to the Kentucky Derby Seattle Slew had won all six of his starts including the Champagne Stakes by an astonishing 9-3/4 lengths.

On the first Saturday in May 1977 all eyes were on Seattle Slew as he entered the starting gate favoured to win this the 103rd running to the Kentucky Derby. His exit from the gate was, however, less than elegant. He stumbled, tumbled sideways, banged into the gate, hit the horse to his right and his rider almost fell off.

Once he regained his balance Seattle Slew shot off in pursuit of the leaders. In a blink Seattle Slew had taken his rightful place at the head of the pack. The others tried to run him down, but to no avail. Seattle Slew, the great dark warrior, did not like to be passed. He won the Kentucky Derby by almost two lengths.

In the Preakness Seattle Slew was out of the gate sharply and hit the ground flying. It turned into a two horse race: Seattle

Slew and Cormorant running in tandem. After seven furlongs Cormorant began to tire. Entering the far turn Seattle Slew began to draw away from his running mate.

Throughout Seattle Slew's training Billy Turner was often criticized for not pushing Seattle Slew harder. Still on Preakness Day the reserve tank of energy Turner had been conserving was there when Seattle Slew needed it most. He soared between the finish post 1-1/2 lengths ahead of his nearest rival.

Despite wind and rain one of the largest crowds in the history of Belmont Park was enticed to the New York track to witness Seattle Slew's Triple Crown attempt. There were so many people flocking to the track that it created a massive traffic jam. Among the vehicles mired in the bottleneck was the horse van carrying Seattle Slew and he was delayed getting on to the racetrack. When he finally got to the gate his supporters backed him as 2-5 favourite. There were only two questions: 1) could he run the mile-and-a-half distance? And 2) since he had never run in the mud, could he handle an off-track?

The race itself was fairly anticlimactic. Seattle Slew splashed to the lead, and stayed there, as was his wont. With a quarter mile to go several horses attempted a challenge, but to no avail. The day, the Belmont, and the US Triple Crown belonged to Seattle Slew.

And horse racing in North America never looked so promising.

Meanwhile back on the other side of the ocean. At the time it is unlikely that there was a not a native Irish woman, man, or child who either descended from horse traders, or were related to horse traders, or at least were familiar with horse traders. It is also unlikely there was a soul alive in the Republic of Ireland who did not know the name Michael Vincent O'Brien, much less recite each and every one of the remarkable horses that had cruised the Ballydoyle gallops and the races they had won and the pride O'Brien and his horses had brought to Ireland, not to mention the wagers that each and everyone had won.

Wind of the great excitement, and presumably the grand profits to be made with the horses, was spreading throughout this land of the horse. And it wasn't long before Patrick Gallagher, twenty-seven year old Irish real estate developer, was compelled to join in on all the fun.

During the 1930's there was scant work to be found in Ireland so Gallagher's father, like so many destitute Irish, traveled to London in search of work. The elder Gallagher laboured long hours and in dreadful conditions. He returned home with a beautiful English bride and enough money to start his own construction business. A shrewd eye for land development opportunities and ambition galore proved the foundation for the sizeable family fortune. When he died in 1974 his son Patrick found himself at the helm of one of Ireland's largest business conglomerates that ranged from real estate development to a merchant bank. Reputed to be a high-flier, young Gallagher was driving his own Rolls Royce before he was twenty. He was also known for his love of horse racing. As a youngster he frequently accompanied his father to The Curragh and was a teenager when the pair followed Nijinsky's every race.

Gallagher got the opportunity to join in this hunt for the next Nijinsky with a horse called Try My Best. (Not to be confused with Diana Mannings' Be My Guest). A son of Northern Dancer out of the mare Sex Appeal, Try My Best made his racing debut in the five furlong Whitechurch Stakes at Phoenix Park. Half-way up the stretch Try My Best blasted free of the pack and won by six lengths. Three weeks later O'Brien entered him in the seven furlong Larkspur Stakes at Leopardstown. Again Try My Best showed blistering speed, this time against Ireland's top two year olds, and won handily. Next Try My Best was shipped across the Irish Sea to Newmarket for the Dewhurst Stakes.

Try My Best was up against stern opposition, but he wasn't fazed and stormed past the crowd to win by a length-and-a half. At the end of the year Try My Best was voted Champion Two Year Old Colt in both England and Ireland. It wasn't long before racing fans were speculating on whether or not he would be the next Nijinsky, or The Minstrel. Or at least another Derby winner in the making.

Shortly after Try My Best's Dewhurst victory Patrick Gallagher approached the Irish syndicate to see how he could become a shareholder. Before long he had paid an astronomical £750,000 for a quarter share in Try My Best. The following spring, in the first of England's Classics, the 2000 Guineas, Try My Best galloped along at the back of the pack and cruised across the finish last in this field of nineteen. He was not the same horse. The fire and blistering speed he had shown at two had dissipated. He would not be a Derby winner, nor would he be syndicated for $9 million. The winner of the big race, Roland Gardens, had cost his owners a mere £3200.

Gallagher was devastated. Several days later Sangster offered him £250,000 for his quarter share. Gallagher's loss was approximately £500,000. Once Gallagher cashed Sangster's cheque, Magnier syndicated Try My Best as a stallion prospect for £2.4 million. The horse would stand at Coolmore for £20,000 a breeding, with shares at £60,000.

The Irish had paid $185,000 for Try My Best at the 1976 Keeneland Sale. Factoring Gallagher's money and now this syndication, they surely had gleaned a tidy profit on this colt. Still, they did not have the 'big' stallion. Nor the next Nijinsky.

Gallagher was not the only investor to be mauled by this, the original Celtic Tiger. When Billy MacDonald was looking for someone to purchase the two year old horse with the shaky knees his friend Monty Roberts was selling he had approached both Sangster and Californian Bob Fluor.

The details of the actual ownership are lost in the shimmering shadows of horse trading. However all this worked, Alleged competed, at least initially, in the racing colours of Fluor. Still it seems that Sangster or MacDonald, or both, also sold a shares in the horse to American millionairess Shirley Taylor.

Alleged was slower to come into his own than The Minstrel and O'Brien only started the colt once as a two year old. The following spring Alleged won several minor races in Ireland quite handily. Despite his questionable knees he was beginning to look like a racehorse. Fluor believed Alleged to be his horse, or at least that he was the major shareholder and as such had some opinion regrading the animal's destiny. Fluor also thought that *his* horse should run in the Irish Derby. To that end he informed O'Brien that he and his family and his friends and Shirley Taylor were all coming to Ireland for the big event. He had gone ahead and booked the accommodations and the flights .

In the meantime the syndicate had decided to run The Minstrel in the Irish Derby. Thus Fluor's idea would hamper their long-term potential profit if Alleged were to beat The Minstrel in the Irish Derby. Since at this point The Minstrel was running on empty and Alleged was just coming to form, there was every likelihood that would be the outcome. So Sangster sashayed into the debate and explained to Fluor that because he, Sangster, owned 40% of the horse, he decreed that Alleged would not run in the Irish Derby.

"This is basically why The Minstrel was allowed to go and win it [Irish Derby]," wrote Patrick Robinson in *Horsetrader*, "and why Bob Fluor spent much of the summer being very brassed off indeed at his colleagues in the Sangster syndicate."

O'Brien had a different game plan for Alleged. He was aiming to send the horse to France for the Prix de l'Arc de Triomphe. The colt's first stop en route to Paris was Yorkshire for the Great Voltigeur at York. Alleged pulverized the field, which included Hot Grove, runner-up to The Minstrel in the English Derby.

Next they entered Alleged in the marathon (almost two mile) St. Leger at Doncaster. In this race he finished second to a filly, Queen Elizabeth's, Dunfermiline, winner of the English Oaks. Following the race, Sangster somehow talked Fluor into selling most of his holdings in Alleged. Possibly Sangster forgot to mention that Alleged was headed to the Prix de l'Arc de Triomphe and that O'Brien had every confidence in the horse. While the amount Sangster paid Fluor was not made public, it is assumed to have been around £250,000.

Fluor returned to California. Alleged went to France where he won the Prix de l'Arc de Triomphe — his jockey now wearing the racing silks of Sangster. The horse won £130,000. Immediately thereafter they valued Alleged at $7 million.

Alleged ran in the Prix de l'Arc de Triomphe again the following year and once again he won. At this point the Irish syndicate sold the horse to Walmac International in Kentucky for a reported $16 million.

Between Alleged's two French victories Sangster got married again (10 March 1978). This time in the Chapel of St. Bridget, where 14 centuries earlier the Irish saint had been bestowed with the veil of virginity.

July 1978. Thoroughbred racing in the United States had been blessed with yet another Triple Crown winner — Affirmed. Prior to Secretariat there had not been a US Triple Crown winner since Citation in 1948. Now there seemed to be a bonanza.

In many ways this year had been the most exciting. In the past, one horse dominated the horizon but in 1978 there were two exceptional horses — Alydar and Affirmed. Both golden chestnut in colour, they seemed to match each other in courage and resolve. In the Kentucky Derby Affirmed prevailed by a length and a half over Alydar. In the Preakness Alydar narrowed the margin to a neck. Scant few North Americans were without an opinion on whether or not Alydar could win the Belmont.

Again thousands flocked to the New York track. Millions watched the race on television. The 1978 Belmont Stakes reigns as one of the most heart-stopping in history of this mile and a half horse race. Down the stretch they flew, Alydar and Affirmed, matching each other stride for stride. Neither giving ground. Neither giving in. Each horse digging deeper for the strength to prevail. At the wire Affirmed had held on to win by the narrowest of margins over the gallant Alydar. In a way they both had won and in the wake of their brilliance the sport of Thoroughbred horse racing had never been so prominent or promising.

Nor had it been so expensive to buy a yearling. In this, the year of Alydar and Affirmed, the Irish crew were back at Keeneland and bought sixteen colts, two fillies, signed chits totaling $5,490,000. As in previous years they were instrumental in pushing the average yearling price up and up. This time by a whopping 45.2 percent.

Still they had not unearthed the next Nijinsky. Furthermore, they missed the 'big' stallion. Not because he wasn't on their *list,* he was. Instead it seems that they may well have tumbled into their own inflationary trap. On one hand they had been driving the yearling prices up into the stratosphere and beyond the reach of ordinary wealthy individuals, but when it came to this one potential stallion, they backed off. Why? The stakes seemed too high.

The one that got away was a compact bay son of Northern Dancer. His dam, a daughter of the Argentinian speedster Forli, was named Special. From the outset the Irish had decided that they must buy every yearling selected by O'Brien. The Kentucky media had begun calling them 'Sangster's gangsters,' and they were — at least some of them — beginning to act like characters in a wild west movie. Their agreed mandate was never to back down, no matter what the price. Of course, they were making the rules up as they went along. Until now they had been basically riding into town, taking what they wanted, and leaving before most people knew what had happened. No one, and certainly not the Kentucky Thoroughbred breeders, challenged their right to buy every horse in the place, should they so wish. O'Brien so wished to have the son of Northern Dancer and Special at Ballydoyle. Sangster was prepared to offer $400,000 of the syndicate's money for the colt.

On Tuesday night of the sale this son of Northern Dancer and Special stood in the tanbark ring beneath the auctioneer's podium. He scanned the audience. His eye, defiant. His physique was much the same as his sire, and presumably because of that the bidding got off slowly. The concept that this Northern Dancer line did not have to be big, to be good, had not yet penetrated the Thoroughbred world.

The opening bid was $20,000. After a protracted series of flicks of catalogues, nods of heads around the arena, the bidding had reached $400,000. The Irish hadn't even entered the bidding yet. Their English money-man had thought they could just step in at the end. He'd simply raise the ante and spirit the colt back to Ireland, as planned, but the price kept going up and up. They hadn't counted on this. This was *their* game, or so they thought. Perhaps it had not occurred to them that the syndication of The Minstrel changed everything.

At this point in the history of Thoroughbred sport, racing communities generally operated within the confines of regional boundaries. There were, of course, exceptions. Canada's Eddie Taylor sent the occasional horse to race in the US, but like most

Canadian owners, preferred to have his horses running close to home. Few Californians brought their horses east except if they thought they had a contender for the major events like the US Triple Crown.

Scant few European horses were shipped to compete in North American races. Even fewer North American horses were sent to Europe to run. Not only was it a terribly expensive proposition, but the training methods, course configurations, and track surfaces on the two continents were entirely divergent.

Other than minimal interest in the major events like the Prix de l'Arc de Triomphe, most North American Thoroughbred racing enthusiasts knew little of the sport and it's horses in Europe. Nor did those on the eastern side of the Atlantic Ocean concern themselves much with what was happening in North America.

This lack of communication between these two very different worlds had worked to the advantage of the Irish and to a great extent proved an important ingredient in the emergence of the original Celtic Tiger. For the first few years the Irish horse traders and their English money man surely had stealth on their side.

This now was changing. News of the syndication of The Minstrel reverberated on both sides of the Atlantic — but more profoundly in Europe. Previously many were of the opinion that North American Thoroughbreds were bred solely for speed, thus lacked the stamina demanded on the European and British courses. Nijinsky had been considered a fluke, but now The Minstrel was the second Canadian-bred son of Northern Dancer to win the coveted English Derby. Perhaps it was time to rethink the theory.

The Irish had struck gold with The Minstrel. As in the Klondike Gold Rush, when the news got out of their big strike, other prospectors were lured to Keeneland, the site where these great riches had been discovered. It appears that a number of them were in attendance at this, the July 1978 Keeneland Select Yearling Sale. It also appears that a number of these new prospectors had their sights set on this bay son of Northern Dancer and Special.

The bidding on the colt was well over $800,000 — twice what Sangster thought they would pay for him. O'Brien wanted the colt and signaled his brother Phonsie to replace Sangster in the bidding. Phonsie bid $860,000. Joss Collins of the British Bloodstock Agency countered with $880,000. Phonsie went to $900,000 and then left his seat to confer with O'Brien and the rest who were congregated in a pack at the back of the sales pavilion.

They thought Collins might be representing Greek shipping magnate, Stavros Niarchos, and reasoned that this colt might prove to be quite expensive. None-the-less they decided to carry on. Collins had just bid $1,000,000. Someone else pushed it to $1,025,000. Collins came back with $1,050,000. The Irish bid $1,100,000 to bring them back into the game.

Someone else upped the ante by $25,000, as did the Irish. Collins calmly went to $1,200,000. He obviously was not backing down.

"One million two, I have," intoned the auctioneer, "Will you give me a million and a quarter?" The Irish agreed. "Okay, lets deal in round numbers," continued the auctioneer, "Give me one million three." Collins immediately nodded.

The Irish and their English money man appeared flummoxed — they didn't know what to do. Up until this moment no one had really challenged their right to buy every horse they wanted. Now the auctioneer was looking across the pavilion at their huddled group, demanding a reply: "one million four, will you go to one million four?"

"Was that a 'No?'" asked the auctioneer. No one from the Irish troop replied. They regrouped further back in the corridor. But the auctioneer was getting impatient. "Is that an emphatic 'No'?" he asked once again. Still no response.

O'Brien then broke from his conversation with Sangster,

turned, looked up at the auctioneer. At that moment the auctioneer was slamming his gavel on to the podium.

They had lost.

The rest is history. Joss Collins was indeed representing Stavros Niarchos. Apparently O'Brien was not the only person bent on finding the next Nijinsky. Niarchos named the colt Nureyev, after the young ballet sensation Rudolphe Nureyev.

The equine Nureyev was an exceptional racehorse and was voted Champion in France in 1980. As a stallion Nureyev was outstanding. He was a sire of sires — Theatrical, Robin des Bois, Soviet Star. Nureyev was also sire of long and distinguished list great champions, including Cartier European Horse of the Year, Peintre Celebre. Nureyev was not the next Nijinsky, but from Magnier's perspectives he was surely the young stallion they had been searching for.

In August of 1978 the Irish traveled to Saratoga for the next round of horse sales and once again they missed out on another extraordinary young stallion. This one would be named Danzig and ultimately be regarded, along with Nureyev and Lyphard, as one of the one of the most outstanding Thoroughbred sires in the world. As with the other two, this colt was also a son of Northern Dancer.

Danzig was purchased for $310,000 by Henry de Kwiakowski who was just getting into horse racing. He named the colt for the Polish City and handed him to US legendary trainer Woody Stevens.

Danzig did not win any classic races. He didn't even win any stakes races. In fact Danzig only raced three times. But he was quick. In his first race he scorched to a 8-1/2 length victory, but he came out of the race lame, bothered by a bone chip in his knee. Surgery was followed by months of rehabilitation which included a regime of daily swims. At three Danzig returned to the track mentally and physically fit and raring to run. He won two allowance races — both by huge margins. Still Danzig was favouring his knee and Stevens was concerned. Further x-rays revealed that Danzig was developing a fracture.

Stevens approached Seth Hancock, boss of Kentucky's Claiborne Farm. Based on Stevens high opinion of the horse, and his own instincts, Hancock agreed to add Danzig to their stallion roster, which included Nijinsky and Secretariat.

It proved an excellent decision. In 1984 the first crop of Danzig foals hit the tracks running. Among them was champion Chief's Crown, winner of the inaugural Breeders' Cup Juvenile race. Every year from then until he was retired from breeding in 2004 Danzig proved to be a prodigious and consistent stallion. He sired horses that were able to run on grass and dirt, over distances or sprints. They ran at two, three and four and on both sides of the Atlantic. And in Australia.

While Lyphard was the first of Northern Dancer's sons to emerge a significant stallion, he was soon followed by Danzig and Nureyev, but none would take up occupancy in the splendid new stalls at Coolmore.

1979 was not a particularly stellar year for O'Brien, the Irish horse traders and their English partner. Success of their horses on Irish and English racecourses was extremely moderate, especially considering the numbers of horses they owned, and the vast amounts of money they had spent.

So far these men had brought sixty-six beautifully-bred young horses back to Ireland for O'Brien to train. Not just any horses. These were the absolute cream of the crop — the finest bloodlines, and physically close to perfection. They were merely one year old when they disembarked from the fleet of horse boxes conveying them to Ballydoyle. Brimming with speed and heart and spirit and courage and curiosity. Yet, what has happened to them?

Out of the sixty-six there was The Minstrel, one of the few to race at three, much less win a Classic. The tiny filly, Fairy Bridge, won a couple of minor races. Two year old colt Solinus won the Coventry Stakes at Ascot and Octavo won a mile race at The Curragh. Lady Capulet won the 1977 Irish 1000 Guineas. Artaius was second in the French Derby. Transworld won the Irish St. Leger.

The spotlight was now on a colt they named Montevardi. He won the National Stakes in Ireland and the Dewhurst in England and was voted champion two year old. Magnier and Sangster valued him at $6 million. The lofty evaluation presumably was based in part, at least, on his bloodlines. Montevardi was a son of Lyphard and several weeks prior to Montevardi's win in the Dewhurst, a daughter of Lyphard, won the Prix de l'Arc de Triomphe. Her name was Three Troikas and she was absolutely brilliant.

Montevardi wasn't. Not at three. The promise had dissipated. The $6 million dollar horse was unable to live up to their expectations. Defeat followed defeat. It was as if Montevardi no longer cared to run. There was no way O'Brien could send him to the English Two Thousand Guineas, which was a good thing as the race was won by Nureyev, the one that got away. Instead O'Brien decided to try Montevardi in the less demanding Irish Two Thousand Guineas. He put blinkers on Montevardi and summed Lester Piggott to Ireland to ride the colt. Had it not been for an aggressive ride by Piggott Montevardi would have cantered across the Curragh finish post at will. Instead he was fifth.

"Useless ..." sneered Piggott, of Montevardi, at the post race press scrum.

Perhaps the horse traders reckoned that no one had noticed that they might, at $6 million, have overvalued Montevardi, because this one comment was enough to get Piggott fired — then for always, hence effectively terminating his long partnership with the horses of Ballydoyle. There can be little doubt that their scheme was floundering, as were its creators.

After all this time and effort and money (over $16 million) they still had not found the next Nijinsky. Nor did not have their 'big' Northern Dancer stallion. Nonetheless each year they continued fly their troops into Kentucky for the Keeneland July sale and then on the Saratoga sale. They bought and bought and bought. And each year the stakes rose higher and higher. Pushed, for the most part, by their obsession.

Losing out on Nureyev was a bitter pill. They vowed that this would never happen again. They *must* buy every horse Vincent O'Brien chose, no matter what the cost. In 1979 they bought 18 more exquisitely bred colts. The price tag: $8,885,000. After the sale Sangster was holding court and explained his philosophy to a small group of confused Kentucky reporters: "A top racehorse, or a top stallion is an international commodity. He has a major value anywhere. He can be moved instantly to where he is most valued. Better still he never answers back."

One of the 18 colts was a son of South Ocean and Northern Dancer. When they got him to Ireland the syndicate named him Storm Bird. Appropriate, for this horse clearly ended up in the eye of a colossal storm.

As with The Minstrel and Nijinsky and so many of the others, this colt was born and raised in Canada at Eddie and Winnie Taylor's Windfields Farm. He was South Ocean's second foal by Northern Dancer. The first was a filly named Northernette and she could run with the wind. She won a slew of races and was voted Canada's champion filly two years running. At four she devastated the field in the Grade 1 Top Flight Handicap at New York's Aqueduct Park.

Her brother was deep bay in colour, with a fine white blaze and white socks capping his two hooves on his near (right) side. He grew into a tall and handsome colt and was shipped with the other Windfields yearlings to Kentucky for the 1979 Keeneland July yearling sale.

When the Irish crew and their English partner arrived in Kentucky this colt was at the top of O'Brien's list. His bloodlines were similar to The Minstrel — and more distantly, Nijinsky. Hence, with this dynamic gene pool, he qualified for one of those luxurious Coolmore stallion stables, should this Canadian colt be inclined to be a racehorse.

Prior to 1979 only two yearlings had been purchased at public auction for $1 million or more. In 1976 a group purchased a son of the two great champions, Dahlia and Secretariat, at the Keeneland Summer Yearling Sales for $1.5 million. While it seemed like an outrageous amount of money to spend on a horse, no one could have asked for any more celebrated parentage.

The first filly in history to be voted Horse of the Year in Europe, Dahlia was a brilliant and formidable speedster. She raced, and triumphed, in France, Ireland, England, Canada and the US. She won the King George VI and Queen Elizabeth Stakes, the highlight of England's Ascot meeting, two consecutive years.

From the perspective of conformation, Secretariat was a perfect horse. From the perspective of disposition, Secretariat and Dahlia seemed such a good and complimentary combination. Secretariat was so laid back and easy-going that in the early days his nickname was 'old hopalong.' Dahlia, on the other hand, was high-strung and terribly impatient. Relaxing was not her natural state. And so they had bred the best to the best.

This first million dollar colt was named Canadian Bound. Unfortunately Canadian Bound was not disposed to horse racing. When his owners finally retired Canadian Bound he had earned a total of $4,770.

Then at Keeneland in 1978 Stavros Niarchos paid $1.3 million for the son of Northern Dancer and Special. This was Nureyev, and he surely was special. But in the summer of 1979, no one obviously had any idea how special Nureyev would become. So at the time when the Irish paid $1 million for Storm Bird there were still many people who thought they were barmy to gamble that much money on one single baby Thoroughbred that had not yet even laid eyes on a saddle. In this case, however, the gamble paid off, but in a very curious manner — and just when they needed it most.

July 1980. The Irish crew were entering the fifth year of their mission, but were not much closer to their original goals now than when they first started out. Still it seemed they were not prepared to quit and off they flew to Kentucky.

In the early years they simply rode into town, took what they wanted and left. But things were changing. The Kentucky horse breeders were getting in on the act and promoting their horses and their sale. They even started hiring celebrities to glitz up the show. Head-liners like comedian, Bob Hope, entertained the guests at Tom Gentry's pre-game gala.

The sales barns were getting fancier and fancier. In one corner of the stable area gentlemen in white livery coats served refreshing cups of lemon ice. In another they were serving delicate finger sandwiches and down the aisle another offered catered plates of clam dip and tortilla chips.

The once staid Keeneland was now beginning to resemble

Disneyland and amid all the hoopla the Irish troop found, much to their surprise and chagrin, that they had competition. Serious competition with serious money. They no longer got what they wanted.

O'Brien had targeted a son of Lyphard, but the Irish folded at $1,650,000. The colt was won by Stavros Niarchos for $1.7 million. The Irish were also the underbidders for a Northern Dancer colt which sold to Dolly Green, the heiress, who's family oil patch, Belridge Oil, had recently been purchased by Shell Oil for $3.5 billion. Nevertheless the Irish still were able to buy 13 yearlings, including two for over a million each and another for $775,000.

It was as if they were caught in a feeding frenzy of their own making. When the Irish began their mission in1975 the average price for a yearling at Keeneland was $53,000. In five short years, at the conclusion of the 1980 sale, the average was $200,000. This was cheerful news if you were a horse breeder. Not so good, if you were trying to purchase a horse. Still, it would get worse. Much worse.

On the home front things weren't all that rosy. To date they had carefully selected and bought at least 100 of the world's finest young Thoroughbreds. They had spent approximately $40 million. The Minstrel had returned to North America. Try My Best had fertility problems. In order to bring Be My Guest to Coolmore they had to buy out Diana Mannings share. While not exactly a brilliant racehorse, still he cost them $1.4 million.

They had pinned their hopes and a $6 million value on Montevardi, but he couldn't live up to their expectations. "This was the lowest point they had ever reached," wrote Patrick Robinson, "... they had failed, if not catastrophically, then certainly resoundingly."

One bit of sunshine in this gloomy scenario was the filly Detroit who won the Prix de l'Arc de Triomphe carrying Sangster's green and blue silks. Detroit was bought as a foal by Hogan for Sangster. It did not seem to cheer Sangster however as in the winners' circle he said: "I wish she had been a colt."

While they were in France, however, O'Brien's son, David, saw a bay colt with three white socks that he knew was special. Hogan agreed and between the two of them convinced Sangster to buy the colt. The price: £16,000.

That fall things started looking up. Storm Bird, their million dollar son of Northern Dancer and South Ocean, galloped to five consecutive wins over Irish and English courses and was rated the top juvenile in Europe. He had won the Erne Maiden Plate, Anglesey Stakes, Larkspur Stakes and National Stakes, all in Ireland.

Then he was shipped to England for the Dewhurst Stakes. Considered one of the of most hotly contested in years, there were only five horses in the starting stalls, but everyone of them was a *real* racehorse. From France there was Miswaki, winner of the Group 1 Prix de la Salamandre. From England there was Kirtling who would emerge the following year as one of the country's top ten-furlong horses. And then there was the promising Centurius, a full-brother to 1975 English Derby winner Grundy.

Storm Bird's main rival, however, was the tall, dark and grand-looking son of Tudor Minstrel, To-Agori-Mou. The colt's British trainer, Guy Harwood, considered To-Agori-Mou to be the best two year old on that side of the Atlantic Ocean.

The Dewhurst Stakes is a straight seven furlongs over Newmarket's undulating lush turf. For the first half of the race the small field rolled along in a pack. The pace was sharp and Storm Bird was galloping easily on the outside while holding a marginal lead as they raced up the hill towards what is known as the

'Bushes,' a windswept clump that had stood as a landmark on this famous course for three hundred years.

When they raced down into the 'Dip' To-Agori-Mou's jockey, Grenville Starkey, went to the whip on his rugged young colt. Within seconds To-Agori-Mou had moved up alongside Storm Bird but the Canadian colt responded instantly to the presence and challenge. In a moment the two horses seemed to burst away from the others. Before long they were six lengths clear of the rest. Both colts were giving all they had, and more. Three hundreds yards from the finish and matching stride for stride, the two courageous horses charged up the hill. Now Storm Bird's Irish jockey, Pat Edderly, went to the whip and cracked Storm Bird three times.

"This was the moment of truth," reported Patrick Robinson in *Horsetrader*," and back in the stands Vincent [O'Brien] visibly flinched as [Pat] Edderly laid into the horse. But Storm Bird responded valiantly. He lowered his head and he laid back his ears and he raced with every last ounce of strength he had. The pace over this ground was killing, but with one hundred yards to go, the Irish horse [Storm Bird], had clawed back that half-length lead."

Starkey continued to pound To-Agori-Mou with his whip, this time right handed, but the exhausted colt had nothing left. Storm Bird flashed across the finish a half length in front.

Storm Bird's reserves were entirely spent. Like To-Agori-Mou, he had been running on empty. The half-length difference between these two valiant colts may well have been genetic — that Storm Bird possessed some of his sire's resolute toughness. Still his five consecutive wins, culminating with the Dewhurst, inspired the statisticians to install Storm Bird as the winter book favourite to win England's Two Thousand Guineas. Storm Bird was voted champion two year old colt in both England and Ireland. Furthermore Storm Bird was also being viewed by many as the prime candidate to win the 1981 English Derby at Epsom.

Finally the Irish syndicate was on the move. O'Brien had a horse that appeared to have the mental and physical abilities to challenge the Classic races. If not exactly the next Nijinsky, Storm Bird was born of Windfields — the dynamic environment that had produced Nijinsky. For Magnier Storm Bird represented a potentially stellar son of Northern Dancer stallion to take up residence at Coolmore. For Sangster Storm Bird presumably symbolized the possibility of a sizable return on investment.

"At that point," reports Raymond Smith in *Vincent O'Brien*, "according to Sangster, he [Storm Bird] was valued at $20 million. He was insured by his owners for $15 million with Hughes, Gibbs & Company for a premium of £208,000."

In a span of twelve years Storm Bird was the sixth of the O'Brien trainees to have won the Dewhurst, considered to be Britain's most important race for two year olds. And how did Storm Bird compare with the others? According to *Timeform*: "... he compares very favourably. The best four of the six — Storm Bird, Nijinsky, The Minstrel and Try My Best — are all sons of Northern Dancer, and of these we rate Storm Bird the highest."

The rationale behind this judgement was that when Nijinsky was a two year old the rivals he faced were considered by the sports media to be a fairly average lot. But then, standing next to Nijinsky, all horses looked fairly average.

Storm Bird on the other hand, battled much fiercer competition: "... in our opinion he's a very worthy favourite to emulate the victories of Nijinsky in the Two Thousand Guineas and of Nijinsky and The Minstrel in the Derby."

Like children on the night before Christmas, racing fans throughout Britain and Ireland were brimming with anticipation at the thought of yet another Nijinsky. That winter, however, the story of Storm Bird becomes quite peculiar and is rife with conflicting information.

There are any number of versions to the tale of what may, or may not, have happened to Storm Bird over the next few months. According to Patrick Robinson in *Horsetrader*, "On one dark winter night, a disgruntled stable lad, fired from Ballydoyle, crept into the yard, found the peerless Storm Bird and hacked off his mane and most of his tail." Robinson also suggests: "The trauma shook Storm Bird badly and he was very down in the dumps for a few weeks."

On the other hand, Raymond Smith in *Vincent O'Brien*, had a different account: "Vincent (O'Brien) maintained at the time that Storm Bird was unaffected by the experience and all seemingly went well for him."

The one thing certain was that something was amiss with Storm Bird. Was he, like so many that had gone before, so spectacular as a two year old that there was nothing left at three? Or was there something else going on?

First Storm Bird was withdrawn from the English Two Thousand Guineas. The reason cited was that he had apparently contracted a virus. Nevertheless, O'Brien continued to assure the media that he would have Storm Bird ready to run in the Irish Two Thousand Guineas, and if not, certainly the English Derby. Many anxiously awaited the return of Storm Bird and thus the rematch of Storm Bird and To-Agori-Mou, who had now won the first of the English classics, the Two Thousand Guineas, by the narrowest of margins. Most simply hoped Storm Bird would fulfill *Timeform's* prophesy and that he was indeed the next Nijinsky.

Two weeks after the English Two Thousand Guineas To-Agori-Mou was shipped to Ireland to face Storm Bird in the Irish Two Thousand Guineas. However O'Brien continued to keep Storm Bird in the wings. The colt had not, apparently, recovered from the virus. In the place of Storm Bird, O'Brien entered King's Lake, the beautifully balanced and beautifully-bred son of Nijinsky and the mare with a most unflattering name of Fish Bar.

King's Lake, To-Agori-Mou, and eleven other three year olds gathered at The Curragh for the 1981 running of the one mile Irish Classic. Pat Edderly, the Irish jockey who had been riding Storm Bird, was now aboard King's Lake. It was his first ride on the colt.

The early running of the race was smooth and uneventful. Two furlongs from home Edderly took King's Lake along the rails to the front of the pack. King's Lake was galloping well and it looked as if the race was his. Briefly. A quick check confirmed that the sound Edderly heard was that of To-Agori-Mou's thundering hooves closing in on them. Under jockey Grenville Starkey's unrelenting whip To-Agori-Mou was tightening the gap with every powerful stride.

For Edderly, it was a scenario not dissimilar to the previous fall's Dewhurst Stakes when he was riding Storm Bird. The pressure was on.

"As the rider of Storm Bird the previous year," wrote Patrick Robinson in the *Golden Post*, "he (Pat Edderly) knew well what that meant as the Golden Post [the finish] was a mere 400 yards away and he was riding one of the best-bred potential stallions in the world. It meant trouble, millions and millions of dollars of trouble."

And so it was that Edderly went to the whip and began pounding King's Lake. Unaccustomed to the punishment, King's Lake became somewhat unbalanced. The horse then tried to escape the whip by ducking to the left. To-Agori-Mou was drawing alongside, also under the whip of his rider. He too swerved and the two colts almost collided.

King's Lake was holding off To-Agori-Mou, but only just, and the two jockeys continued pounding the obviously tiring horses. Both were no longer traveling in a straight line and brushed into each other several times. Mere strides from the wire, Grenville Starkey stood up in his stirrups, a dramatic gesture meant to convey that he had been wronged and he continued to stand in his stirrups as King's Lake crossed the finish a neck ahead of To-Agori-Mou.

The stewards at The Curragh immediately reacted by announcing an inquiry and retreated to watch taped replays of the final furlong and to discuss rule number 214 which calls for disqualification of a horse whose rider "has intentionally crossed or jostled another horse or rider or been guilty of any form of foul riding."

Eventually the stewards disqualified King's Lake. The Irish horse racing community was stunned. They could not imagine Irish stewards demoting one of their own and thereby giving the glory of winning an Irish Classic to English invaders. Instantly the air over The Curragh was rife with protestations. O'Brien was outraged and challenged the decision of the stewards. The pleading, cajoling, and shouting between the owners and trainers of King's Lake and To-Agori-Mou and the Irish stewards lasted six long hours.

Then, in yet another unbelievable break from tradition, the stewards overturned their initial ruling and King's Lake was reinstated as the winner of the Irish Two Thousand Guineas.

By this point blood was boiling and tempers were flaring among many of those involved. The senior officiating steward at The Curragh and former Senior Steward, Major Victor McCalmont, resigned from the Irish Turf Club in protest. This was an even greater blow to the Irish racing community and now everyone became embroiled in the controversy. For McCalmont to resign from this important post was considered untenable among Irish racing's elite. Eventually he was persuaded to withdraw his resignation. In the meantime, the British racing media were incensed and wrote scathing reports on the matter of the Irish and the apparent manipulation of the rules of racing.

Added to the King's Lake brouhaha was, of course, the controversy over Storm Bird. People were still waiting for him to make an appearance. O'Brien continued to utter assurances that he would have Storm Bird ready for the English Derby at Epsom. Then, after sending Storm Bird out for his final prep prior to the great horse race, O'Brien withdrew Storm Bird from the Derby.

By this point any number of fans and media were beginning to wonder what really was amiss with Storm Bird. It was hard to imagine that the apparent shaving of his mane and part of his tail would have traumatized Storm Bird to such an extent that he would never be able to race again. If the horse had been out in the wild, or simply turned out all the time, and this had happened in the summer when flies and other insects are most bothersome, it was possible that not having a mane and very little tail to swish away the pests would be worrisome. But Storm Bird's alleged assault occurred in the winter.

Some wondered if the Dewhurst Stakes had exacted such, both physically and mentally that the horse was finished. Others suggested the beating taken the heart out of him.

Storm Bird's sire, Northern Dancer, despised the whip as did his dam, Natalma. Both flatly refused to step a hoof on a track in the aftermath of a jockey using a whip on them. Natalma's sire, Native Dancer (thus Storm Bird's grandsire), also hated the whip — really hated the whip. If anyone was obtuse enough to hit Native Dancer, the strapping 16.3 hand, powerful steel grey colt, was reputed to grab the rider by the boot and fling him to the ground.

Whatever was wrong with Storm Bird did not seem to factor into the value Magnier and Sangster placed on the colt as a potential stallion. Storm Bird was, after all, their first million dollar gamble. That the Irish horse traders managed to sell Storm Bird for twenty-eight times his original purchase price, is even more incredible.

Nonetheless, events in the young life of Storm Bird become even more convoluted.

July 1981. Almost a decade had passed since the Irish troop and their English money-man began making an annual pilgrimage to the Keeneland Summer Sales in search of Nijinsky and those potential baby stallions to fill the barely occupied stalls at Coolmore.

Possibly because the Englishman was the most visible player in the group, onlookers and the media alike were referring to the Irish brigade as *Sangster's gangsters.* What they saw were a group of foreigners who came to town with a seemingly bottomless war-chest of money and steely determination. When they set their sights on a particular horse they raised the price beyond the reach of ordinary millionaires and generally left town with exactly what they wanted. Until the previous year, most other prospective buyers had learned just to step out of their way. The Kentucky Thoroughbred breeders simply went back to their farms and counted the colossal amounts of money they were receiving for their animals.

Then one July afternoon in 1981 a mysterious stranger came to town. His name was Sheik Mohammed bin Rashid al Maktoum, of Dubai. Out on the runway of Bluegrass Field airport and directly across the road from the entrance to Keeneland, stood the United Arab Emirates Boeing 727 which had conveyed the thirty-one year old Arab prince, his two brothers and their advisors to Kentucky.

There were five Northern Dancer offspring being offered at the Keeneland sale. The stars of the show were two colts: a son of South Ocean and a son of Sweet Alliance. Both colts were bred and born at Windfields Farm.

Near the top of O'Brien's shopping list was the son of South Ocean, and thus full brother to Storm Bird. As in the past O'Brien led his troop to the turquoise and gold Windfields Farm stable area. When the groom led the colt down the path in front of the shedrow O'Brien liked what he saw. He informed Mangier and Sangster they *must* buy the colt.

Later, when the amphitheatre filled with the buyers and sellers and agents and the merely curious, there was a different aura to the cavernous arena. The highly-charged level of anticipation was created, for the most part, by the presence of the Arab prince. Sheik Mohammed and his team of advisors sat in their allotted row of seats near the front, while O'Brien and his group stood huddled near the back of the amphitheatre.

Soon after the bidding began for this good-looking son of South Ocean and Northern Dancer everyone but Sangster and Sheik Mohammed had dropped out of the game. No matter how bold Sangster was with the syndicate's money, Sheik Mohammed blithely raised the stakes. One million. Two million. Three million. Three million four hundred thousand, offered Sheik Mohammed. Three million five hundred thousand, signaled Sangster.

At that moment, having pushed the Irish crew into paying more than twice the previous record for a Thoroughbred yearling, Sheik Mohammed stood up and calmly walked out of the building.

That evening Sangster bragged to a Kentucky reporter that he had been prepared to go even higher for the colt: "When we shoot, we hit. He's a full brother to a champion colt and a fantastic filly. Like anything else in the world, the best things in life have a value. We estimated that he will make at least $2.7 million at the track as a racehorse."

Optimistically they named the colt Ballydoyle, after O'Brien's training centre. Ballydoyle, the horse, however did not follow in the hoof prints of his brother and sister, Storm Bird and

Northernette. Nor, of course, Nijinsky. Nor did he earn $2.7 as a racehorse.

Sheik Mohammed returned later to the sale. He purchased the son of Sweet Alliance and Northern Dancer. He named him Shareef Dancer and the colt was indeed a racehorse. At the close of 1983 Shareef Dancer was declared champion three year old colt in both England and Ireland and syndicated for $40 million.

The deal to sell Storm Bird was surely an exercise in horse trading 101 — graduate studies. The transaction occurred in early July 1981, during this same Keeneland Summer yearling Sale. Storm Bird had not yet even started in a race, much less won a classic, in this his three year old season.

This very fact caused considerable speculation. There were those who suggested that the Irish syndicate didn't want to run Storm Bird unless they thought that he had a chance of winning. No doubt they hoped to capitalize on the great promise Storm Bird had shown at two. Yet, for whatever reason, that promise had faded. To the casual observer it appeared that Storm Bird was not going to race, much less win at three. This reality, however, had little bearing on the value the Irish horse traders placed on Storm Bird.

O'Brien and company were staying at the Hyatt Regency Hotel in Lexington during the Keeneland sale. As the story goes, one morning at breakfast they were approached by George Harris, yet another Irish horse trader and acquaintance of Magnier. Harris apparently asked if they would consider selling Storm Bird and if so, for how much. Without hesitation the answer was $15 million.

As luck would have it, Harris had a client who was looking to pay $15 million for a stallion. Harris' clients were based in North

America, so there is every chance they might not have been quite as suspect of Storm Bird as British racing journalists and fans. But then, the key to successful horse trading is to give the client what he or she wants.

At this point in the saga it would look as if the synergy created by this most disparate team of Irish horse traders and their English partner truly coalesced. It would also appear that ultimately they were far more astute at selling horses than they were at buying horses.

No doubt sensing that Harris' clients were eager to get in on this Thoroughbred carousel they pushed the horse-trading game to its limits, and beyond. The first thing they did was raise the stakes. The previously mentioned $15 million was simply a starting point — the minimum they would accept for Storm Bird.

In *Horsetrader*, Patrick Robinson suggested that Harris then decided to consult with John Magnier, whom he had known all of his life. Harris had never laid eyes on Storm Bird, so he asked Magnier for his valuation of the colt.

It is unclear if the subject of why, exactly, Storm Bird was in a stall at Ballydoyle instead of the starting stalls at Epsom. What was reported is that Magnier advised Harris that Storm Bird was worth $20 million and apparently pointed out that Storm Bird's brother fetched $3.5 million the previous evening. It is also not known if he remembered to say that the Irish were the ones who bought the brother for $3.5million.

Harris's client was Robert Hefner, an oil man from Oklahoma who had harvested a hefty bonanza from oil and gas in the 1970s. Now, in the 1980s, Hefner decided to conjure his next fortune from Thoroughbreds. His partner in his horse vision was Dr. Bill Lockeridge, owner of the stately Ashford Stud, and considered one of the leading bloodstock experts in Central Kentucky.

Hefner wanted in at the top of the game. The horse he and Lockridge set their sights on was Shergar — conceivably the most outstanding Thoroughbred in the world at the time. Shergar was certainly far more accomplished than Storm Bird. Actually there was little comparison between the two horses. Where Storm Bird had been a sensation at two, Shergar instead started late and raced only sparingly.

Shergar's first two year old start was 19 September 1980 at Newbury. The one mile maiden event attracted a herd of twenty-three starters. Shergar won easily by two-and-a-half lengths and set a course record. His second race was the William Hill Futurity Stakes where he finished second to Beldale Flutter by two-and-a-half lengths. And that was it for the year. The spotlight in the British Isles was on Storm Bird. He was the talk of the turf. Shergar was barely mentioned.

The following year, while Storm Bird was ambling around O'Brien's Ballydoyle gallops, Shergar was steadily making a name for himself on the racecourses of Britain. In the spring at Sandown, in the Guardian Classic Trial, he won the race in a canter and by ten lengths. Less than a fortnight later Shergar traveled north to Chester where he won the Chester Vase by twelve lengths. Again with great ease.

At the end of May and into early June, the south of England was deluged with harsh and persistent rain. On Derby Day at Epsom the famous turf course had the consistency of a soggy sponge. The previous day racing at Salisbury had been canceled because of the conditions.

The 1981 English Derby will always be remembered with reverence for the great Shergar who turned Derby into a parade, with himself cantering elegantly ahead of the procession. After three furlongs, Shergar bounded into the lead and then began to draw further and further away from his followers. He galloped past the fabled winning post ten lengths ahead of his nearest rival — the widest margin in the history of the English Derby. Three weeks later Shergar traveled to Ireland where he won the Irish Sweeps Derby by four lengths. Again with seemingly little effort.

Lockeridge and Hefner offered the Aga Khan $28 million for Shergar. Unfortunately the Aga Khan turned down their offer. Unfortunately, because had Shergar gone to North America he might have lived. Instead Shergar was retired to the Aga Khan's Ballymany Stud in Ireland's County Kildare. On 9 February 1983 Shergar was kidnaped from his stable by members of the Irish Republican Army. The Aga Khan refused to meet their demands. Within the week it was reported that the terrorists had slaughtered Shergar.

It would appear that the original Celtic Tiger spawned countless opportunities for Irish horse traders around the globe, but it is unlikely any conducted the business with such flair and acumen as George Harris. He was born Christmas Day 1942 in County Tipperary's Golden Vale horse country and not too many furlongs from Coolmore. His uncle, Sir Ian Harris, was master of the family stud farm at Ballykisteen. His father, Percy, presided over Athassel House Stud. Added to a family tree studded with horse breeders, George Harris collected an Arts degree majoring in economics and then a Bachelor of Science degree in Agriculture. Harris went on to manage a series of stud farms in Ireland and the United States before hanging up his shingle as a Thoroughbred broker.

Harris was, from all accounts, a very high-end horse trader. His office was not in Kentucky, nor Tipperary, nor Newmarket. Not where the horses were. No, Harris set up shop in New York City, on the 15th floor of a 54th Avenue office tower.

Patrick Robinson in *Horsetrader* describes the operation of George Harris:

"Upon the door, at the end of a cool, silent corridor, are the words: 'George I. E. Harris, Bloodstock Associates.' And behind this door, in deep-carpeted, air-conditioned isolation, sits the man who arranged the sale of Storm Bird ...

"... strictly Wall Street. It was a brokerage in everything but name. And George Harris was the only no-nonsense stockbroker in the entire industry of Thoroughbred bloodstock trading. There were pretenders, part-timers, and agents who might dabble in anything. But there was no one who was at his desk at 8:30 every morning and who traded stocks in racehorses and stallions all day long, taking a quick sandwich at this desk, and working until after 7:00 p.m. in order to accommodate clients in California."

Harris seldom left his 15th floor office. He rarely got his highly polished shoes dusty while wandering from barn to barn at the yearlings sales. Instead he carved out a new niche — a commodities market for horses. A market, no doubt, that would have astounded horse traders of yore.

"Some thirty percent of George Harris's clients were men with money but no horses, and many of them were from Wall Street. They were in there buying shares and nominations like stocks and bonds. There were men buying a 'service' to a major stallion, hoping to trade it through George's office for a profit a few months later."

According to Robinson, Harris was single-handedly trading stallion shares to the tune of $25 million a year. And he soon would be adding Storm Bird and his high-priced shares to his Thoroughbred commodities market offerings.

Now, but weeks after Shergar's Irish Sweeps Derby, and their attempts to buy Shergar denied, Harris' clients Hefner and Lockeridge were headed in a new direction. This time they would get the horse. Briefly. And it would cost them dearly.

George Harris had come down from his office tower and was

in Keeneland, as were his Irish friends — and two fellows looking to spend $28 million on a horse. Before long it was decided that the Irish syndicate might indeed have a horse for sale in that specific price range. A meeting was arranged at the Hyatt Regency hotel.

The terms of the sale of Storm Bird were convoluted, complicated and required several days to negotiate. They concluded the transaction in Ireland, where, presumably Hefner and Lockridge had the opportunity to see Storm Bird, their $28 million stallion prospect, for the first time.

In negotiating the terms of the purchase of Storm Bird, Hefner had surely met his match when he ran up against the Irish horse traders. Hefner wanted the payments for Storm Bird to stretch out over four years. Magnier insisted Hefner pay for the colt in three years. He also wanted the option to hold on to ten breeding shares in Storm Bird. Based on syndication terms of forty shares in Storm Bird, this meant that the Irish horse traders would own one-quarter of the stallion. So while they agreed to part with Storm Bird for $28 million, they would only be getting $21 million in cash, or three-quarters of his value, from Hefner.

Magnier also demanded an uncommonly severe penalty clause: following their initial $7 million payment, should the partnership of Hefner and Lockridge subsequently default, the ownership of Storm Bird would instantly revert to the original partners, but Hefner and Lockridge would continue to owe the money on the second payment. They would not, however, have to pay the final installment. In other words, if Hefner and Lockridge were unable to meet their financial obligations, they would not only lose Storm Bird, they would also lose $14 million. At the time, it appeared as if money was not a problem, so they signed the contract.

They also agreed to leave Storm Bird in the care of O'Brien until the end of the1981 racing season. There was still talk about getting Storm Bird back racing. Now O'Brien was apparently aiming Storm Bird at the fall meets. But whatever did, or did not happen on the race course, Storm Bird would be shipped to Ashford Stud Farm at Versailles, Kentucky, a short drive to the west from Lexington. Storm Bird would cover his first season of mares in 1982.

Storm Bird remained in training at Ballydoyle. O'Brien was talking about targeting the colt for the Prix de l'Arc de Triomphe at Longchamp the first week of October. Popular opinion was that should Storm Bird win the Prix de l'Arc de Triomphe, then all would be forgiven.

Storm Bird finally made his long-awaited appearance 20 September 1981 in a lesser event at Longchamps, the Prix du Prince d'Orange. There are several versions of why this race was chosen. One account was that it was meant to be a prep race prior to the Prix de l'Arc de Triomphe. Another was that it was meant to satisfy the insurance company who were holding a huge $15 million policy on the horse — a policy that Sangster had negotiated back in Storm Bird's juvenile year.

In this, the long-awaited debut of Storm Bird, French racing fans sent the colt to post as the 7-4 favourite. Storm Bird was in the lead after the first half mile, and then he started to fade. The brilliance and tenacity he showed the previous year was long gone. Storm Bird finished a clearly uninspired seventh behind Vayrann, owned by the Aga Khan and ridden by Yves Saint-Martin.

In his biography *Vincent O'Brien: The Master of Ballydoyle*, Raymond Smith interviewed Sangster about Storm Bird: "I never saw Vincent so shattered after any failure as he was that afternoon in Paris," said Robert Sangster (following the Prix du Prince d'Orange). "I recall about twenty pressmen crowding around me, asking me what had gone wrong. All I could say was: ' I do not know. I don't own the horse any more. I cannot explain it.'"

Perhaps, in the heat of the moment, Sangster had forgotten

that he and his partners did actually have a vested interest in Storm Bird. They owned ten shares, or one-quarter of Storm Bird.

Standing before a United States Senate Committee in the 1970s, Hefner had revealed $2 billion in assets. Much of these so-called assets were in the form of oil and gas reserves beneath the plains of Oklahoma, to which Hefner had negotiated the rights. It seemed impossible that his fortunes could tumble so rapidly, but they did. And right at the height of the Thoroughbred game's wildest bull market. At least the wildest bull market — to date.

Hefner's personal financial collapse occurred in 1984. The crash was spectacular. It was also devastating and far-reaching. The first victim was Penn Square Bank in Oklahoma City, which fell simultaneously with its valued client, Robert Hefner. Two of Hefner's other banks, the Continental Illinois and the Seattle First, barely survived the after-shocks resulting from Hefner's enormous indebtedness. Mobil Oil had invested $200 million in Hefner's Oklahoma drilling operation and now were wondering where at least $40 million of their investment had disappeared.

The value of Hefner's assets had plummeted. Such is the transitory nature of the commodities market. Natural gas, once valued at $9.50 per one thousand cubic feet was now, in 1984, commanding a meagre $1.50 per one thousand cubic feet.

Robert Hefner, the man who had boldly offered $28 million for Shergar, and who had eventually promised to pay $21 million for Storm Bird, had declared debts of $770 million. Furthermore, two of his three $7 million payments for Storm Bird were in arrears.

For Lockridge the news must have been utterly calamitous. When the Texas-born veterinarian purchased Ashford it was a cattle farm. Over the years he had built it up into a stately Thoroughbred breeding operation, and certainly a grand showpiece among Kentucky's beautiful stud farms. Over a period of four years, Lockridge employed twenty stonemasons full time in order to create the intricate stonework of the principal buildings. Ashford Stud had been a labour of love for Lockridge — a dream come true. Before Hefner walked into his life Lockridge owned the farm and its horses outright and had secured assets of $15 million, with a $3 million debt.

According to their agreement, Hefner and Lockridge were to be full partners. To that end, in the spring of 1981 Lockridge sold a half interest in his palatial Ashford Stud to Hefner for $4 million. When Hefner's 'house of cards' came crashing down, it was discovered that Hefner had pledged Ashford Stud against his multifarious debts which ran close to a billion dollars.

If things weren't bad enough for Lockridge, on top of everything else, other claims against his short-lived partnership with Hefner were over $55 million. And then there was Storm Bird. Hefner had made only the initial $7 million payment on Storm Bird. There was $14 million owning on Storm Bird.

Rather than be party to the huge debts created by this 'partnership from hell,' Lockridge opted to hand over his half-share in his beloved Ashford Stud plus his holdings in Storm Bird to Hefner.

Although Hefner came to arrangements — paying pennies to the dollar — with his many creditors, when it came to the Irish syndicate Hefner chose to settle this debt in full. He *gave* them Ashford Stud along with most of the shares in Storm Bird.

"Bill Lockridge walked away," wrote Patrick Robinson in *Horsetrader*, "to pick up the shattered pieces of his life and to spend nine long years building up another breeding operation, during which time he would repay his original shareholders in the farm every last dollar they were owed.

"They loved Hefner in County Tipperary though. Every cent

he owed for Storm Bird was, after all, repaid. And now Robert Sangster and his men owned the most wonderful new stud ... The craftsmanship and splendor of the stallion area would have filled the eye of Louis XIV. The address, Ashford Stud, Versailles, would surely have thrown the Sun King into total confusion."

Storm Bird stayed at Ashford where he served his third season at stud in the spring of 1984. The following year he was shipped to nearby Pegasus Stud and then returned to Ashford for the 1986 breeding season. Ashford was then listed as being owned in the name of one of the Sangster Group's related companies, Bemak NV, an off-shore operation registered in the Netherlands Antilles and run under the auspices of Magnier's Coolmore management.

Today it is home to Coolmore America.

The original Celtic Tiger had, inadvertently, generated up a huge demand for Northern Dancer offspring. In the fall of 1981 a wire arrived at Windfields Farm offering $40 million for the now aging stallion. The wire was signed Horse France, a Paris bloodstock agency. Northern Dancer had been syndicated in 1970 for $2.9 million. Eddie Taylor had kept seven shares and the rest were purchased by prominent Canadian and US racing families. After some wrangling and infighting amongst the shareholders, the offer was rejected.

Meanwhile back at Ballydoyle a procession of two year olds were being dispatched to various Irish race tracks. Lords, a million dollar colt, won a maiden race at Leopardstown. At The Curragh, The Minstrel's full brother, Pilgrim won his first attempt. Chronicle fought to win by three-quarters at Naas. Punctilo prevailed by four lengths over 15 others at The Curragh. They were worthy young horses and with time perhaps they would develop, but the Irish syndicate appeared to be in a hurry. Possibly they needed the money, or perhaps it simply reflected Sangster's *return on investment* mantra.

Then at Leopardstown on 19 September, O'Brien started a tall, grand-looking son of Nijinsky in his first race. Named Golden Fleece, the colt romped to an easy four length victory. Among his challengers was Assert, the colt David O'Brien had convinced Sangster to buy following Detroit's Prix de l'Arc de Triomphe the previous year.

Golden Fleece had cost $775,00 at Keeneland. Assert £16,000 at the Paris sale. Assert was one of the first horses David O'Brien would train during his brief, however successful, career as a trainer. Born and raised at Ballydoyle, the younger O'Brien was an excellent horseman. He had an eye for a good horse. He knew that Assert was a horse with immense potential.

Golden Fleece surpassed Assert so easily in the Leopardstown race. Did this mean that Golden Fleece, like his sire Nijinsky, was outstanding? Or even better, the next Nijinsky? The *Timeform* correspondent was certainly impressed with Golden Fleece: "... it was obvious from the time the runners swung into the straight that he was going to win. Rounding the turn Edderly asked him to quicken and the horse immediately lengthened his stride, cruised into the lead and was going on in great style at the finish."

The article is accompanied by a photo of the great strapping Golden Fleece towering over his lad. The caption beneath the photo reads: M. J. P. Binet's "Golden Fleece."

Monsieur Jean-Pierre Binet was one of the stream of individuals who, for one reason or another, became financially involved in the Irish syndicate. King's Lake, the horse involved in the melee at The Curragh, carried the Binet racing silks. As did Golden Fleece. At least initially.

When Golden Fleece marched on to the track in the spring of 1982 he was carrying the racing silks of Robert Sangster. The grand colt surely had so much riding on his powerful shoulders. It seems they decided to point the colt at horse racing's holy grail — the English Derby. And they would not give him too many races between the maiden race at Leopardstown and the English classic. Two, in fact.

Where his sire, Nijinsky, raced four times in Ireland and once in England as a two year old, Golden Fleece only started the one time. The reason given was that Golden Fleece was claustrophobic. A big rangy horse, Golden Fleece had the build of a steeplechaser. Following his lone two year old race he apparently developed a dislike of enclosed spaces — particularly horse boxes and starting stalls. This might not bode well for the destiny they had carved out for the horse.

Golden Fleece made his first start of the 1982 season 17 April in the Ballymoss Stakes at The Curragh. Once again Golden Fleece romped to an relaxed victory. Next, the Nijinsky Stakes on 8 May at Leopardstown. Golden Fleece won by 2-1/2 lengths. His nearest pursuer was Assert. Three races down. One to go. All he had to do was win the Derby and Golden Fleece would be their Golden Goose.

According to all reports O'Brien was enthusiastic over Golden Fleece: "I know a thousand things can go wrong, but this fellow is very special. I'm not sure I've ever seen the horse who I might back to beat him."

Yet no sooner had O'Brien deemed Golden Fleece 'special,' when things started to go wrong. First there was the colt's dislike of starting stalls and enclosed spaces. Then one morning out on the Ballydoyle gallops, Golden Fleece whipped around, dropped his rider and went careening off on his own. The hopes and dreams and prayers of O'Brien went out the window as Golden Fleece was last seen flying across Ireland's Golden Vale, the reins dangling dangerously between his front legs.

Golden Fleece was eventually corralled with no apparent damage. It seemed, however, that he had inherited Nijinsky's nervous disposition. According to his jockey, Pat Edderly: "Golden Fleece was a highly-strung horse; he didn't like patting on the neck or being fussed with. Riding out, if he did anything silly you wouldn't want to give him a slap, or he wouldn't go well. You had to coax him along. He was a horse you had to watch all the time. You couldn't ride him with a long rein or you'd be on the floor! Very quick at spinning around he was. For a big horse he was very sharp."

With less than a fortnight to the Derby Golden Fleece pulled up lame. There was swelling in his off-hind hock. It looked as if their Golden Goose was unlikely to leave the nest. O'Brien's vet, Bob Griffin, was called in. As was the blacksmith. The blacksmith forged special horse shoes that would take the pressure off the colt's hock. Jacqueline O'Brien sought advice from a team of physiotherapists at King Edward VII hospital in London. They prescribed ice-packs and ultrasound.

The swelling was reduced. The Derby back on target.

O'Brien abandoned his regular Skyvan horse transport and hired a chartered air bus with much more headroom for his claustrophobic horse. He also put plugs in the colt's ears; a hood over his head; and sent his stable horse, General Custer for company.

Because of his swollen hock, Golden Fleece missed valuable days of exercise, so O'Brien was able to get permission to work the rangy colt over the Derby course. Jockey Pat Edderly rode Golden Fleece. The colt's lad rode General Custer. The first day all went well. The second day Golden Fleece had coughed a number of times. There was less than 30 hours to the Derby.

O'Brien phoned Griffin, who was back in Ireland. After running through all possible symptoms they opted to wait and see if the colt coughed any more. Since the rules of racing dictate that no medication can be used within 36 hours of the Derby, there was nothing they could do but monitor Golden Fleece.

No doubt the Irish camp was rife with tension. Sangster chose to avoid the crisis by staying home on the Isle of Man and playing golf. He and his second wife, Susan, flew in the day of the race.

The day began with a crashing thunderstorm, leaving the turf soft, the air humid. The eighteen Derby horses were all glistening with sweat as they jogged to the starting stalls. Golden Fleece fretted slightly in the gate. Finally the last horse was in. The gates sprang open and off the colourful field galloped. Golden Fleece was easy to spot. The leggy colt was cruising languidly near the pack of the field. Then, as if he suddenly remembered he was late for an appointment, Golden Fleece came charging along the outside. Edderly drew up his whip and cracked him twice on the left. At the bottom of the hill to the finish there were still four horses ahead of Golden Fleece. Again Edderly hit the colt. And continued. Golden Fleece flashed past the famed finish post three lengths the better of his nearest opponent.

It was a heady, however hollow victory. In less than a fortnight Golden Fleece was sick. This time it was not Griffin that was called in, but Demi O'Byrne, the Irish vet after whom Sangster named his horse Dr. Devious. Patrick Robinson referred to him as the "the mercurial and inventive vet from the village of Kilenaule near Coolmore ... there was little he did not know, or could not somehow fix, about a Thoroughbred horse. He could treat any injury, cope with any problem. And if the condition was 'impossible' he'd still come up with a way of getting the horse sound."

O'Byrne was Magnier's Coolmore veterinarian, hence it can be assumed that Golden Fleece had been re-designated — from racehorse to stallion. But the Tipperary vet was unable to work his magic on Golden Fleece. The grand colt's cough lingered and lingered. When Golden Fleece's cough cleared up his near-hind leg began swelling. A year and a half later Golden Fleece was dead.

When Golden Fleece was retired to stand at stud at Coolmore Magnier valued him at over £16 million and had insured him for over £12million. The insurer, Lloyds of London, balked at paying.

Not long after Golden Fleece's Derby celebrations Robert Sangster hosted an even grander party. This one to fete his second wife's fortieth birthday. The gala took place in Newmarket. The staid Jockey Club subscription rooms were ablaze in hot pink tablecloths and napkins. The price for the flowers alone was reported to be in excess of £6,000. Horse's heads created by a topiarist adorned the alcoves. Which somehow seemed fitting.

The event began with dinner for the Sangster's closest friends and associates. Several hours later the next wave of guests, several hundred more, converged upon the hot pink party. Dancing and cavorting, apparently, went on until dawn at which time those still up and partying were served buck's fizz, caviar and scrambled eggs.

Susan's birthday gift from her husband was a house. In Australia. It was a $6 million, six bedroom home in Point Piper, the most exclusive (and expensive) part of Sydney Harbour. Built into the hillside on three levels, the dwelling offered spectacular views of the Harbour, Opera House and along the shore to the Sydney Boat Club. Called Radford for the people who built it, the

Sangster's renamed the house Toison d'Or — Golden Fleece — for the horse that had paid for it. Shortly after her birthday party Susan Sangster flew to Australia to consult with her architect about changes she would make to the house. Once organized she planned to fly out her London interior decorator. In the meantime, her husband would be doing some re-designing of his own. In fact in the not distant future Sangster would not only find himself a third wife, he would take back Susan Sangster's birthday present and banish her from the house.

The 1982 Keeneland sales catalogues arrived in Ireland not long after Golden Fleece's English Derby. On one hand the Irish syndicate were, no doubt, relieved and pleased that they had managed to get Golden Fleece to the Derby — and that the grand courageous colt had won this, the holy grail of Thoroughbred racing. And made them millions in the process.

Still to stay in this game, they were going to need much more money. Up against the petroleum based wealth of Dubai, Sangster's inheritance was but pocket change. One of seven sheikdoms that form the United Arab Emirates, Dubai was second to Abu Dhabi in oil reserves. At the time crude oil was selling for $35.93 a barrel and Dubai was producing between 300,000 and 400,000 barrels daily.

The Irish syndicate needed someone with an abundance of money and an abundance of nerve to join them in this high stakes gamble. The man to step up to the plate was Danny Schwartz, proprietor of one of the largest construction firms in California, Schwartz had retired a very wealthy man. At one time he owned a horse called Mr. Right in partnership with Frank Sinatra. An ardent gambler, Schwartz was reputed to have once won $1 million playing the tables at a Reno, Nevada casino.

Schwartz had been introduced to the Irish syndicate by Billy MacDonald back in 1976 when he was attempting to generate interest in Alleged. Now, in 1982 Schwartz was about to celebrate his 60th birthday and was persuaded to turn his back on the gaming tables in favour of gambling on potential stallions.

When the Irish arrived at New York on 15 July 1982 a private Learjet was fueled and ready to ferry them to Kentucky. There were two other Learjets, with identical Lexington flight-plans, waiting on the tarmac: one for Prince Khalid Abdullah and his advisors; and the other for Sheik Mohammed's brother, Sheik Maktoum al-Maktoum.

The three Learjets landed, one after the other, at Lexington's Bluegrass Field. Sheik Mohammed's Boeing 727 was already parked on the edge of the runway. Soon Stavros Niarchos' Boeing 727 would join the lineup.

Over the years Sangster's profile had become more and more baronial. The Englishman appeared to enjoy his minor celebrity status, but possibly not more than the afternoon he sashayed into the lobby of Lexington's Hyatt Regency Hotel with super-model, Jerry Hall, on his arm. To the casual observer it seemed an unusual departure for Hall, former girl friend to rock star Bryan Ferry and most recently partnered with Rolling Stone's Mick Jagger.

Furthermore, Hall and Sangster presented a curious couple — a squat forty-six year old Brit with this glamourous leggy blonde who not only towered over him, but was young enough to be his daughter. Apparently the relationship had been percolating for several months.

The Kentuckians were no longer surprised at any of Sangster's antics: "... these were people who considered Sangster something of a playboy anyway," surmised Roy David in *Robert Sangster: Tycoon of the turf*, "people who had seen him in the company of beautiful women before knew about his fun philosophy of having 'the best time in life one can possibly have.'

"It brought a wry smile, too, to the faces of those who had heard Sangster often repeat with grim determination that there was nobody in the world who could outbid him at the sales. They thought that he usually got what he wanted."

When the colt with hip number 30 was led into the ring the Irish syndicate thought they might try outmaneuvering the opposition. Each one of the group was positioned at a different point in the sales pavilion, except for Sangster who was outside in the passageway feigning disinterest — which was the furthest thing from the truth. The animal bearing Hip number 30 was a grand bay son of Nijinsky out of the beautifully bred and accomplished mare, Spearfish. O'Brien wanted this colt. He was at the top of his list of choices: "I could not fault him."

The bidding began slowly, but before long was at $1.5 million. Then O'Brien's man, Tom Cooper entered the game and casually upped the ante by $250,000. Sheik Mohammed's representative, Colonel Dick Warden, standing by the auctioneer's rostrum at the front of the pavilion and in constant eye contact with the Arab prince, immediately struck back at $2 million.

It was a bit like watching a championship tennis match at Wimbledon. Back and forth they went. Cooper in the rear of the building, Warden in the front. As soon as Cooper served yet another big bid Warden countered it with an equally powerful salvo. Before long the bidding had reached $3.5 million. Cooper called a 'time-out.' They were now over their limit.

After a brief chat with his team, Cooper returned with a bid of $3,750,000. Warden looked to Sheik Mohammed. There was no sign of surrender in the Prince's dark eyes, so Warden powered back with $4 million.

The hundreds of people crammed into the rows of pavilion seats rose as one and began applauding and cheering. Another record price. But it wasn't over. Even before the noise of the crowd had totally subsided, Cooper shot back with $4,250,000. An almost imperceptible nod of Sheik Mohammed's head signaled to

Warden that this match was now over. Sheik Mohammed would allow the Irishmen to take the colt to Tipperary, yet once again he had ensured that they would pay dearly.

This million-dollar baby son of Nijinsky and Spearfish was joined on the flight to Ireland by eleven other Thoroughbred yearlings. The horses had cost the Irish syndicate over $14 million. Sheik Mohammed had spent close to that amount on nineteen yearlings. Between his purchases and those of his brothers the tab was about $20 million.

The Keeneland sales spectacle was fast gaining momentum. This year a total of eighteen year old Thoroughbreds sold for more than $1 million each. Kentucky horse breeders were reveling in the bonanza. The average price for a yearling had soared to $337,734, up thirty per cent over the previous year. Never in their wildest imaginations could they have dreamt of such wealth. Some of the horse breeders began acting like sultans — buying expensive cars, hiring limousines and chauffeurs and spending lavishly entertaining themselves and friends. The market for their young horses would tumble. They would lose their homes, their farms, their horses, but for the moment the hunt to find the next Nijinsky and fetch potential baby stallions to Ireland had a few more furlongs to run.

June 1983. There were but mere weeks prior to the annual Keeneland July sale. While mares and foals lazily grazed in Kentucky's bluegrass paddocks, the finishing touches were being applied to the Thoroughbred yearlings. These potential million-dollar babies were having their young hides groomed over and over until they glistened in the warm sunshine. They were being taught to walk, turn and pose properly — like aspiring fashion models prior to their first big show. The owners of the yearlings eagerly awaited the next influx of millions the foreigners would spend on their horses.

Thousands of miles away, their two biggest buyers were about to clash, this time at a racecourse. The event was the Irish Derby. O'Brien had his hopes pinned on Caerleon, the compact son of Nijinsky that they had bought at the 1981 Keeneland sale for $800,000. At two Caerleon had won his two starts handily and at three he triumphed the French 2000 Guineas over L'Emigrant, a son of The Minstrel who had won the French Derby.

O'Brien presumed that Caerleon would face his toughest competition from Teenoso, reigning English Derby winner. The somewhat unknown factor in Ireland's big horse race was Shareef Dancer, the Northen Dancer colt Sheik Mohammed bought at the 1981 Keeneland sale for $3.3 million.

Sheik Mohammed had named the colt for the descendants of the Prophet Muhammad — the Hasemite Shareefs who ruled Mecca for centuries. He then presented Shareef Dancer as a gift to his eldest brother, Sheik Maktoum al-Maktoum. Shareef Dancer had won the King Edward VII stakes at Ascot. In May, Wassl, a colt Sheik Mohammed had given to his youngest brother had won the Irish 2000 Guineas. Now it appeared that their adversary in the sales ring was, once again, challenging the Irishmen — this time on their own turf.

No doubt there must have been a collective moan of discouragement rise up from O'Brien, his son-in-law, and the rest when Shareef Dancer blasted to victory three lengths ahead of second-place Caerleon. Teenoso finished third, two lengths back of Caerleon. The triumph of Shareef Dancer, and thus his owners, found Sangster contemplating the forthcoming annual Keeneland foray.

"I suppose this will have inspired the Arabs to take us on even more bloody belligerently," brooded Sangster in the Turf Club after the race .

In anticipation of the 1983 edition of the yearling sale, and no doubt intoxicated by thoughts of all the money the Europeans were going to spend, the atmosphere at Keeneland and environs was taking on the dimensions of a Disney theme park for adults.

The motif of Kentucky horse-breeder, Tom Gentry's, annual pre-sale party was, appropriately, *Carnival.* Guests were serenaded by Sergio Mendes. They were offered rides on the back of a large and ancient elephant named Myrtle. Gentry had even rented a camel from a circus in Atlanta, Georgia, which he tethered nearby Sheik Mohammed's table at dinner.

Throughout the weekend before the sale Lexington radio stations implored their listeners *not* to go to the sales. They, of course, came in droves. It was like a modern day re-enactment of Ben Hur with all the citizens rushing to the Coliseum and the Kentuckians were there to witness the spectacle. Beyond all the beautiful horses, the show now featured a star-studded cast that included Arab princes, Greek shipping magnates, US heiresses, a troop of Irish horse traders and at least one wealthy British gambler. Nothing at the cinema could top the entertainment.

The spectators didn't have long to wait. The moment the colt brandishing hip number 27 was led into the ring the game was afoot. The colt was a son of Nijinsky and Sheik Mohammed won this early round with a final bid of $4.1 million. At the conclusion of the first session eleven yearlings had been sold for $1 million or more. The big buyers were, as expected, Sheik Mohammed and the Irish. Possibly spurred on by the presence of Sheik Mohammed, Sangster was now taking a more and more prominent profile at the sales. And he was becoming more aggressive.

The star of the 1983 summer sale, the youngster many presumed would sell for the top price, was a son of Northern Dancer. A short-coupled bay with white socks and a white blaze, he was reminiscent of Northern Dancer, who, by this point, was well on his way to being declared Thoroughbred sire of the century. The life expectancy of Thoroughbred stallions is twenty-two years — Northern Dancer was twenty-one years old. How many more opportunities would there be to purchase one of his frequently outstanding offspring?

Furthermore, the colt's mother, My Bupers, was dam of eight foals, seven of which were winners, including the 1976 champion sprinter, My Juliet. Everyone was talking about this good-looking colt. He wore hip number 308 which meant he was nearly at the end of the sale. Based on his stellar pedigree people were predicting buyers might go for as much as $5 million, maybe even $6 million.

This auction was, however, no longer about horses. Instead it had become a test of egos and bank balances. The yearlings lineage, it's conformation, were incidental. It was a game — one that bore absolutely no relation to reality — no relation to the sport of Thoroughbred racing. The first thing the players did was hide from one another — or at least find places in the complex where they thought one group could not see what the other was doing.

Shortly before 11:00 p.m. Sheik Mohammed made the first move. He slowly rose from his seat in the amphitheatre and headed toward the entrance to the holding area behind the auctioneer's stand. Members of his entourage solemnly followed. At the back of the pavilion the forces from the opposing team began to gather. In order to combat Sheik Mohammed's vast resources, this group had grown in numbers and international in scope. There was O'Brien and Magnier and the rest of the Irishmen. The Englishman, Sangster. Danny Schwartz from the US. Off to one side stood Greek shipping magnate, Stavros Niarchos, who had agreed to lend his support to the Irish mission. Niarchos brought his own bloodstock advisors, Joss Collins of the British Bloodstock Agency in England and Sir Philip Payne-Gallwey. Collins would do the bidding.

It was hot and muggy. It was late into the evening. But the

huge crowd remained crammed into the building. This is what they had come to see. The showdown.

Finally the son of Northern Dancer and My Bupers was led into the ring and the announcer spoke very briefly about the colt's lineage and then stepped aside.

"All right, *let's go!*" sang auctioneer Scott Caldwell, "Who'll give me a million?"

"*Yip!*" shouted a bid-spotter, raising his right arm skyward.

Dick Warden, Sheik Mohammed's man jumped into the game at $4 million and upped the ante to $4.5 million. A new record! The crowd cheered with the fervor of baseball fans witnessing a home run. When the bidding went to $5 million, they cheered again. *Another home run!*

Joss Collins now joined the game with a bid of $5.3 million. Sangster had thought the stakes would be between $5 and $6 million. His plan was to enter the game late, bid high, and win. He had tried that strategy before with Sheik Mohammed and it hadn't worked. Once again he not only underestimated his opponent, he didn't consider that he might be challenged from elsewhere. Backed by a group of his owners US trainer Wayne Lucas had been in the early running, only to fade out around $4 million, but a syndicate that included John T Jones Jr, owner of the Kentucky farm, Walmac International, was still in the game.

The bids continued quickly in $100,000 increments. When the ante sailed past $6 million the crowd ceased cheering. Instead they watched in disbelief as Jones and company went to $7 million. Then as Collins raised the bid by $150,000 Jones pulled out of the game and joined the rest of the crowd on the side-lines. This left Sheik Mohammed vs the Irish brigade.

At $7.5 million Collins huddled with Sangster and the rest. Tension had set in, but Sangster appeared determined to win. Nerves were beginning to fray. There was no possible way they could compete with the Arab oil money. They knew they weren't going to win. One-by-one members of the team were ready to concede. Everyone but Sangster.

"It was not that Robert (Sangster) wouldn't stop," wrote Patrick Robinson in *Horsetrader,* "He couldn't. Something had taken hold of him. His face was set tight. He believed that Vincent O'Brien had invented Northern Dancer, that it was Nijinsky and The Minstrel who had made his reputation. And Storm Bird added to it. This little horse in the ring belonged in County Tipperary and he, Robert, was damned if he was going anywhere else. 'Go to nine,' he told Joss. 'And if that won't do it, go to ten.'"

The crowd let out a great cheer when the bidding hit $9 million. *Another home-run!*

The Irish troop were trying to pull Sangster out of the fight, but he wouldn't quit. It was if he had become obsessed. At $9.6 million he took over the bidding from Joss Collins. Glaring down at the bid-spotter and he raised his two open hands to signify a bid of $10 million. He had raised Sheik Mohammed's bid by $400,000. To add to the drama, at that very instance the lights on the scoreboard went out. The price had literally "gone off the board." The seven-digit electronic board could not accommodate an eight-digit bid and there was a slight delay while they rolled the board back to zero.

The crowd rose to their feet and cheered and applauded Sangster. Many thought he had won. He thought he had won. His glory was brief. Once the board had been reconfigured and the crowd settled down Warden came back with $10.2 million. Sangster had been defeated. Keeneland no longer belonged to him and his Irish associates. No longer could they simply ride into town and take what they wanted.

The average price paid for a yearling had vaulted to over half-a-million dollars. Nine years earlier, when they launched their first assault on Keeneland, the average price for a yearling was a little over $50,000. At the 1983 Keeneland July sale a total of twenty-four yearlings were sold for a million or more under the auctioneer's hammer.

Meanwhile back in Ireland. In the fall of 1983 O'Brien started a colt that would provide the Irish mission with more money than they could spend. He was not, however, one of their million-dollar yearlings. He was, instead, a fluke.

His mother was the little filly the farm manager at Claiborne had confided to Billy MacDonald was always first to the gate. She was the filly none of them were inclined to even look at, much less purchase. They were only interested in colts. Yet presumably to placate MacDonald they bought the filly at the 1976 Keeneland sale for $40,000.

Perhaps had they not been so focused on buying colts and looking for immediate return on investment they would have discovered that the world's leading breeders of Thoroughbreds focused all their efforts on amassing mares — the very best mares their money could buy. Which is, of course, where all their outstanding horses came from.

The little filly was named Fairy Bridge. She too was born of a stellar line of broodmares. Her great-grandmother, Rough Shod II, was a cornerstone of Claiborne's ongoing success. Her most prominent offspring, both on and off the track, was champion filly Moccasin. Another daughter was Thong. While not an inspired racehorse she was dam of Thatch, an O'Brien-trained champion and of a filly named Special. The filly only raced one time, but Special is distinguished as the dam of Nureyev, one of the leading Northern Dancer sons.

At two Fairy Bridge won a couple of insignificant sprint races at Phoenix Park, one by a head, the other by 5 lengths. Curiously Fairy Bridge was considered the fastest two year old filly cantering around Irish tracks that year and then seemed to disappear from the radar. *Timeform* reported that Fairy Bridge: " ... clearly had training troubles and was retired to stud at the end of her two year old days."

In 1980 Fairy Bridge ended up in North America where she was bred to Northern Dancer. Eleven months later she gave birth to a bay colt with a white blaze that began with a great white patch beneath his forelock and tumbled down his face like a paint spill as it ran out and across his nostrils. The colt was not sent to auction. Instead, when he was a yearling he hitched a ride to Ireland with the batch of young horses O'Brien and company had harvested from the 1982 Keeneland sale.

While so many of the Northern Dancer offspring were named for famous dancers, this one was named Sadler's Wells for the famed London dance theatre. The colt made his racing debut in September 1983 at Leopardstown. He was sent out up against fifteen other two year olds and he won by six lengths. Three weeks later he was shipped to The Curragh. This time there were only four horses. Again he won by six.

In the meantime, his stable-mate, El Gran Senor, was making a name for himself. Also a son of Northern Dancer, El Gran Senor appeared to run a bit green and all over the place in his first races. He won every event but it wasn't until the Dewhurst that El Gran Senor finally found his running legs. It was the first time the bay colt had faced serious competition and he showed he had the heart for the game.

In April 1984 O'Brien sent Sadler's Wells and El Gran Senor to The Curragh for the Gladness Stakes. El Gran Senor won by two lengths. From there on O'Brien sent the two colts on divergent flight plans.

"Sadler's Wells is a good horse," explained O'Brien, "but El Gran Senor is exceptional." According to *Timeform*: "His trainer's much publicized view that El Gran Senor might turn out to be the best horse he had handled heightened anticipation of El

Gran Senor's appearance at Epsom, as did a report that a staggering eighty million dollars had been offered for him by a group of American breeders — subject to his winning the Derby."

And so it was that El Gran Senor headed toward the English Derby; Sadler's Wells on a less demanding schedule. El Gran Senor was electrifying in the Two Thousand Guineas. The performance inspired his trainer to announce: "I believe his Guinea's performance to be on a level with Nijinsky's and Sir Ivor's."

June 1984. The English Derby at Epsom. Not one, but two Northern Dancer colts — El Gran Senor and Secreto — were flying up the stretch, matching each other stride for stride, will for will. Their heads bobbing on every other beat, they were soaring toward the finish in such perfect harmony that they appeared to be one horse. Neither would concede. And when they flew past the world's most famous finish post these two extraordinary animals, were indeed, one.

After contemplating the photo of the finish, the racing stewards eventually declared Secreto the winner — Secreto's muzzle showed to be jutted out fractionally higher than El Gran Senor's.

Although Secreto's name was inscribed in the ledger as the winner of the 1984 Derby, both horses had won. Traditionally the Derby winner's owner, trainer and entourage are invited to the Royal Box. This year the Queen Mother extended her invitation to everyone involved with both horses. It surely was a family affair. Not only were El Gran Senor and Secreto sons of Northern Dancer, they both had been bred and born at Windfields Farm. El Gran Senor was trained by Vincent O'Brien and Secreto was trained by O'Brien's twenty-seven year old son, David.

El Gran Senor went on to win the Irish Derby and didn't race again. Apparently he was suffering from a mysterious foot problem and after treatment in Ireland proved futile he was sold to back to Windfields Farm. Not for the once-touted $80 million, but for about half that amount.

As a racehorse, it seems that less was expected of Sadler's Wells. When El Gran Senor was flown to England in May for the Two Thousand Guineas, Salder's Wells and stable mate Capture Him were vanned down the road to The Curragh for the much less demanding Irish Two Thousand Guineas. Ballydoyle's retained jockey, Pat Edderly, had first choice of the two and opted to ride Capture Him. The stable jockey was left with Sadler's Wells.

"Strongly pressed by the French-trained Procida throughout the last two furlongs, Sadler's Wells — displaying an unusually high head carriage as in all his races — kept on very bravely to win a battle royal by a neck." *Timeform*

Capture Him was sweating noticeably prior to the race and finished fourth. He was said to have suffered sore shins and was pulled off racing for four months and was next seen in the Hollywood Derby (California) in November.

Sadler's Wells, however, was kept marching to the tune of Coolmore stallion syndication parade. In June Sadler's Wells was dispatched to France for the Prix du Jockey-Club (French Derby). The colt ran gallantly in the mile and a half French Classic, but was unable to match the closing speed of Darshaan. Sadler's Wells was second, a length and a half behind Darshaan.

Since Sadler's Wells had won both the Irish Derby Trials and Irish Guineas, the next logical stop would be the Irish Derby, but instead they had rerouted El Gran Senor to that one. Perhaps they still had their sights on the $80 million syndication.

What does seemed apparent is that they continued ensure the paths of El Gran Senor and Sadler's Wells would not converge. So while El Gran Senor raced over the Irish turf, Sadler's Wells was sent to England for the Group One Coral Eclipse at Sandown.

Pat Edderly knew what he had to do. He had been here many times before on a Coolmore stallion prospect. Coming down to the wire, the grand champion mare, Time Charter, was flying, narrowing Sadler's Wells modest lead with each flowing stride.

Edderly went to the whip and managed to pound Sadler's Wells across the wire, a scant neck to the good.

El Gran Senor was now benched with his foot ailment so Sadler's Wells was designated to represent the Irish syndicate in the major summer and fall races. The colt's next race was the King George VI and Queen Elizabeth Diamond Stakes at twelve furlongs over Ascot's royal turf. Sadler's Wells finished a respectable second, two and a half lengths behind Teenoso. It was a powerful field of horses: "... one of the most strongly-contested and strongly-run all season."

With only three weeks to recover from that very tiring exertion, Sadler's Wells was entered in the Benson and Hedges Gold Cup at York. This time he was fourth, five lengths behind the winner. The *Timeform* reporter then suggested: "We shouldn't have been surprised if Sadler's Wells's performance in the Benson and Hedges had signaled the end of his racing career."

The prediction was totally off the mark. Instead of retiring Sadler's Wells, his handlers went in quite the opposite direction. They decided to run him in the Prix de l'Arc de Triomphe in October. It was a curious decision. At twelve furlongs over Chantilly's sweeping turf, Europe's most demanding and prestigious race is for exceptional horses.

The expression *horses for courses* suggests that horses, like their human custodians, have their strengths and weaknesses. Some horses are disposed, both physically and mentally, to running distances. Others are sprinters. Some are exceptional. Most are not. Hence the challenge when dealing with horses is to discover what is best for them and where they will excel. Conventional wisdom dictates that a horse should be entered in an event that it has a chance of winning, or at the least, being competitive. Thoroughbreds run on heart and lungs. It is critical not to break its spirit.

En route to France Sadler's Wells was back in Ireland at The Curragh for the Champion Stakes. "He wasn't an impressive winner, but he did what was needed, running on strongly and holding on courageously near the finish." He won, but as in all his other victories that year, not by much. This time, three quarters of a length.

There could be little doubt that Sadler's Wells was a courageous horse. What he lacked in physical scope, he more than compensated in sheer grit. Still all the while, in every one of his races he ran with an usually high head carriage. His grandsire, Nearctic, carried his head very high, but he galloped skyward up off his hocks. Sadler's Wells raced with his white muzzle jutting out and gave the appearance that either he was fighting his rider, or simply troubled by something.

In October Sadler's Wells was among the twenty-two starters in the Prix de l'Arc de Triomphe. As was his wont, Sadler's Wells galloped along with the leaders for the first mile, but when the pack swept into the home stretch, try as he might, he was left behind. According to *Timeform*: "... he showed he was well past his best for the season, fading disappointingly into eighth."

When Sadler's Wells returned to Ireland he was moved to Coolmore. He stood his first season in 1985 for £125,000 (Ire) a sizeable fee for an unproven stallion. Five years later Sadler's Wells was declared champion sire, a designation he would be awarded eleven times between then and 2001.

The fee for stud services to Sadler's Wells was raised to £200,000 a session and then later listed as private. It has been reported that Sadler's Wells was bred to approximately 200 mares in a season. He was also one of the few stallions that stayed in Ireland and was not shipped off with the rest to Australia or Japan or South America to breed mares in the Southern Hemisphere. Still, it is entirely conceivable that during the 20 years between the time Sadler's Wells was led into his box stall at Coolmore and 2005, this one horse enriched Coolmore in the neighbourhood of £500,000,000. (Tax exempt) A wholesome return on investment considering the mere $40,000 paid for Fairy

Bridge and Northern Dancer's stud fee of $100,000 in 1980.

The 1984 Keeneland sale was basically more of the same antics. Parties were taking place all about the Lexington area. This year, instead of rides on Myrtle the elephant, Tom Gentry was offering his guests hot air balloon rides. Which seemed appropriate

For onlookers the annual horse safari was high entertainment and the local Kentuckians continued to flock to the scene of all the excitement. They watched in astonishment as the Irish went to $8.25 million for a Windfields-bred son of Northern Dancer and Ballade. They were mesmerized as the auctioneer continued to prod the combatants to up the ante on another Northern Dancer colt. This time Sheik Mohammed was victorious. The winning bid was $7.1 million. Then he went to $6.5 million for a Seattle Slew colt.

The next three most expensive million-dollar babies were all Northern Dancer progeny. The Irish snared the son of Truly Bound for $5.4 million, but lost out to Sheik Mohammed in the duel for the Queen Sucree colt at $5.1 million. Sangster and Niarchos joined forces to win the son of Mississippi Mud for $4.6 million.

The twelve Northern Dancer yearlings at the sale brought $41 million — an average of $3,446,667 each. The over-all yearling average had risen to $601,467. Sheik Mohammed and his brothers spent $46 million. The Irish and company spent $36 million.

The disparity between Thoroughbred racing and Thoroughbred breeding had never been greater. The jockeys and the trainers and the lads and the grooms and the hot walkers — the people who were generally up before dawn, in all weather, caring for, and working with the race horses — were earning but a pittance compared to what the *Sultans of Kentucky*, the horse breeders, were gleaning. Not only was the whole scenario totally out of kilter, it was reckless.

While many of the Kentucky Thoroughbred breeders were rolling around in their new-found fortunes like intoxicated cats bouncing about in a field of catnip — saner minds knew things were getting precarious. In order to help shore up some of the inequities, Kentucky stalwart, John Gaines, owner of Gainesway Farms, spearheaded the group that created the Breeders' Cup day of championship races. The purses to range from $1 million to $3 million.

Gaines brought Eddie and Winnie Taylor's son, Charles, into the operation and he in turn was instrumental in raising the purse money by imposing a 'tax' on stallions. Each farm was asked to annually contribute the cost of one nomination to each of their sires. Windfields, with twenty of the top stallions, which included Northern Dancer and The Minstrel, was the first to sign up to the program. The other farms couldn't refuse. If they did their stallion's offspring would not be eligible to compete in the Breeders' Cup races. This in turn would have a negative impact on the prices breeders would receive for their yearlings. In the fall of 1984 the inaugural Breeders' Cup race day was held at California's Hollywood Park.

The wrap-around cover of the 1985 Keeneland July Yearling Sales catalogue was a copy of a painting of Epsom Downs. In the background — the colourful fairground. In the foreground — El Gran Senor and Secreto, in neck-and-neck battle to the finish in the 1984 English Derby. It portrayed Thoroughbred racing at one of its finest hours — the drama, excitement, glamour, and the glory.

The painting on the cover, no doubt, was designed to seduce

potential buyers into dreaming that, they too, with a bit of luck and a Keeneland yearling, might one day find themselves a part of this portrait. And on top of that, with a bit more luck, your Keeneland yearling will not only shower you with great glory when it wins the English Derby, it will become a great stallion and you will reap millions. At least that was the theory.

There can be little doubt that El Gran Senor and Secreto gave their owners, and everyone else who watched the 1984 English Derby, one of the most memorable and exciting races in the long history of the event. At the end of the racing season both horses were retired to stud. Like everything else in the Thoroughbred business at the time, they were both hugely over-valued.

Secreto went to stand at Calumet Farm, almost next door to Keeneland. He had been syndicated (at least on paper) for $40 million. El Gran Senor went to Windfields and was syndicated for $1 million a share. That spring he had been bred to over fifty mares at $200,000 each — live foal guaranteed. Only a fraction of the mares were shown to be in foal. El Gran Senor proved to be sub-fertile and Secreto did not prove to be a top sire.

Thus the cover of the 1985 seemed curiously symbolic. On one hand it heralded that buying a Keeneland yearling could put you in the English Derby winner's circle as Secreto did for Luigi Miglietti. From Caracas, Venezuela, Miglietti purchased Secreto at the 1982 Keeneland sale for $340,000. Yet, having an English Derby winner in your barn did not guarantee that the horse would emerge as a great stallion.

The era of million-dollar Thoroughbred yearlings and outrageously inflated prices which would come to be known as the "Bluegrass Bubble" burst in 1986. The average price of yearlings sold at Keeneland plunged 24 percent over the previous year.

In any market this would be a serious downturn. For commercial Thoroughbred breeders it was devastating. Thoroughbred yearlings of 1986 had been conceived in the spring of 1984, which meant that their owners paid stud fees at the peak of the boom. During the 1980s breeders expected to sell their yearlings for 2.5 times the stud fee. Now, in 1986, they could throw that formula out the window. A breeder may have paid a stud fee of $200,000, spent at least another $40,000 to raise the youngster and get it to the sale — only to discover that in this crashing market, people were only prepared to pay $60,000 for the yearling. If that.

A further complication was, that for the most part, breeders were expected to pay for the services of the stallion up front. Generally the fee is payable upon the birth of a live foal. Other times payment is accepted in installments.

Now breeders were facing the inevitable. Prices were more than likely to continue to spiral downward, creating a domino effect. Stallion fees would start to fall, thus devaluing their horses and their entire operations even further. It would only be a matter of time before the banks clued into the fact that the worth of the horses that had been used for collateral was starting to slide at the rate of bobsleds at the winter Olympics.

Another aspect of the crisis was overproduction. Up until the band of Irish horse traders set out to find the next Nijinsky and subsequently unleashed this, the original Celtic Tiger, Thoroughbred breeding was not considered big business. Many farms like Windfields, Calumet, Walmac, The Meadow, were built and funded by money earned elsewhere. Their owners, wealthy and successful business people in ventures that had nothing to do with horses, only hoped that their farms would break even. The farms and the horses were their hobby — albeit an expense hobby, but a hobby nonetheless.

Commercial breeders had a similar mandate — they hoped that their farms would pay for themselves. Staff, expenses, veterinary bills, feed, equipment, fences constantly in need of repair. The overhead is enormous. Prior to Sangster's commercialization philosophy, it was unlikely that anyone in North America went into Thoroughbred breeding to get rich.

In the 1980s few commercial breeders could resist the lure of the huge amounts of money being offered for their yearlings. The demand seemed infinite so they began to produce more and more yearlings. The result, of course, was overproduction.

In 1973 there were 26,810 Thoroughbred foals registered with the US Jockey Club (including foals born in Canada). In 1980 there were 35,613. In 1986 the figure had jumped to 51,293. So, in this era of rampant inflation, the number of Thoroughbred foals had practically doubled.

Nonetheless the scent of money, big money, attracted a lot of new people to the world of the Thoroughbred. Passion for horses had been supplanted with lust for money. Even those who had been breeding Thoroughbreds for decades, those who, theoretically, knew better, tumbled into the greed trap. Or perhaps they had forgotten that breeding Thoroughbred champions is a long-term investment — not only in terms of money, but of careful planning, intuition, commitment and luck. It is not a game for speculators.

Still, suddenly it seemed as if almost everyone was thinking short-term. Patience, the operative ingredient in the breeding of Thoroughbreds had been replaced by panic. And then there were the bank loans. Some of the farms had borrowed money using their stallions as collateral. Now that the value of the stallions was crashing along with the yearling market, the banks were starting to get nervous. To make matters worse, some of the banks had been lending against stallion shares. Tom Gentry owed the Citizens Fidelity Bank and Trust of Lexington over $14 million. Money that he did not have.

Others had mortgaged their farms. While the boom was on, real estate prices soared along with everything else. Now FOR

SALE signs began popping up on the fenceposts of in the Lexington area. By the end of the decade there were over eighty horse farms on the market in Kentucky's Bluegrass area.

In the fall of 1986, came the news of an auction of a different sort, but one that would send a cold shiver through many of the Kentucky Thoroughbred breeding establishments. John Ryan Gaines, master of the magnificent Gainesway Farm on Paris Pike, was selling his treasured art collection. And he wasn't just selling off two or three of his collection of Old Masters drawings to raise enough money to get him through a minor cash flow problem caused by the crashing Thoroughbred market — he was selling the entire collection.

It didn't seem possible. Gainesway was one of the most solid and sound Thoroughbred operations in Kentucky. Gaines was a pillar of the Thoroughbred community. His farm was home to one of the finest herd of stallions in the world. The list included Lyphard with forty stakes winners from only six crops; Prix de l'Arc de Triomphe champion, Vaguely Noble; the amazing Exceller; French miler Riverman, sire of the brilliant racemares Triptych, Detroit and Gold River. There was Blushing Groom and Sharpen Up and Icecapade and Bates Motel and Green Dancer and Czaravitch, Nijinsky's first son to make a hit in North America. Forty stallions in total. Forty stallions whose stud fees were being devalued.

The Gaines art collection included drawings by Rembrandt, Cézanne, Edouard Manet, Picasso, Vincent Van Gogh, Claude Monet, Turner, Raphael, and Edgar Degas. Three sketches by Leonardo da Vinci, drawn on a small, five-by-eight inch paper, dated from around 1500 and entitled *Child with a lamb* sold for a record $3.6 million to a London art dealer on behalf of the J. Paul Getty Museum in California. A Henri Matisse drawing called *Dance* brought $935,000. The sketch *Little Jump* by Edgar Degas sold for $1,100,000 and went to Tokyo. When the numbers were added up at the end of the sale, the international art dealers in attendance at Sothebys had spent $21,280,000 for John Gaines prized collection. Fourteen months later Gaines sold his beloved farm, apparently for a lot less than his Old Masters drawings.

Also, in the fall of 1986, at about the time of the auction of Gaines art collection, Spendthrift, the only farm to stand more stallions than Gainesway Farm, was about to go under. Shares in Spendthrift Farm, listed on the New York Stock Exchange in November 1983, had collapsed — nose-dived from $12 a share to $2 a share.

Over the years, Leslie Combs developed Spendthrift's stallion roster into one of the finest on the continent. Inspired by the mania gripping the yearling sales created by the Irish invasion in the early 1980s, Combs and son Brownwell formulated a grand plan to turn Spendthrift into the largest and most profitable commercial Thoroughbred breeding operation the world had ever seen. To that end they decided to turn the farm into a public corporation and used their stallions, mares, foals, yearlings, real estate, as collateral.

At the time these assets included the farm on Ironworks Pike outside Lexington and a training centre in Florida — a total of about 2000 acres. There were forty-three stallions (most of which were owned by syndicates), one hundred and seventy-five broodmares, one hundred and thirty-eight foals, and approximately eighty horses in training at various destinations around the globe. There were also seventy-five yearlings being prepared for the summer yearling sales.

Brownwell Combs awarded himself a salary of $500,000 a year. He leased private aircraft and limousines, entertained his friends lavishly, and insured Spendthrift quite heavily with an insurance company that he partially owned.

In 1985 the average price at Keeneland slid seventeen percent. The slide was actually worse, but was buoyed by the $13.1 million paid by the Irish for the son of Nijinsky and My Charmer. Of all the consigners at Keeneland that summer Spendthrift was probably the hardest hit. Now a publically traded company, Spendthrift grossed less than $2.5 million for six yearlings. This decline in income of over fifty-four percent would not look good on the annual report to shareholders. Yet that wasn't the worst of it. In fact, the revenue from the yearling sale wouldn't even cover the interest payments on the money the younger Combs had been borrowing.

In 1984 Spendthrift paid $3.4 million in interest and still had outstanding debt of $18 million. Combs continued borrowing in 1985 and now the annual interest had risen to $6.3 million. He then negotiated a $28 million line of credit. His Visa bill was reported to be in excess of $90,000 by the end of 1985.

In November 1986 the farm's colossal debt of over $50 million became public knowledge and shares in Spendthrift sank. The original private investors who each had $1 million tied up in Spendthrift were enraged. There ensued lawsuits, court cases, accusations of fraudulent behaviour and alleged securities violations.

The syndicate that controlled Seattle Slew had already moved him out of Spendthrift and down the road to Three Chimneys Farm. Affirmed's owners, Mr. and Mrs. Louis Wolfson, decided that their horse had also better be re-located to another farm before the banks started holding the stallions as collateral against Brownwell Combs' gargantuan debt. Brownwell was fired. But it was too late. Nothing could save Spendthrift.

By mid-April 1987 Northern Dancer had covered twenty-four mares. Only four were shown to be impregnated. Two of the mares would produce foals. Alas, the time had come to retire Northern Dancer from his stallion duties. Still his run had proven quite remarkable, especially considering that in the world of the

Thoroughbred, age twenty is considered old. But then it would appear that the feisty Canadian stallion was born to breed and to pass on his tenacity and his bold heart to generations to come. On 14 April 1987, six weeks shy of his 27th birthday, Northern Dancer was pensioned off. Thoroughbred horse breeding does not subscribe to artificial insemination. There would be no more Northern Dancer babies. Thus that part of the game, the pursuit of Northern Dancer's progeny, was over.

And so were the parties — in more ways than one. Tom Gentry, famed for his lavish pre-sale parties with exotic themes and famous celebrities and the occasional elephant or camel — was bankrupt. In the five previous years Gentry's yearlings had fetched him $35 million, yet Gentry was not only broke, he was indebted to Citizens Fidelity Bank for $14.4 million. The bank eventually seized his assets — the horses.

It seemed somewhat ironic that the Keeneland pavilion, setting for all the excitement over the past decade, would now play host to the sorry aftermath. On the morning of 9 January 1988, the entire bloodstock holdings of Nelson Bunker Hunt went under the auctioneers gavel. The Texas oil billionaire had boasted the largest collection of Thoroughbred horses in the world. All five hundred and eighty horses located at his Bluegrass Farms outside Lexington, including the outstanding international champion mare, Dahlia, were auctioned off.

Several years later Keeneland sales ring was the scene of yet another tragic image: "On a late October morning (1991), 126 Thoroughbred horses, their coats glistening in the sunlight, were led single file across Calumet's rolling fields." wrote Anne Hagedorn Auerbach in *Wild Ride: The rise and tragic fall of Calumet Farm, Inc., America's Premier racing dynasty.* "Through openings in the white fences and along winding back roads, the funeral-like process slowly walked a three-and-a-half-mile path to the barns behind Keeneland."

The reason that the mares and foals were being walked through fields and back roads to Keeneland is that the once mighty Calumet Farm — home to Citation and Alydar and Bull Lea and so many great legends of the sport — was now bankrupt. The cost of transporting the horses in vans the short distance between Calumet and Keeneland was $40 per horse. The farm could not afford it.

The image of these noble mares and their unsuspecting babies being led, and in this way, to be auctioned at Keeneland symbolizes the tragedy and ignominy resulting from the decade of avarice. While disastrous for nearly all involved — horses and humans alike — it surely worked in the favour of the Irish for they had effectively, if not inadvertently, wiped out the competition. In the near future the Irish would fairly rule the world of the Thoroughbred.

Meanwhile back in Ireland. 1987 also reflected stark contrasts on the Irish horizon. The year marked the beginning of the third Haughey government and things were looking grim. Fifteen years after joining the European Union Ireland was facing double-digit unemployment, mass emigration and public debt of over 120% of the GDP. Yet aspects of Irish economy were in fine mettle. The previous year the Irish horse traders paid $13.1 million for a yearling son of Nijinsky at the Keeneland sale. This brought the total they had spent to date to about $200 million on approximately 200 of the world's most beautifully-bred Thoroughbred yearlings they harvested from the US sales.

They had, of course, not found the next Nijinsky. Nor had they filled Coolmore's stalls with the world's greatest stallions. Not yet. Coolmore's star performer, Sadler's Wells, stood his first year in 1985. In 1987 his first crop of foals were yearlings. Most would begin racing in 1988, but it wouldn't be until 1989, when that first crop were three year olds, that Sadler's Wells prominence as a sire would be determined. At the time no one knew that he would turn out to be a significant stallion.

Furthermore, some of their backers had taken their losses and ran. After contributing about $10 million to the operation, Californian Danny Schwartz decided to take his leave: "There was no properly thought-out agreed budgets ... When Robert went up over $13 million for that yearling, I was beginning to think seriously that the entire world might be going crazy. And that's a bad attitude for a gambler!"

Undaunted the Irish horse traders devised a new proposition. This one was a little closer to home and could involve friends and neighbours. With counsel from Irish financier Dermot Desmond they hatched a public company and called it Classic Thoroughbreds. At the time the population of the entire island was little more than five million. It seems unlikely there were many unaware that this band of Irish horse traders had set forth to America to find the next Nijinsky. The racing media reported on the plane-loads of horses being brought back to Ireland and they wrote about the colossal stallion syndications and the fine profits gleaned in the process. Now, with Classic Thoroughbreds, everyone in Ireland could get in on the horse game.

On 22 October 1987 amid much fanfare Classic Thoroughbreds was introduced on the Dublin Stock Exchange. Vincent O'Brien was installed as chairman. He would also continue to train the horses. O'Brien's equity in the enterprise was listed at £1million. Magnier and Sangster at £600,000 each, as was Michael Smurfit, who's pulp and paper empire stretched as far as Columbian rain forests. County Cork meat wholesaler, John Horgan, was said to have invested £250,000. Financial institutions lending support to the enterprise included Citibank, Shield Insurance, Allied Irish Investment Bank and Irish Life.

Television programs, publicity galore, and an innate love of horses and horse racing inspired a large crowd of Irish men and women to gallop to their stock brokers. Before the starting bell had rung 2,500 had ventured £750 each for a stake in an issue that was over-subscribed four times. Before the end of the year Classic Thoroughbreds had invested £7.6 million for 'interests' in thirty-eight yearlings (29 colts and 9 fillies).

In mid-1988 while the *Economist* was sounding the alarm that Ireland was scorching headlong into the great abyss of financial disaster, another stock issue was heralded. Despite the bleak economic forecast Classic Thoroughbreds raised an additional £5.7 million. The directors appointed Smurfit as chairman of the finances and as such he had allocated a budget of $4 million for O'Brien to spend at the Keeneland sale. The Irish were no longer traveling in a pack. O'Brien was on his own now, accompanied solely by his son, Charles, who was being groomed to assume responsibility for the running of Ballydoyle upon O'Brien's retirement.

The original group of horses owned by Classic Thoroughbreds were now two years old and, in theory, of an age to begin racing. Still the results were not exactly stellar. While 23 of the 38 young horses started in races over a number of Irish courses, there were but six winners. And there certainly was no Nijinsky among them.

The lone star of the show was Saratogan, a handsome son of El Gran Senor. At two Saratogan ran only twice. In his first race, a minor event at The Curragh, Saratogan got off to a slow start but managed to find his running legs and rolled across the finish a length behind the winner. Next he was dispatched to England for the Dewhurst Stakes at Newmarket. The race was won by Prince of Dance and Scenic in a dead heat. In their wake, and half a length back, was Saratogan carrying the Kelly green with a gold sash racing silks of Classic Thoroughbreds.

According to *Timeform*: "Had he (Saratogan) not been so short of racing experience he might well have given O'Brien his eighth victory in the Dewhurst instead of failing narrowly to wear down

Prince of Dance and Scenic ... His principal objective is reported to be the Two Thousand Guineas, for which he merits serious consideration, with a tilt at the Derby a possibility ..."

Over the winter months and in the pubs from Shannon to Dublin, Saratogan and *a tilt at the Derby* was surely a topic of conversation among Irish horse racing fans, especially those who were shareholders in Classic Thoroughbreds. In anticipation of Saratogan's sweep of the English Classics, common shares in Classic Thoroughbreds, originally listed at 30p rose to 41p.

Saratogan finished ninth in the English Two Thousand Guineas and crossed the finish line nine lengths behind the winner. O'Brien brought Saratogan home to Ireland and entered him in the less demanding Irish Two Thousand Guineas. He also fitted the colt with blinkers, hoping this would help Saratogan stay focused. Shareholders in Classic Thoroughbreds were surely chagrined as they witnessed Saratogan and their Kelly green and gold colours finish a dismal sixth.

"Saratogan's comprehensive defeat at Newmarket was the turning point in the company's fortunes. Optimism gave way to despondencey as results on the racecourse didn't pick up and by mid-summer Classic Thoroughbreds' share-price had settled near its previous low." *Timeform*

Indeed, none of their other horses seemed to be inspired racehorses. Classic Frame was sixth in the English Derby. Classic Secret, a $1.4 million purchase and full brother to 1984 Derby winner Secreto, won his only start at two, a maiden race at Leopardstown. The beautifully-bred colt, according to *Timeform* was "highly regarded. And is sure to go on to better things."

He didn't. There is no record of him racing at three.

Puissance, another Classic runner, was "held in high regard

(possibly a 2000 Guineas contender) and," prophesied *Timeform*, "is sure to go on to much better things." He too failed to live up to the prediction. Puissance had won a minor race at two. The following year the colt was meant to strut his stuff before the humans strutting their stuff at Ascot, but it was announced that Puissance was injured. He had suffered a fractured knee. Maritzadoon, purchased for $1.25 million, never even saw a racecourse.

At the annual meeting at the end of the year shareholders were advised that the company had sold seventeen of the horses. Saratogan was among that group. There was no momentous syndication deal as in the past. Instead Saratogan was banished to California.

According to *Timeform*, shareholders in Classic Thoroughbreds "will want to forget the 1989 Flat racing season as swiftly as the market value of their stock depreciated during the year. Based on the promise of Saratogan shares reached an all-time high of 41p, but by December they'd crumpled dramatically to11p on the stock market."

The pressure on O'Brien was colossal. In the early days it was challenge enough to have the horses in his care win races for their owners. Now there was the added stress of getting those million dollar yearlings to stay sound and perform and provide return on investment to the expectations of syndicate members. More recently there were all these shareholders — Irish men and women who had staked a bit of their savings on his ability to bring a horse up to a race.

And it wasn't working.

Yet no sooner had the promise heaped upon Saratogan faded, a new star galloped on to the scene and into the hearts and hopes of shareholders in Classic Thoroughbreds. It was a horse O'Brien should not have purchased for Classic Thoroughbreds. But he did. The horse *'spoke'* to him. So O'Brien ran the risk.

Since the crash of the US Thoroughbred yearling market, sales prices were tumbling rapidly and O'Brien reasoned he could purchase six or eight well-bred horses with his $4 million budget. "His views however changed dramatically when he went to visit a Nijinsky colt from the mare Crimson Saint." wrote Patrick Robinson in *Horsetrader*. "He was alone now, except for his son and assistant, Charles, but he needed no encouragement from anyone for this most striking individual. He had the look of Nijinsky about him, a big bold eye, and the short elegant head of his sire, right down to the white star on his forehead."

Was this the one? The next Nijinsky? Was this the horse O'Brien had been searching for over all these years? O'Brien thought the horse would sell for $2.5 million. Tops. When this grand-looking son of Nijinsky was led into the ring O'Brien knew he had to have him. He was not the only one in the arena with the same intent. The bidding was brisk. In a blink it had soared to $1.8 million. O'Brien caught the eye of the bid spotter. He offered $1.9 million. A group of Californians countered with $2 million. O'Brien answered with $2.1 million. Back and forth they went at $100,000 increments. In no time the bidding had hit the $2.5 million limit O'Brien had put on the colt.

The Californians were not backing off. O'Brien couldn't quit. They were now at $3 million. The auctioneer was looking for $3.1 million. This was no longer the wild west show of yesteryear with his brother and his troop cheering him on. This was no longer about his son-in-law's potential 'baby stallion' obsession. Nor was this was a contest between the Irish and the Arabs, or anyone else for that matter. It was no longer a game. No, O'Brien was charged with finding a racehorse. His sole obligation was to the investors in Classic Thoroughbreds. In his heart he believed this colt was the one. After all those years of combing the horse sales with his son-in-law and the rest O'Brien had stumbled upon a young horse that most evoked memories of the magnificent Nijinsky. Finally. He couldn't stop now.

O'Brien looked at the horse. He looked at the auctioneer. And nodded his head. $3.1 million. The Californians hit back with $3.2 million. O'Brien went to $3.3 million. The Californians immediately bid $3.4 million. O'Brien was well aware of his fiscal responsibility. He was, after-all, chair of a public company. The auctioneer cajoled him to try one last bid. Just one more point. Another hundred thousand.

O'Brien continued staring at the colt. The auctioneer was exclaiming: "I'll sell him now. I'll sell him for three point four million dollars." His hammer raised, about to slam down on the podium. In that moment the colt looked at O'Brien, flicked one ear back. O'Brien raised his catalogue.

"Yip!" whooped the bid spotter.

"Three and a half million!" replied the auctioneer. "Going once! Going twice! Sold to Mr. O'Brien!" The gavel cracked on the podium. Vincent and Charles O'Brien left the amphitheatre to make arrangements to bring the colt home to Ireland.

This grand-looking son of Nijinsky was given the name Royal Academy. In his first race, a maiden event at Phoenix Park, Royal Academy sashayed past the finish an astonishing 10 lengths ahead of his nearest rival. Irish eyes were smiling once again and on the stock exchange shares in Classic Thoroughbreds began to rally as anticipation grew that Royal Academy would become the seventh horse trained by O'Brien to win the Dewhurst Stakes at Newmarket. "The increasing confidence behind Royal Academy, boosted by impressive gallop reports, ensured that he started an even-money favourite at Newmarket," reported *Timeform*."

Royal Academy finished sixth in the Dewhurst, four lengths behind the winner. Once again the hopes and dreams of shareholders in Classic Thoroughbreds were dashed. O'Brien, however, was not ready to give up. Royal Academy looked every inch a racehorse, but a very young racehorse. He was tall and lean with legs that seemed to go on forever — like a teenage lad that had recently experienced a growth spurt. O'Brien believed that the colt had what it takes and suggested that Royal Academy was simply inexperienced and immature and that the colt would mature over the winter.

This was, of course, a reflection of O'Brien's ongoing dilemma. Horses, like their human custodians, mature at different times and according to varying tempos. When it comes to horses the challenge is further complicated by the fact that physically they are not even fully grown until they are five years old. Yet in flat racing the animals are expected to start blasting out of starting gates as two year olds and the most important races are written for three year olds. These are decisions borne, no doubt, of economics and owners looking for return on investment.

Michael Vincent O'Brien rules as the greatest horse trainer in history, but he was neither a magician nor alchemist. He possessed all the gifts to assist a horse to become the very best it could be, but he could not make a horse into something it wasn't. No matter how much the owners of the horses wanted him to.

The following spring it looked as if the Master of Ballydoyle was right. Over the winter Royal Academy seemed to have grown and filled out and was ready for his first start of 1990, the Tetrarch Stakes at The Curragh. Once again shareholders in Classic Thoroughbreds flocked to the ancient track and much to their delight Royal Academy won. Instead of shipping Royal Academy across the Irish Sea for the English Two Thousand Guineas, O'Brien opted to keep the horse in Ireland and entered him in the Irish Two Thousand Guineas. Yet it seems when O'Brien decided not to go to England, England came to him. The owners of Tirol, winner of the English Guineas, dispatched their horse to Ireland to challenge Royal Academy.

A furlong from home Royal Academy was in the lead and it looked as if he would, once again, be carrying the Classic Thoroughbreds Kelly green and gold racing silks to glory. Tirol, however, was not prepared to concede and moved up alongside Royal Academy. The two young warriors began matching each other stride-for-stride. Royal Academy was gallantly digging in and holding on to his slight lead but Tirol continued inching ahead. A nod of the head at the wire showed that Tirol had prevailed over Royal Academy by the narrowest of margins.

Royal Academy had shown that he surely had the heart for the game so O'Brien decided to enter him in the one mile St. James's Palace Stakes at Royal Ascot. Designated as a Group One, or top tier horse race, the conditions suited Royal Academy. While the colt may not have inherited his sire's extraordinary brilliance, it seems he did inherit one aspect of Nijinsky's disposition — the mercurial part. No matter what, Royal Academy refused to enter the starting stalls. The race went on without him.

Nonetheless O'Brien had not given up on the colt and this time decided to enter Royal Academy in another Group One event. This time he chose the July Cup. A slightly shorter race run over Newmarket's undulating and demanding terrain, the course is surely a test of stamina and sheer grit.

Not long out of the gate the horses face a steep three furlong climb before the course flattens out. At the bottom of the hill Royal Academy began his charge. At the crest he had taken command. With the others in fervent pursuit Royal Academy won the July Cup by almost a length over Great Commotion. It was a brilliant victory.

The Kelly green and gold racing silks of Classic Thoroughbreds were paraded in Newmarket's hallowed winners circle.

Their horse had won a Group One, top drawer race! It was certainly cause for celebration and that evening in pubs across the Irish countryside, a pint or two was raised to the grand and courageous Royal Academy.

O'Brien chose the Ladbrookes Sprint Cup (formerly Vernons) at Haydock Park as the next destination on Royal Academy's calendar. This time Royal Academy was up against Dayjur, considered one of the fastest European sprinters in history. The event unfolded as a two-horse race — Royal Academy and Dayjur. Royal Academy finished second, a length and a half behind Dayjur. The next horse was a distant five lengths back. At the end of the season Dayjur would be named 1990 champion sprinter and Horse of the Year.

For Royal Academy to vindicate his $3.5 million purchase price and boost value as a stallion, O'Brien calculated the horse needed one more race. A big race. The biggest one on the horizon was the million dollar Breeders' Cup Mile scheduled for late October at New York's Belmont Park.

It was a huge gamble. Still, the colt was steadily improving and if the gamble paid off it certainly would be worth the risk. Not long after O'Brien made up his mind, Royal Academy's regular rider took a spill and broke his collarbone. O'Brien was going to have to find a new jockey.

He also needed one more miracle.

27 October 1990. It is unlikely there was a television set in Ireland that was not tuned into the Breeders' Cup. A little after 8:30 p.m. the program showed the horses in the saddling enclosure at Belmont Park. There was Ireland's horse — Royal Academy, son of the great Nijinsky. Vincent O'Brien was not there. He was at

home at Ballydoyle sick with the flu. Representing Ireland's greatest horse trainer was his wife Jacqueline and their son Charles. Once Charles checked Royal Academy's girths in swanked Lester Piggott clad in the Kelly green and gold racing silks of Classic Thoroughbreds.

Piggott had been retired from race riding for five years. Several of those years were spent in jail for income tax evasion. Now that he was out he wanted to return to riding. Vincent O'Brien needed a rider he knew, one who had something to prove. And so it was that 54 year old Piggott came out of retirement to ride Royal Academy at the Breeders' Cup.

Charles O'Brien tossed Piggott up on to the colt's back and Royal Academy trotted toward the racetrack. The colt had drawn the number one post position, next to the rail. At the sound of the bell Royal Academy skipped out of the gate slowly and swerved to the right at about the moment the rest of the field were veering to the left. After avoiding a near collision Piggott moved Royal Academy to the back of the 13 horse field and there they cruised for the first half of the race. The other horses were running in a pack so when Piggott decided to make his move he had to steer Royal Academy out and around the wall of horses. Many watching the race were immediately reminded of Piggott's questionable ride of Nijinsky in the Prix de l'Arc de Triomphe. Once again surely he was asking too much of the horse.

Coming into the turn Royal Academy was about half a dozen lengths behind the leaders. The horses had now taken flight and it seemed impossible he could make up the ground.

"Down the stretch they come," hollered the track announcer. "Its Expensive Decision out front ... followed by Isallgreektome ... then a wall of horses ... Lester Piggott and Royal Academy are on the outside and launching their challenge ... that's Royal Academy down the centre of the track ... and he's flying."

At the three-sixteenth pole Piggott went to the whip and began pounding Royal Academy. And pounding. Where his sire,

Nijinsky, balked at the sting of Piggott's whip, Royal Academy kept trying.

At the wire Royal Academy prevailed by a long neck over Itsallgreektome. When the decision was declared official, the hooting and hollering and partying in the pubs from Tipperary to Cork to Dublin to Waterford could be heard across the Irish countryside. Royal Academy was the first Irish-owned horse to win a Breeders' Cup race. The most excited were, of course, shareholders in Classic Thoroughbreds. That their horse had won a million dollar race no doubt meant that he would be syndicated as a stallion for many more millions. Others suggested that because Royal Academy was getting better and better with every race he should continue racing at four and maybe even five. However this worked out, the future looked very bright indeed.

The euphoria was, however, brief. Apparently shareholders in Classic Thoroughbreds only held a 40% minority interest in Royal Academy. The lions share, the controlling 60%, according to the directors, belonged to the directors and they decreed that the Breeders' Cup was Royal Academy's final race. Shortly thereafter he was immediately retired to stud. Magnier valued him at $3.5 million, the price O'Brien paid for him as a yearling on behalf of Classic Thoroughbreds. There was no big overinflated syndication fee. No hoopla. Instead, Royal Academy was the first stallion in this saga to be under-assessed. Instead of keeping him in Ireland, Royal Academy was shipped to Ashford Stud, Coolmore's US base.

Royal Academy became designated as a traveling stallion and was dispatched from Kentucky to Australia and South America and back again. One year they flew him to Japan for a Northern breeding season. According to a 2005 Coolmore America stallion promotional brochure: "Royal Academy has reached a significant milestone, joining the likes of his three-parts brother Storm Cat, sire Nijinsky, and grandsire Northern Dancer in the elite club of world-leading sires with 100+ Stakes winners."

Royal Academy sired winners of the top races around the Globe — Hong Kong, Brazil Australia, England, Ireland, France and North America. These offspring include Classic winners Sleepytime (English 1000 Guineas), Val Royal (Breeders' Cup Mile) and Oscar Schindler (Irish St. Leger twice). Over the years Royal Academy's stud service fee fluctuated. Coolmore charged $30,000 in 1998; $45,000 in 1999; $20,000 in 2004.

In December 2007 it was announced that Royal Academy would no longer be traveling. Instead he would remain at Coolmore's Australian base in Hunter Valley, NSW. Royal Academy had sired over 1800 foals. Suffice to say Royal Academy enhanced the coffers of Coolmore by many, many millions.

While Royal Academy was being spirited off to Coolmore America the directors of Classic Thoroughbreds announced that there would be one more horse. This one was named Sportsworld. Perhaps to compensate for losing the only good racehorse to carry the Kelly green and gold silks, it was decreed that the shareholders would own Sportsworld outright. There were but six horses in the 1991 Irish Derby. Sportsworld, finished fourth.

Several months later the directors called an Extraordinary General Meeting to be held at the Berkeley Court Hotel in Dublin. Approximately 100 shareholders showed up. O'Brien, Magnier and Smurfit sat at the front of the room. Eventually they were joined by Sangster who arrived late, after the meeting had begun.

"After three disastrous years we have come to the conclusion," intoned Smurfit, "that enough is enough. This noble and unique experiment has not been a success ... There is little point in proceeding with the purchase of any further horses."

There is scant information on what ultimately happened to the massive herd of young Thoroughbreds that were part of the *noble and unique experiment.* The one horse that can be traced is, of course, Royal Academy — the one horse that surely offered return on investment — at least to some.

Interestingly the two most important horses to occupy the stalls at Coolmore were not among the herds of young Thoroughbreds the band of horse traders brought home to Ireland during their search for the next Nijinsky. The first was Sadler's Wells. The other principal performer to aid in the extraordinary economic renaissance created by this, the first Celtic Tiger, was a horse named Danehill.

Where Sadler's Wells never left Ireland, Danehill was among the troop of Coolmore stallions that were expected to perform stallion duties on several continents. Danehill was also a prodigious source of revenue.

Foaled 26 March 1986 at Juddmonte Farms in Kentucky, Danehill raced in England, France and Ireland carrying the colours of Prince Khalid Abdullah. "He had great speed, but it was difficult to harness," recalled Juddmonte farm manager, Dr. John Chandler. Danehill was started twice at two. He won his first race, a maiden event at York by 1-1/2 lengths, but only really got going in the final furlong. Danehill was then shipped to France in September for Prix de la Salamandre at Longchamp. Danehill fought his rider throughout most of the race and finished eighth in a field of nine. *Timeform* however, described Danehill as a "strong, good-bodied colt" with "quick fluid action," the "sort to improve with racing."

And improve he did, but not until Danehill was ridden the way *he* wanted to be ridden — and over the distance *he* wanted to run. The seven furlong Free Handicap at Newmarket seemed to suit Danehill. Jockey Pat Edderly held the colt at the back of the pack in the early stages, then let him stretch out to win by two lengths.

His stellar performance inspired his handlers to enter him in the first of England's Classics, the Two Thousand Guineas at Newmarket. The race was eight furlongs. Once again his rider employed the previous strategy of holding Danehill to the back of field, but this time it didn't work and the wilful colt reverted to wrangling with his rider. When it was time to challenge the leaders, Danehill had once again used up his energy. He finished third.

The next race on his card was the Irish Two Thousand Guineas. The performance was the same. The outcome: fourth. According to *Timeform*: " ... the cost of attempting to settle him finally proved too great. Danehill again fought for his head, behind and between horses ..."

It wasn't until he raced in the Cork and Orrery Stakes at Royal Ascot that Danehill's splendid swiftness came to the fore. The race was six furlongs. It suited his scope and disposition: "Danehill's next race saw a new trip, new tactics and a resounding success." Danehill won by three lengths.

His next stop was the July Cup at Newmarket. The race was the same distance, yet once again Danehill and his rider were out of sync. They finished third. *Timeform* considered Danehill's performance "a creditable effort but with fast conditions (which resulted in another course record) and that the "step up in company too much for him."

Danehill's final race was the six furlong Group One Ladbroke Sprint Cup at Haydock Park. The report from *Timeform* suggests: " racing on an easy surface for the first time since the spring, Danehill produced an impressive effort in the absence of those who had beaten him at Newmarket. "... he couldn't be so forcefully ridden as on his previous two outings but it didn't matter; Danehill was always traveling supremely well."

Danehill won easily and by two lengths. Shortly thereafter he was retired due to an injury. Some time later it was announced that Danehill had been sold for a reported £4 million to a partnership between Coolmore and the leading Australian Thoroughbred farm, Arrowfield Stud in New South Wales, owned by John Messara.

This meant Danehill, now owned by an Irishman and an Australian, was slated to be a traveling stallion. The regime they mapped out for Danehill was that beginning in the spring of 1990 he would spend the Northern Hemisphere breeding season in Ireland, then be flown to Australia for the Southern Hemisphere season.

After four years John Messara began to have concern over the effect the accelerated breeding program and the long flights were having on Danehill. Massera wanted to give the horse time out to recover and recharge. Presumably he thought this reasonable. Furthermore, he controlled over 50 percent of Danehill. Coolmore, only 13.5 percent.

As in the case of Robert Hefner and Dr. Bill Lockeridge and others in this saga, John Massera might have done well to have examined the fine print. Magnier, while a minority shareholder, had written into their agreement that he had 50 percent control over the management of Danehill. It seems he saw no reason to rest the horse, nor of compromise. The two men went toe-to-toe. The feud turned nasty and before long was reported on in the press.

"John Magnier doesn't do climbdowns," wrote Ed Micheau in the *Irish Examiner*, "Conflict resolution comes in the shape of complete and utter victory for the normally publicity-shy Corkman. Get in the way of the Coolmore boss and you are likely to get trampled upon ..."

A professional mediator and former judge, Sir Laurence Street, was hired to preside over the clash between the Messara and Magnier. The weapon of choice: money. The game: an auction. But this was a private auction. Limited to two players. Messara vs Magnier. There would, however, be no physical contact. The former judge ensconced the men in separate rooms and asked them to present their bids in sealed envelopes. Over the next few hours Sir Laurence Street shuttled back and forth across the hallway nearly thirty times before Magnier was declared victorious.

His winning bid of Aus $23 million would prove but a pittance relative to the amount of money Danehill would earn for Magnier and Coolmore.

Danehill emerged as the leading stallion in Australia year after year. Eventually Coolmore was charging a stud fee of Aus$200,000 per session and Danehill was breeding close to 200 mares a year. Thus, in a single season, Danehill brought to Coolmore's coffers, almost twice what Magnier had paid.

Not only was he annually shunted the 12,000 kms between Ireland and Australia, in 1996 Danehill was dispatched to Japan for a breeding season. In 1999 Danehill covered 164 mares in Australia. This resulted in 124 foals. He was only thirteen, but there was every chance, as predicted by Messera, the travel was taking a toll and his mighty sperm was losing its potency. In June 2002 Coolmore announced that Danehill would no longer be flown to Australia for the Southern Hemisphere breeding season. It wasn't exactly the 'time-out' Messara had prescribed all those years before. Still Danehill's progeny continued to command attention.

The skirmish over Danehill was but a warm-up act compared to the battle over one of the stallion's offspring — a colt named Rock of Gibraltar. And none more bloodied than his co-owner, Sir Alex Ferguson, legendary manager of Manchester United.

When Sir Alex bounded into a horse deal with the Irishman he possessed no idea of what lay ahead. Horse racing he presumed offered a splendid diversion from the pressures of managing the football team. The dream that rapidly plummeted into Sir Alex's worst nightmare began in March 1997 when he was invited to sit in JP McManus' box at the Cheltenham Festival — the rollicking finale to Britain's National Hunt season. Among the other guests that fateful day was McManus' good friend and business partner, John Magnier. From there a friendship grew between the Scottish footballer and the Irishmen. They played golf. Went to the races. Indeed, Magnier confided to a journalist that in his opinion Sir Alex Ferguson should be Britain's next Prime Minister.

Somewhere along the line Sir Alex acquired the services of Mike Dillon, a part-time Irish bloodstock agent. According to Brough Scott in *The Sunday Telegraph*, "Dillon would keep me posted on our friend's latest racing adventure ... "I said that Ferguson would be joining the Coolmore team in no time. "Not yet," said Dillon, "John [Magnier] says he wants to wait until he is sure he has a horse to suit."

The *horse to suit*, Rock of Gibraltar, was a racy-looking bay son of Danehill and the mare, Offshore Broom. As the story goes, Sir Alex Ferguson entered into an ownership agreement with Magnier prior to the running of the 2001 Gimcrack Stakes at York. "My first real memory of Rock of Gibraltar was the Gimcrack Stakes at York in August of last year." wrote Sir Alex in *The Observer* (6 October 2002) "I had bought him a couple of months earlier."

Dillon concurred and was quoted as saying that Sir Alex had paid £120,000 for a 50% stake in the horse. Later on the precise arrangements for the ownership of Rock of Gibraltar became somewhat shrouded — but then such is the nature of horse deals.

Back in the times of the ancient Irish horse trading markets a transaction was confirmed with a spit on the palm, followed by a handshake. Things haven't really changed all that much. Documentation, signed contracts or conventional agreements in any form seldom find their way into a horse deal. Instead, a sort of gentleman's agreement frequently prevails, as if for some curious reason it is presumed that all will be conducted in a fair and honourable manner. While in some cases this may be true, the buying and selling of horses is often cloaked in arcane rituals and practices.

In this particular arrangement what was clear was: 1) Rock of Gibraltar was duly registered with the Irish Jockey Club in the name of Sir Alex Ferguson and Magnier's wife, Susan; 2) the horse ran in Sir Alex Ferguson's red and white racing silks; 3) Sir Alex Ferguson had no idea of what he was getting into.

Initially the whole affair seemed quite miraculous. Perfect, in fact. No sooner had the two men shook hands when this horse, Rock of Gibraltar, began to rocket to victory upon victory over English, Irish and French turf. And in the most lofty Thoroughbred events.

Few horse owners savour such incredible success. Not in an entire lifetime. Yet here was Sir Alex, a relative neophyte, strolling the winner's enclosures with his grand champion. Perhaps it was due to the *luck of the Irish.* He was after-all, the lone Scot in a pack of Irish horse dealers. Sir Alex was effusive in praise of his Irish partners and their Irish trainer and his Irish racing consultant. Those were heady days and the champagne bubbled and spilled and flowed.

Suddenly the party was over. Almost as quickly as it had begun. In November 2002 Magnier announced that the time had come to retire Rock of Gibraltar to stud. That same week Rock of Gibraltar was named Horse of the Year at the Cartier Awards ceremony in London. Sir Alex was unable to attend the event. Instead he was in the dugout at Old Trafford supervising his team's game against Bayer Leverkusen. Everyone, including the Cartier organizers, were well aware that Sir Alex represented a marvelous spokesperson for horse racing.

Capitalizing on his popularity they presented Sir Alex with the award for Rock of Gibraltar prior to the big night and had his acceptance speech videotaped for the assembled black-tie crowd: "As a relative newcomer into ownership I cannot adequately express the pleasure I have derived from the association with such a great horse," enthused Sir Alex, "Whilst I will be saddened not to see Rock of Gibraltar in action on the racecourse I will look forward to the future with keen anticipation and I have every confidence that he will transmit his amazing talent and courage to his offspring." Befitting the Oscar cinema awards, Sir Alex went on to thank his racing manager, the jockeys and his partners.

"It is wonderful that Sir Alex Ferguson, through Rock of Gibraltar, has shone at the very highest level in a different sport," offered Cartier's racing consultant, Harry Herbert, "He has been a great ambassador for racing ..."

Surely Sir Alex thought he had tumbled into a field of four-leaf clovers. He now would share in the bounty of Rock of Gibraltar's glorious stud fees. Or so he thought. But the rules of the game had changed. In January 2003 Magnier apparently declared that Sir Alex no longer was a partner in the horse.

In March 2003 Sir Alex sued the Irishman. A statement issued on behalf of Magnier and Coolmore Stud farm in County Tipperary by public relations firm Murray Consultants declared: "We wish to point out in response to the lodging of legal proceedings against our clients by Sir Alex Ferguson in Dublin, that our clients consider them to be without merit, and that they will be vigorously contested."

The Irishmen would bring a new depth of meaning to the expression *vigorously contested.* The brouhaha raged on for an entire year. When the fight over Rock of Gibraltar was in full fury it received more publicity than the Derby and football finals combined. The almost daily skirmishes dominated sports pages and front pages of newspapers and tabloids published anywhere on the planet where there is a passion for football or Thoroughbred racing. The battle played out like a brutal serve and volley tennis match. For the most part the spectators — the media, football fans, general public and the entire Manchester United conglomerate (from the millions of supporters to board members) — appeared at times bemused, confused, outraged and basically stupefied.

The media were particularly stymied. Every time Rock of Gibraltar, or *The Rock* as he was now known to his legion of fans, won a race he was led to the winners circle by a beaming Sir Alex Ferguson. Hence, it seemed reasonable to assume that this was *his* horse.

In May 2003 Rock of Gibraltar's sire, Danehill, died in what was described as a 'paddock accident.' Danehill was seventeen. The Australian Stud Book states Danehill covered 1479 mares in the Southern Hemisphere. Appending his breeding seasons in Ireland and one stint in Japan, Danehill sired over 2,200 foals. In contrast his grandsire, Northern Dancer, was retired from breeding at twenty-seven and died at twenty-nine. He sired 635 foals, but then Northern Dancer was not a traveling stallion and was born into an era where these animals were not expected to breed with more than fifty mares in a season.

Fortunately for Coolmore they had a stallion to replace Danehill. His son, Rock of Gibraltar, was deemed appropriately fertile and in his first season at stud was bred to 100 mares in Ireland. Then he was loaded on to the Coolmore cargo plane and flown to Australia where he was bred to another 130 mares at $A132,000 a covering. By the end of the 2003 Northern and Southern Hemisphere breeding seasons Rock of Gibraltar had, according to Brough Scott in the *Sunday Telegraph*, enhanced the Coolmore bank balance by over £13.8 million.

All the while the battle over who exactly owned Rock of Gibraltar raged on and on. Back when Sir Alex and his new Irish friends were playing golf and going to the races, a company called Cubic Expressions, that was registered in the British Virgin Islands, had begun buying shares of Manchester United on the open market. The identity of who was behind the company was a mystery. Eventually the football club had to issue a Section 212 to discover that Cubic was Magnier and his friend, JP McManus. By July 2001 Cubic owned 6.77% of the football team. It had cost the Irishmen £28 million.

By this point in the tale the group that ignited the original Celtic Tiger had dispersed. Vincent O'Brien was no longer at Ballydoyle. In his stead was Aidan O'Brien, Magnier's trainer and no relation to the Ireland's greatest horseman. Nor was Sangster at Coolmore. He'd bought his own farm, the historic Manton stable in Wiltshire for which he paid £18 million. He then hired Michael Dickinson, the young successful National Hunt trainer, to run the operation. A clash of philosophies ensued and before long Dickinson was replaced with Barry Hills. After a year Manton returned to being a public stable and eventually was put up for sale.

In the meantime Sangster married once again, this time to Susan Lilley, wife of heir to Lilley & Skinner shoes. In1987 an article in *Business* magazine not only suggested Sangster's finances were precarious but revealed details of some of the indebtedness. Before long banks began calling his loans. He sold Vernons for £90 million and was able to pay down the £60 million the banks were demanding. By the time Sir Alex Ferguson entered the scene Sangster was spending more and more time in Australia.

Magnier's new partner, John Patrick McManus, was born in Ireland's County Limerick where his family managed a dairy farm. He was also born, it appears, with an instinct for gambling. According to legend, McManus placed his first bet when he was but a lad of twelve. By the time he was twenty he had set up shop as an on-course bookmaker at Limerick's greyhound track. McManus swiftly gained a reputation for his daringly big money gambles — a reputation that earned him the nickname 'Sundance Kid.'

McManus was 26 when he bought his first racehorse, Cill Dara, and now had more than 100 horses in training, the most famous, Istabraq, won the Champion Hurdle at Cheltenham three consecutive years 2001 - 2003.

Besides their shares in Manchester United, McManus and Magnier also held investments in a UK nursing home operation and a chain of sports clubs. In 1997 Magnier and McManus teamed up with Dermot Desmond to buy the Sandy Lane Hotel in Barbados. Built in the 1960's by Ronald Tree, former advisor to Churchill, the Irish trio paid a reported £38 million for the hotel and invested millions more to refurbish the complex.

Internationally renowned as a destination for its celebrity guests and golfing elite, the most famous event to take place at their exclusive resort was the wedding of Elin Nordegren and Tiger Woods in 2004.

Sir Alex Ferguson did not emerge one of the most successful and respected football managers by being a push-over. It was clearly not in his nature, but his opponents had no intention of backing off. When Sir Alex started rattling his sabre the Irishmen retaliated by buying up even more Manchester United shares. By October 2003 they had amassed a whopping 23.15%. It had cost over half a billion dollars. They did not yet have control of Manchester United, but their almost quarter interest gave them immense influence.

The enemy was at the gate. Sir Alex responded by boarding a plane to Dublin and issuing a writ against Magnier over Rock of Gibraltar's ownership and subsequent stud fees. The Irishmen countered by purchasing even more shares. By 19 January 2004

Cubic Expression had increased its holdings to over 66.5 million shares and beyond the 25% mark. Along the way the Irishmen began posing questions concerning the running of the club and its manager.

By now Manchester United fans were fuming and decided to strike back at the Irishmen by targeting British racecourses. It began with a small group at the Hereford race meet carrying banners which they strung across the open ditch jump. After delaying the races they were escorted from the track by security staff. The stunt did, however, get the attention of the news media and the threat of escalating actions at Britain's race courses ensued. In response the Irish bought eight million more shares. They were mere fractions short of the 30% stake wherein they were required to make a formal takeover bid. The reaction of Manchester United supporters was fierce and instantaneous.

And so it was that the place where all this began, the Cheltenham Festival, in five weeks hence, became the target. A group of football devotees applied for a permit to hold a *peaceful but vocal* demonstration 18 March 2004, the day of the Cheltenham Gold Cup. That weekend a leaflet entitled 'Just Say Neigh' listing addresses, phone numbers and email details of Coolmore's Irish, US and Australian farms was handed out to supporters. The pamphlet suggested that fans 'Go to horse races they are attending or wherever they have horses running and let them know how you feel.'

This was followed by a newspaper report hinting that some of the more indignant fans were planning to throw footballs in front of runners owned by either Magnier or McManus. Magnier did not own steeplechase horses, but his son, JP, was a steeplechase jockey. The situation was close to a boiling point and becoming potentially dangerous for the horses and the riders.

On the final day of February 2004, at the urging of Sir Alex, the fans agreed to call off their planned demonstrations at Cheltenham. On 8 March 2004, ten days prior to the Cheltenham

Gold Cup, Sir Alex announced that he had abandoned his fight for Rock of Gibraltar. He agreed to drop the court case and accepted Magnier's offer of £2 million — a mere drop in the bucket, it would seem, considering the millions the horse would earn for his owners.

On 18 March 2004 the Cheltenham Gold Cup was run without incident and won by the hugely popular Best Mate — for the third consecutive year. One of the most beloved horses in the history of horse racing in the UK, the remarkable bay gelding joined Arkle and Cottage Rake in that long list of courageous Gold Cup champions bred and born in Ireland.

Epilogue

By the time Best Mate bounded to glory at Cheltenham, Ireland was well on the road to once again ruling the world of the horse. There can be little doubt the path to this extraordinary resurgence began the moment Nijinsky first galloped across the lush green turf of The Curragh. And somewhere along the route the Celtic Tiger began to roar—initially in reverence and later with pride of triumph.

A clue linking the horse and the tiger can be found in the observations of John Maynard Keynes. The noted British economist coined the term 'animal spirits' to describe the illusive human emotions that influence consumer confidence and stimulate economic growth: "... of our decisions to do something positive, the full consequences of which will be drawn out over many days to come, can only be taken as the result of animal spirits - a spontaneous urge to action rather than inaction."

In this case, Keynes' animal spirits were indeed inspired by the spirit of an animal—the noble Nijinsky. For this one horse surely spurred Michael Vincent O'Brien and the troop of Irish horse traders with a spontaneous urge to action. They did not find the next Nijinsky, but then its highly unlikely there will ever be another so brilliant. Still their bold quest clearly impacted not only Ireland's economic growth, but her future. In bringing the horses back to Ireland they revitalized an industry, rekindled the ancient art of horse trading and created prosperity beyond their wildest dreams.

When Nijinsky stepped off the plane at Shannon airport in the fall of 1968 Ireland was an impoverished nation and sport with horses was but a shadow of its original prominence. Where once upon a long time ago Ireland enjoyed far more horse racing than all other societies of the medieval world, except for the Irish Sweeps Derby, purses were meagre and the country's important horse races were insignificant on the world stage.

Thirty-five years later, Ireland's Thoroughbred racing and breeding was booming. There were twenty-seven racecourses (25 in the Republic of Ireland and 2 in Northern Ireland)—hence more courses per capita than any other country in the world. One track, County Kildare's Punchestown, had been recently demolished and totally rebuilt to accommodate this horse racing revival.

In decade spanning 1994 - 2004 the number of annual race meetings in Ireland multiplied by 20% to upwards of 300. While any number of North American tracks were struggling for survival during the same period, attendance in Ireland mushroomed over 25% all the while contributing an estimated several billion euros to the government purse.

Furthermore almost half of Europe's Thoroughbreds now had **Ireland** printed in the nationality column of their passports and this tiny island nation had risen to third largest producer of Thoroughbreds world-wide. The only countries ahead of Ireland were the United States and Australia. England, considered the home of the Thoroughbred, had been left in the dust. As had Canada, home of the world's foremost Thoroughbred bloodlines.

Then there was the Coolmore empire. By 2004 it had evolved into a massive multi-national and Coolmore stalls were filled to over-flowing with blue-blood stallions. Lounging beneath the Mountain of the Women outside the village of Fethard and sprawling across10,000 acres of the Golden Vale Coolmore headquarters was home to 33 stallions. There were another 17 stallions residing at Coolmore America, their Kentucky operation. Following the Northern Hemisphere breeding season 14 of the Irish-based stallions were loaded into the company's transport plane and flown to Coolmore's Australian station in the Hunter Valley. Including their National Hunt stallions, those considered for one reason or another, without credentials or marketability at the prominent sales, the total number of Coolmore stallions stood at just under sixty. All but one were descendants of Nijinsky's sire, Northern Dancer. It was safe to say that Ireland's Coolmore dominated the world of the Thoroughbred like no other.

Success breeds success and Coolmore's enormous financial success coupled, no doubt, by Charlie Haughey's declaration of no taxes on stallion fees, encouraged others, both Irish and foreign, to establish stud farms. Before long any number of stately, prosperous-looking horse breeding farms had begun surfacing throughout the countryside. The tax holiday that began with the appearance of Nijinsky in Ireland finally came to an end in August 2008. But by then Irish dominance was well entrenched and Irish horse traders, now known as bloodstock agents, had become a recognizable force the world over.

This Irish horse renaissance cascaded beyond the rarified world of Thoroughbred breeding and racing. There was also a renewed popularity of horse fairs across the Emerald Isle. In County Gallway, for example, the Ballinasloe Horse Fair, which traced its origins back to the High Kings of Tara, was attracting over 80,000 horse buyers and spectators during the week-long festivities and injecting millions of Euros annually into the local economy. Other tourists were flocking to Ireland to go trekking or simply make the acquaintance of the famed Irish horses and their illustrious caretakers.

So to leave horses out of the debate over what actually sparked the Celtic Tiger is akin to an orchestra without the percussion section. The steady rhythm of horses hooves dancing and prancing along dusty roads or pounding across soft green turf has long been music to the Irish soul. Tigers may come and go—but the horses are here to stay.

Sources and References

1. Baerlein, Richard. *Nijinsky Triple Crown Winner.* London. Pelham Books, 1971
2. Baerlein, Richard. *Shergar and the Aga Khan's Thoroughbred Empire.* London. Michael Joseph, 1984
3. Crick, Michael. *Many Sides of Alex Ferguson.* Simon & Schuster. New York, 2002
4. David, Roy. *Robert Sangster Tycoon of the Turf.* London. William Heinemann Ltd, 1991
5. Hagedorn Auerbach, Ann. *Wild Ride: the rise and fall of Calumet Farm, Inc., America's premier racing dynasty.* New York. Henry Holt, 1994
6. Herbert, Ivor and O'Brien, Jacqueline. *Vincent O'Brien's Great Horses.* London. Pelham Books, 1984
7. Robinson, Patrick with Robinson, Nick. *Horsetrader: Robert Sangster and the rise and fall of the sport of kings.* London. Harper Collins Publishers, 1994
8. Sampson, Lesley I. *Nijinsky: Blue Riband Sire.* London. J.A. Allen, 1985
9. Smith, Raymond. *Vincent O'Brien: Master of Ballydoyle.* London. W.H.Allen, 1990
10. Stewart, Ian. *Does God Play Dice: The New Mathematics of Chaos.* Oxford. Blackwell Publishing, 1989

And countless magazines and newspapers including *The Economist, MacLeans Magazine, The Racing Post, Manchester Guardian, Thoroughbred Times, The Independent, Irish Times, The People, Sunday Telegraph, and The Observer.*

Acknowledgments

The trail leading to this story took me on a merry chase. Indeed it seems I have been traveling it forever. Perhaps I have. I suspect it began with my grandpa, Herbert Lennox. For this is surely where I inherited my passion for horses.

Grandpa's father emigrated to Canada during Ireland's Great Hunger, or potato famine, in the late 1840s. He and his brother managed to survive the Atlantic crossing in one of the barely seaworthy vessels. Because so many died during the voyages the boats became known as coffin ships. They finally stumbled off the ship and on to the Canadian shore only to discover that at the time the Irish were not exactly welcomed with open arms. Unable to find work the two young men enlisted in a local militia and were eventually rewarded with the choice of £100 or land. They eagerly chose the land.

Far from the lush green fields of Ireland the acreage, located near the Magnetawan River in Northern Ontario, straddled the massive rocks of the Canadian Shield. The dense and dark forests of the region were populated by black bears, black flies and gigantic moose. My ancestors first task was to clear what would be known as 'the acre of light,' a patch of land upon which they could erect their homes. Before long they, and other Irish immigrants, had carved out a sustaining farm community.

My grandparents followed suit by building their own farm, raising seven children and tending to countless grandchildren each and every summer. It was like going to camp, but better. Especially the food. Our parents simply dropped us off at the start of the summer. We all were expected to help with chores, but more important we had the opportunity to spend time with our grandparents.

When the activity in the homestead became too much for

grandpa to tolerate, he took refuge in the barn with his horses. He sat on an overturned bucket, often for hours on end. Even when the weather was bitterly cold and damp, he preferred the company of his beloved horses. I suspect it brought him to a state of peace. I know it works for me.

Of my grandfather's many horses the one that stands out in my childhood memory was a sleek black roadster named Johnny. On the most magical winter afternoons my grandfather would disappear to the barn only to reappear at the front door with Johnny all harnessed and hitched up to the cutter. In the meantime my grandma had stuffed me into my snowsuit and donned herself in heavy coat and boots. Then we'd wait to hear the harness bells that jingled and jangled when Johnny trotted smartly down the road. Even today the memories of those outings touch my soul and make me smile.

It appears that my ancestors were bent on putting the bitter and painful memories of Ireland far behind them. Back then being Irish did not have the cache it has in the 21st Century, especially on St. Patrick's Day. Instead my forebears were focused on survival and assimilating into Canadian culture as quickly as possible. Hence we grandchildren knew little if anything of our Irish heritage. Nor did it seem important until I was lured into this story of the horse and the tiger.

It wasn't long before I became curious and that was what sustained me through the difficult task of reading Irish history—particularly the famines, the injustices and the suffering—in order to provide a background to this tale.

This book grew out of a series I was commissioned to write for *Gallop*, the leading Japanese magazine. So I owe a debt of thanks to Kunio Serizawa, editor-in-chief, for offering me the assignment and for giving me free rein and to my translator, Jiro Ohara, for his patience and assistance. Writing for *Gallop* offered me the opportunity to revisit and reexamine this world of horses and horse racing, a world I had inhabited for such a long time.

The book itself went through any number of incarnations and titles and perspectives and rewrites. All along the way any number of people stepped up to offer their support, insights, and expertise. Thanks to all of you and most notably Jenny Dereham for lending her assistance in the early days. Author Gail Hamilton read the continually shape-shifting manuscript many, many times. As did Judy Mappin and Bridget Bimm. Their support over all these years was unwavering. And then there was my dad. Always available by phone, he simply listened and cheered me on with stories about my grandpa and his horses.

LaVergne, TN USA
01 November 2010
203108LV00003B/4/P

9 780969 902553